THE
LABOUR
PARTY
IN CRISIS

PAUL WHITELEY

THE LABOUR PARTY IN CRISIS

METHUEN · LONDON AND NEW YORK

First published in 1983 by
Methuen & Co. Ltd
11 New Fetter Lane,
London EC4P 4EE

Published in the USA by
Methuen & Co.
in association with Methuen, Inc.
733 Third Avenue, New York,
NY 10017

Typeset in Great Britain by
Scarborough Typesetting Services
and printed by
Richard Clay, The Chaucer Press,
Bungay, Suffolk

*British Library Cataloguing in
Publication Data*

Whiteley, Paul
The Labour Party in crisis.
1. Labour Party (Great Britain)
I. Title
324.24107   JN1129.L32

ISBN 0–416–33860–7
ISBN 0–416–33870–4 Pbk

*Library of Congress Cataloging in
Publication Data*

Whiteley, Paul.
The Labour Party in crisis.
Bibliography: p.
Includes index.
1. Labour Party (Great Britain)
2. Great Britain – Politics and
government – 1945–   I. Title.
JN1129.L32W48   1983   324.24107
83–13176

ISBN 0–416–33860–7
ISBN 0–416–33870–4 (pbk.)

To Susie, Helen, Tom and Alice

Contents

List of figures		viii
List of tables		ix
Acknowledgements		xi
1	The Labour Party in crisis – an overview	1
	Part I The political sociology of the crisis	
2	The ideological crisis	21
3	The membership crisis	53
4	The electoral crisis	81
	Part II The political economy of the crisis	
5	Labour's policy goals	111
6	The Labour Party and economic policy	131
7	Labour's social policy – the case of poverty	163
8	The future of the Labour Party	188
9	Postscript: The 1983 General Election	208
	Appendix I A non-technical review of the statistical methods	220
	Appendix II A review of the surveys used in Part I	226
	Bibliography	229
	Index	244

List of figures

1.1 The decline in Labour Party individual membership,
1950–78   7
1.2 The relationship between the Labour and Conservative
shares of the total vote and time, 1945–79   11
2.1 Distribution of respondents along the left–right ideology
scale   38
3.1 The decline of Labour's published individual membership,
1950–78   54
3.2 The relationship between individual party membership
and inflation, 1950–78   72
3.3 The relationship between individual party membership
and unemployment, 1950–78   73
4.1 A theoretical model of voting in Britain   90
6.1 A multiple interrupted time series analysis of a
hypothetical economic series   156

List of tables

2.1 The factor analysis of the issue indicators for Labour
    identifiers in 1979   27
2.2 Responses of pooled sample to attitudinal indicators   33
2.3 The factor analysis for the Labour elite, and correlations
    between factors   36
2.4 The relationship between attitudinal indicators and the
    first principal component   37
2.5 Occupational status by ideology for the pooled sample   42
2.6 The relationship between ideology and political status in
    the Labour elite   44
2.7 Social background, political status and attitude saliency as
    predictors of ideology   46
2.8 The discrepancy between the attitudes of the Labour elite
    and the Labour government's performance in office   48
2.9 Attitudes of the Labour elite (Members of Parliament,
    parliamentary candidates and councillors) to the public
    ownership of industries and services in the long run   49
3.1 Membership and activism in constituency Labour parties,
    1978   56
3.2 The relationship between social class and motives for
    joining the Labour Party   59
3.3 The relationship between ideology and political orientation
    for party conference delegates   65
3.4 Factor analysis of the attitudes of middle-class conference
    delegates   67
3.5 Factor analysis of the attitudes of working-class conference
    delegates   68
3.6 Economic variables as predictors of Labour's individual
    membership, 1960–78, controlling for confounding
    influences – ordinary least squares estimates   75

4.1   The relationship between social attributes, affective,
      prospective and retrospective evaluations and Labour
      voting, 1979   97
4.2   Social attributes, affective, prospective and retrospective
      evaluations as predictors of the probability of voting
      Labour   101
4.3   Social attributes, affective, prospective and retrospective
      evaluations altogether as predictors of the probability of
      voting Labour   103
4.4   Correlations between affective, retrospective and
      prospective evaluations of issues   105
6.1   The main economic indicators, 1959–79   133
6.2   Generalized least squares estimates of the influence of
      Labour incumbency on economic time series   157
7.1   The social security budget in 1982–3 – the main elements   164
7.2   The distribution of individuals, by household income
      relative to the supplementary benefits line and type of
      family, 1975   169
7.3   The distribution of individuals, type of family by
      household income relative to the supplementary benefits
      line   169
7.4   Changes in numbers of beneficiaries, 1960–79   171
7.5   The changes in real terms in social security benefits,
      1964–79   173
7.6   Social security benefits as a percentage of average earnings
      for last increases of various governments, 1951–79   174
9.1   The results of the 1983 General Election in Great Britain   209
9.2   Levels of party support at key times from 1979 to 1983   210
9.3   The electorate's evaluation of party performances in the
      1983 General Election   212

Acknowledgements

It is always difficult to acknowledge the intellectual debts one owes to individuals within and outside academic life. Many people have helped me to write this book. I should like to thank particularly Ian Budge of the University of Essex for his valuable comments on earlier drafts of Part I; Steve Winyard of the University of Leeds for his help in organizing in my mind the mass of material summarized in Chapter 7; and Norman Schofield of the California Institute of Technology, formerly of the University of Essex, for his stimulating conversation and his profound insights into the nature of collective action. I should also like to thank friends in the Department of Political Science at the University of Kentucky, particularly Mike Baer, who provided a stimulating academic environment in which to work whilst the structure of this book was being developed. I should also like to thank Steve Kelly of the Computer Centre at the University of Bristol for his help with software.

I am grateful to the Volkswagen Foundation and the European Community for financial support in processing the Party Conference Delegates' survey, which is part of the European Middle Level Elites' Project of the European Consortium for Political Research. Finally, I should like to thank the British Election Study, particularly its director, Ivor Crewe, for providing the data from their 1979 survey of the electorate.

The 1983 General Election occurred while this book was in proof; Chapter 9 was added at this late stage to consider the results of the election and their significance as well as possible future developments.

Paul Whiteley
Bristol
July 1983

1
The Labour Party in crisis
– an overview

The Labour Party is in serious trouble, and faces a series of crises greater than it has experienced since the 1930s. The faction fighting of recent years over the party constitution and policy are only visible indicators of underlying problems which go deep, and which have been with the party for many years. There are three major crises facing the party at the present time which stand out particularly. Firstly, there is an ideological crisis manifest in the battles over the constitution, the split with the Social Democrats and the problems of entryism from the revolutionary Left. Secondly, there is an electoral crisis manifest in the long-term decline in the Labour vote, producing a vote share of 28.3 per cent at the 1983 General Election, the worst result since 1918. Thirdly, there is the less conspicuous but nevertheless damaging decline in the individual membership of the party, the component of total membership not tied to trade union affiliations. This can be described as the membership crisis, which in turn has produced major financial problems plunging the party deeper and deeper into debt.

These three crises, together with the debilitating problem of finance, put the future of the party at risk as the main alternative party of government. Any organization which faces multiple crises will at some stage reach a point of no return, at which the problems become so great that it can never overcome them. This has not already happened to the Labour Party, and it is certainly not inevitable that it will happen. But we shall argue in this book that it could easily happen if nothing is done to reverse the decline.

The main thesis of this book is that these interrelated crises all have a common origin in the failure of the Labour Party, particularly in office, to achieve its goals. Failures of policy performance are at the heart of the crises of the Labour Party. The party shares in the wider failure of British institutions, and British society, particularly in the field of economic management. But we shall argue that the party has made a considerable contribution to these failures, and this ultimately explains its present travails. In saying this, we must recognize that the Conservative Party shares in this failure, particularly since 1979, together with the other major institutions of government, such as the civil service, Parliament, industry and finance, and the trade unions. But our theme is not the decline of Britain, a subject ably discussed elsewhere (Alt, 1979; Gamble, 1981). Rather our focus is on the role of the Labour Party in that decline, and the consequences of that role for the party.

At the centre of the analysis is the implicit notion that the Labour Party is just a key component of the wider political system, which in turn is linked to the wider economic and social systems. Its performance in the political system influences the performance of these other systems, which via a process of feedback influences the fortunes of the party. The idea of a political party being a component in a complex and wider social system is not, of course, new. The systems approach to political analysis was fully, if rather abstractly, developed by Easton (1953, 1965) and Deutsch (1963). As it stands, systems theory is merely a conceptual framework for organizing ideas, and in the absence of detailed analysis and empirical evidence explains little of importance on its own. But, in the case of the crisis of the Labour Party, it provides a very useful device for organizing our discussion. Roughly speaking, Part I of this book is concerned with analysing the consequences of the policy failure for the Labour Party, and Part II is concerned with examining Labour's contribution to this failure in the key areas of economic management and social security policy.

To set the scene, we shall briefly examine the nature of these three crises facing the Labour Party in this chapter before discussing them in more detail later. We shall also set out the main conclusions concerning Labour's policy failures before discussing them in depth in Part II.

The ideological crisis

There have always been ideological divisions within the Labour Party, and periodic rows over ideological questions during its history. However, since the defeat in the General Election of 1979 the party has faced three major battles, all of which were at root ideological. These were the conflict over internal party democracy, particularly the question of mandatory reselection of MPs and a wider franchise for the election of party leader; the split with the Social Democrats, which led to the formation of the Social Democratic Party in March 1981; and the problem of entryism by the revolutionary Left, particularly the Militant Tendency.

We shall argue that each of these had its origins in the failures of policy performance of the Wilson and Callaghan governments, particularly the conflict over intra-party democracy. The starting point of the campaign by the Left to change the constitution was the defeat in the General Election of 1970. After the defeat the party swung to the Left and radical new policies were developed to avoid what was seen as the failure and drift of the Wilson government (Hatfield, 1978). The Left worked initially through the elaborate network of policy subcommittees set up by the National Executive Committee to develop policies especially for economic management and industrial intervention. These were incorporated into *Labour's Programme for Britain, 1973* (Labour Party, 1973), which was the most radical restatement of party policy since the war. In office these proposals, particularly the ideas on industrial policy, were quickly abandoned and after 1976 the party in government resumed the policies of economic management by deflation, characteristic of much of the postwar era.

The Left grew in strength in the 1970s, as the economic orthodoxy produced an ever-increasing slump, but after the defeat in the General Election of 1979 it changed strategies. It realized that controlling party conference, the forum for initiating new policy, was not enough. It had to obtain control over the parliamentary party and the leadership. This produced the campaigns over mandatory reselection, the control of the Manifesto, and the election of the leader. The campaign by the Left was spearheaded by the Labour Co-ordinating Committee, originally set up in 1978, and the Campaign for Labour Party Democracy, set up in 1973 following the refusal by Harold Wilson to accept the conference decision to nationalize twenty-five leading industrial companies (Kogan and Kogan, 1982). The former was concerned with questions of policy, and the latter with questions of constitutional change.

The Campaign for Labour Party Democracy pursued three aims: the mandatory reselection of MPs by constituency parties during the lifetime of each parliament; the introduction of an electoral college for the appointment of the party leader, containing representatives from the unions, constituencies and the parliamentary party; and, thirdly, the vesting of the right to draw up the Manifesto in the National Executive Committee, and the removal of the veto on the contents of the Manifesto of the leadership. This campaign was given a crucial boost by the defeat in the 1979 General Election. Following this election, the Left was able to turn an argument, previously used by the Right, against their opponents. This was the argument that 'extremist' policies produce electoral defeat, and 'moderate' policies electoral success. As we show in Chapter 5, Labour fought the 1979 Election on a very anodyne Manifesto following Callaghan's refusal to accept a number of radical proposals, such as the abolition of the House of Lords. The 'moderate' Manifesto produced the worst electoral performance since 1931, a uniquely crisis election. In fact, the contents of the Manifesto have little influence on the electorate, as we point out in Chapter 4, but the argument that 'moderate' policies were required for electoral success was widely accepted in the party before 1979. The other important aspect of the electoral argument was that in 1978–9 the Callaghan government had ignored TUC and party conference decisions in incomes policy and gone ahead with the 5 per cent pay norm, which led to the so called 'winter of discontent'. The Left were quick to point out that, if the government had followed conference decisions, the winter of discontent would not have occurred and Labour would probably have won the General Election. These two arguments gave a big boost to the Campaign for Labour Party Democracy.

Ultimately the Left achieved two out of the three objectives. In 1979 the annual conference accepted mandatory reselection of MPs. It also obtained a crucial victory in getting the abolition of the three year rule, the device which prevented the raising of policy or constitutional issues again for another three years after they had been discussed at a conference. This enabled the question of the electoral college and the writing of the Manifesto to be raised again in 1980, following their rejection in 1979. At the 1980 conference the election of the leader was deferred to a special conference in January 1981, and after much wrangling the party decided at this conference that the electoral college should consist of 40 per cent trade union delegates, 30 per cent constituency party delegates and 30 per cent parliamentary party delegates. The control of the Manifesto by the NEC was not accepted, but instead joint control was vested in the NEC and the Shadow Cabinet. The Left had won two out of the three objectives.

Jim Callaghan resigned from the party leadership in October 1980, immediately following the annual conference, but before the special conference. This meant that the election for leader was conducted under the old system. Many people regarded the timing of this resignation as a manoeuvre designed to ensure the election of a leader from the Right of the party before the new system could be introduced. If this were true, the plan misfired, since Michael Foot was elected leader. But the new electoral college was soon tested when Tony Benn challenged Denis Healey for the deputy leadership. The campaign for the deputy leadership was long and drawn out, and was clearly damaging to the standing of the party in the country. The year 1981 was a particularly bad one for Labour since all three ideological disputes over conference democracy, entryism and the SDP were going on at a time when the party was arguing over the deputy leadership. In December 1980 the party received the support of 47.5 per cent of the electorate in the Gallup Poll (Webb and Wybrow, 1981, p. 168). By December 1981, after a year of internecine warfare, support was down to 23.5 per cent, a uniquely low level for the main opposition party (Gallup Polls, 1981, p. 2). Denis Healey ultimately won the deputy leadership by a hairsbreadth, which ended this particular source of division.

The creation of the SDP was a major influence on the political standing of the Labour Party. The split which led to the emergence of the new party had been building up ever since the swing to the Left in the Labour Party in the early 1970s (Bradley, 1981). The first organizational evidence of the split was the creation of the Social Democratic Alliance in 1975 immediately following the EEC Referendum. The SDA was made up of pro-Common Market zealots, but it never attracted the support of any major figures in the party and soon degenerated into McCarthyite smear tactics of opponents on the Left. The Limehouse Declaration which inaugurated the Council for Social Democracy, the immediate forerunner of the SDP, was made the day after the special conference of January 1981. The formal breach with the Labour Party came finally in March 1981, when the SDP was launched.

The immediate cause of the split was thus the victory of the Left over the electoral college system for electing the leader. But the underlying long-term cause was the increasing isolation of the revisionist and Gaitskellite wings of the party in Parliament. We review the main doctrines of revisionism in Chapter 5, but in the present context the major problem was that revisionism in practice failed to deliver the goods. It failed really on two grounds. Firstly, there was no distinctively Social Democratic economic policy other than orthodox Keynesianism. When this failed in the 1960s, partly because it was misapplied – as we shall see in Chapter 6 – the rest of the revisionist programme failed too. Crosland most clearly articulated revisionism in his classic book, *The Future of Socialism* (Crosland, 1956), in which he set out a vision of an increasingly egalitarian society made possible largely by redistribution from economic growth. When the economic growth was not achieved, neither was the greater equality. Shortly before his death, Crosland found himself, much against his will, supporting large cuts in public expenditure which had the effect of increasing inequality. Thus the second failure of revisionism was the failure by its advocates to stick to the ideals of equality when the going became tough. The acceptance of a kind of weak monetarism by a Labour Cabinet in 1976, a Cabinet which contained a majority of revisionists, represented the final death knell of the doctrine. This produced the increasing isolation of the Social Democrats in the Labour Party, which in turn produced the SDP.

The question of entryism was the third manifestation of the ideological crisis in the party, which again has its origins in the failures of the party in office. The Labour Party has always contained Marxists, and it has frequently suffered from entryism from the revolutionary Left. Before the Second World War, and in the 1950s, the threat came from the

Communist Party, and increasingly over time from the Trotskyite Fourth Internationale, which periodically attempted to take over the Young Socialists. One of the apparently innocuous decisions taken in 1973 as a result of the swing to the Left in the party was the decision to abolish the list of proscribed organizations. Membership of such organizations rendered the individual ineligible for membership of the Labour Party. This gave the Militant Tendency an opportunity to take over the Youth Movement, as had a previous Trotskyite organization in the 1960s. But, unlike this earlier case, nothing was done to prevent it, and Militant began to make inroads into the adult party, particularly in inner city areas which often had decrepit local parties. Essentially the failure of the Social Democratic case and the ever-increasing economic crisis provided an ideal breeding ground for the simplistic, messianic vision of the Militants. Finally, in 1981 the newly elected party leader supported the idea of an investigation into the activities of Militant, which was duly carried out by Ron Hayward, the General Secretary, and David Hughes, the national agent. This report found that the Militant Tendency was in breach of Clause II of the party constitution, which proscribes all groups 'having their own Programme, Principles and Policy' (Labour Party, 1982a, p. 13). At the 1982 annual conference the party constitution was amended in order to set up a register of non-affiliated groups within the party. Groups which do not conform to the party constitution will be ineligible for membership of the register and will in theory be expelled from the party. The register was aimed primarily at Militant, but at the time of writing it is not clear how many Militant supporters will actually be expelled from the party. However, the introduction of the register represents a decisive defeat for entryists like Militant, and it seems likely that their influence in the party will be reduced in the future.

The ideological crisis is perhaps the most visible of the current crises in the party. The membership crisis is less obvious, and has been going on for so many years that it attracts little public attention. But it poses a real threat to the future viability of the party.

The membership crisis

The decline in the published individual membership of the Labour Party over the years 1949 to 1979 can be seen in Figure 1.1. The correlation between individual party membership and the number of years since 1949 is a near perfect −0.91. Thus on published figures the party has been losing on average more than 11,000 members per year, and, since the published figures exaggerate the true membership, the actual loss of membership may well be higher than this. The published figures exaggerated the true membership, particularly up to 1979, because until 1980 the constituency parties were required to affiliate with at least 1000

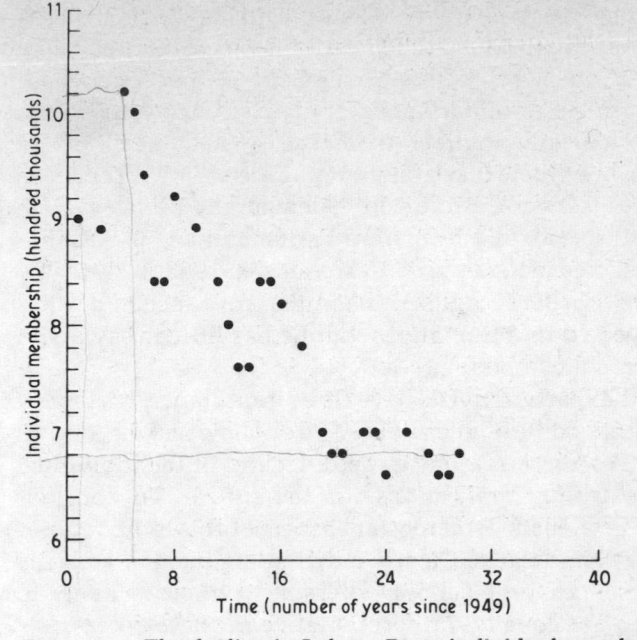

Figure 1.1 The decline in Labour Party individual membership, 1950–78 (Correlation between individual membership and time = –0.91)

Sources: Butler and Sloman (1980, p. 143) and Labour Party headquarters.

members. When this rule was dropped individual membership fell from 666,091 in 1979 to 348,156 in 1980 (Labour Party, 1980, p. 84). However, constituency parties can still buy more individual membership cards from the central office than they actually issue so, as we argue in Chapter 3, these figures still exaggerate the true membership.

We shall examine the reasons for this dramatic decline in the membership in Chapter 3, but for the moment we shall ask, why should this be a matter of real concern for the Labour Party? Are individual members actually important? In discussing individual members it is necessary to distinguish between the activists who keep the party going at the local level and the passive card-holding members. As we shall see in Chapter 3, the former are a minority of the total membership. As far as a passive membership is concerned, it is really only important to the party as a source of funds. Also it might be argued that passive party members will be more likely to vote Labour in an election than non-members, although this is debatable. Thus the real focus of attention in discussions of the importance of party members must centre on the activists.

The literature on political parties in Britain has tended to play down the importance of party activists, often arguing that their only important role is to support the party leadership. For example, in his classic study of British political parties McKenzie argued that the local parties were primarily servants of their respective parliamentary parties, whose function was 'to sustain teams of parliamentary leaders, between whom the electorate is periodically invited to choose' (1963, p. 66). More recently, McKenzie has argued that grassroots influence over policy in British political parties is incompatible with a democratic British system of government, since it removes power from Parliament and places it in the hands of an unelected outside group (McKenzie, 1982, p. 195). By contrast, Blondel (1963, p. 88) recognizes the important function of local parties in selecting elected representatives, but he has little to say about the role of activists in policy making.

We shall argue that party activists have three important roles to play in the Labour Party: in political recruitment, in policy making and in mobilizing the vote. For these reasons a rapid decline in the individual membership has disturbing implications for the future. To consider political recruitment first, the most important aspect of this is the recruitment of parliamentary candidates. Clearly a dwindling band of activists increasingly unrepresentative of Labour voters as a whole is likely to select candidates who are equally unrepresentative of these voters. We note in Chapter 2 that the activists who make up the party conference delegates are overwhelmingly middle class, as are the parliamentary candidates. The trend towards an ever-increasing number of middle-class professionals selected as parliamentary candidates may be partly a reflection of the fact that activists are predominantly middle class, and are reluctant to select manual workers, who often lack the communication skills of the white collar professionals. Yet again, the selection of up to nine members of the Militant Tendency as parliamentary candidates during 1981 and 1982 reflects the problem of entryism referred to earlier. Militant's programme is almost completely at odds with the programme and beliefs of the mainstream Labour Party, let alone Labour voters, and yet local parties selected such candidates. Obviously entryism would not be possible if local constituency parties had large numbers of activists representative of the views of Labour voters as a whole.

The role of activists in policy making is also important. They have little or no role in the process of policy implementation, but they are important in defining the agenda of debate within the Labour Party and setting priorities to issues once they are on the agenda. The constitutional changes discussed earlier were initiated by activists in the Campaign for Labour Party Democracy who put mandatory reselection on to the agenda, and finally had it accepted by the conference as a whole. A similar point can be made about unilateral nuclear disarmament. This was almost entirely a grassroots issue, both in its original form in the early 1960s (Parkin, 1968) and in its resurgent form as the European Nuclear

Disarmament Campaign. In 1982 a unilateralist motion received the necessary two-thirds majority at the annual conference to place it in the party programme. In many important areas activists influence policy making even if they are not in a position to affect policy implementation directly. But even in this area it is possible to see activists having an indirect influence. For example, the decline in the percentage of gross national product spent on defence by the Labour government after 1964 was partly a product of the low priority given to defence spending by many of them. Similarly, the revolt over incomes policy by rank and file trade unionists in 1978–9 was strongly supported by Labour activists. A future Labour government will probably have to adopt an incomes policy, but it has become impossible for the party leadership to proclaim openly that they are in favour of such a policy. Rank and file opposition in the trade union movement, and in constituency Labour parties, has made this issue very delicate, so that the party leadership has to approach it by stealth rather than directly. These examples illustrate the influence rather than the power of the grassroots activists expressed through party conference.

Thirdly, we shall argue that activists have a significant role to play at election times, which has been enhanced by the decline in party allegiance in the electorate (Crewe, Särlvik, and Alt, 1977). Influence over elections comes about in two ways. Firstly, party activists have a kind of negative influence, which emerges when there is a great deal of visible faction fighting, as in 1981. When this occurs it damages the standing of the party in the polls. Thus a party leadership which ignores or opposes the rank and file, and thereby precipitates internecine conflict, is likely to put the electoral position of the party at risk. Such considerations must loom large in the minds of the leadership immediately prior to a General Election. Thus party activists have a kind of negative power, an ability to help lose an election, which the leadership ignores at its peril. The second influence of activists on elections is their role in mobilizing the vote. An ingenious experiment in canvassing was carried out in Dundee by Bochel and Denver (1972). They showed that an intensive local campaign of canvassing and leafletting made a difference of 10 per cent in the turnout at a local election. They used two blocks of flats in a strong Labour ward, one acting as an experimental block and the other as a control. Obviously the impact of the local campaign is greater in a local election than it is in a General Election. But in 1979 87 per cent of respondents to a post-election survey said they had received leaflets from the Labour Party, and 23 per cent said they had been canvassed (Crewe, 1981, p. 270). The latter figure would obviously be higher in a marginal constituency, where the party puts in a special effort. In these circumstances if the local campaign improved the turnout of Labour voters by as little as 2 or 3 per cent this would be decisive in a number of key marginal constituencies. This is increasingly true at a time of declining partisanship.

Finally, party activists have an important role to play in political education, which has an indirect influence on electoral behaviour and which has been almost completely ignored by political scientists. This is the function of transmitting political ideas within their local communities, and at the workplace. There is a large and complex network of interest groups of all kinds at the local level, many of them not directly concerned with politics (Newton, 1976). A few Labour activists scattered amongst these groups can have a disproportionate influence in relation to their numbers in putting the Labour case. This is particularly likely to be true in interest groups which directly impinge on politics, such as housing associations, tenants' rights groups and parent–teacher associations. Discussions of the processes which form public opinion have been almost entirely concerned with the influence of the mass media (Worcester and Harrop, 1982). But there is evidence to suggest that the media have a rather weak influence in determining voting behaviour (Crewe, 1981, pp. 270–1). Face to face contacts between individuals in voluntary groups and at the workplace are probably more important than is commonly thought. Thus party activists have a role in carrying out political education, in the widest sense, in the community.

For a number of reasons we have seen that party activists have an important role to play in politics. At its most general, it is true to say that any democracy requires the active participation of ordinary citizens in political action, broadly defined, if it is to survive (Almond and Verba, 1963). This means that the decline of individual membership in the Labour Party is a serious problem both for the party and for the wider political system.

The electoral crisis

The decline in voting support for the Labour Party is particularly disturbing. The Labour and Conservative shares of the popular vote in the eleven General Elections between 1945 and 1979 are graphed in Figure 1.2.* In this figure the correlation between the Labour vote share and the number of years since 1944 is −0.85, and the equivalent correlation for the Conservatives is −0.37. Thus the decline in the Labour vote is much more rapid and predictable than that of the Conservatives. At the 1983 General Election, the decline in the Labour vote continued on trend, and the party received 28.3 per cent of the vote. This is a matter of grave concern for all party members.

Moreover, there were some features of the 1979 election which are particularly disturbing. There was an 11 per cent swing to the Conservatives amongst skilled manual workers, a 7 per cent swing amongst trade union members and a 9.5 per cent swing amongst young voters, the 18 to 22 year olds (Crewe, 1981, pp. 280–1). But perhaps the most striking

* See Table 9.1 in the postscript for a breakdown of the 1983 election results.

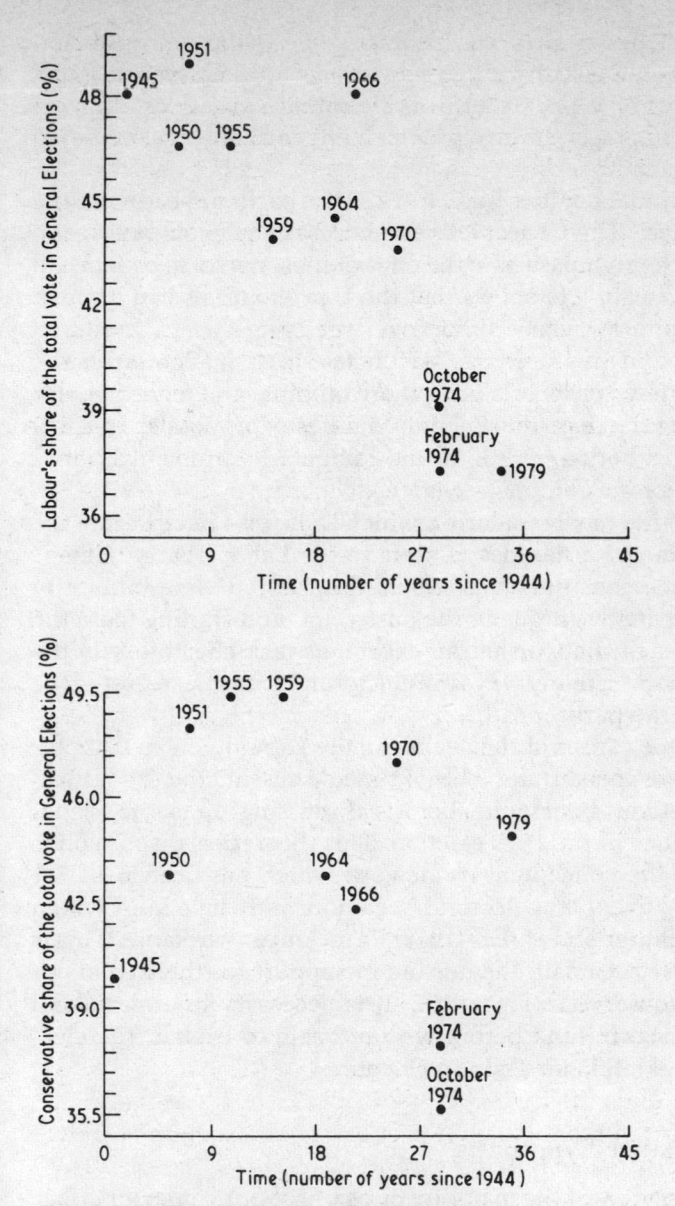

Figure 1.2 The relationship between the Labour and Conservative shares of the total vote and time, 1945–79

Correlation between Labour's share and time = −0.852 and between Conservative's share and time = −0.370.

Source: Butler and Sloman (1980, pp. 208–9).

figure was the 14.5 per cent swing amongst voters who had been unemployed under Labour. All these figures compare with an overall swing
to the Conservatives of 5.2 per cent. It is clear that Labour lost support
disproportionately amongst the groups which are normally considered to
make up its core constituency.

There is additional evidence that in 1979 the party did badly on the
issues. Crewe argues: 'The Conservatives' success came from saying the
right things about the right issues – the ones of most personal concern to
the voters' (1981, p. 283). He shows that the Conservatives had a much
stronger advantage in popular opinion over the issues which favoured
them than Labour did in the issues which favoured it. Similarly, the
Conservative Manifesto proposals were more credible and more popular
amongst the electorate than the Labour Manifesto proposals. In 1979
Labour suffered from both a credibility and a popularity problem as far as
the political issues of the campaign were concerned.

The new constituency boundaries, which came into force before the
1983 election, produced a net loss of seats to the Labour Party. This is
because many of the constituencies which disappeared were inner city
Labour strongholds. As we argue in the postscript, and starting from the
base of the 1983 result, Labour has an enormous task ahead to win the
next General Election. In many ways the electoral crisis is the worst of the
three crises facing the party.

We examine the causes of the decline in the Labour vote in Chapter
4. In that chapter we spend quite a bit of time discussing the theoretical
literature on electoral behaviour before discussing in some detail
Labour's performance in the 1979 election. This theoretical discussion is
necessary because the conceptual framework which has been used for
nearly fifteen years to explain electoral behaviour in Britain, and which
was developed by Butler and Stokes (1974), is no longer workable. This is
because it is unable to explain the decline in support for the two major
parties, which we observe in Figure 1.2. It is necessary to undertake a
substantial theoretical rethink before we can begin to explain the electoral decline. We take this up again in Chapter 4.

The performance hypothesis

In the light of this review of the major features of Labour's present crisis,
it is useful to restate the basic hypothesis underlying this book. The
hypothesis is that the failure of the party to achieve its policy goals,
particularly in the area of economic management, is the underlying cause
of these crises. This relatively straightforward idea is justified using
evidence from a wide variety of sources. The ideological disputes are
examined using survey evidence of the attitudes of the Labour elite, that
is Members of Parliament, parliamentary candidates, local councillors

and party conference delegates. The membership crisis is examined with time series data on party membership, together with indicators of aggregate economic performance, unemployment and inflation. The electoral crisis is examined using the 1979 British Election Study Survey of the electorate, focusing on the role of social background and attitudes as predictors of the vote.

The most visible of the three crises facing the party is perhaps the ideological crisis, since it has produced so much faction fighting in public. We examine this in Chapter 2. Discussions of ideology are plagued by the variety of meanings attached to the concept by different writers. So we start this chapter by defining ideology. We use it to mean roughly attitude coherence, that is the extent to which political attitudes are interrelated and mutually reinforcing in the minds of individuals. An individual with a reasonably diverse and interrelated set of political attitudes would be an ideologue in these terms, whereas an individual with fragmented and inconsistent attitudes would not. One of the key issues which is examined in Chapter 2 is the scope of ideological divisions within the party. In general we conclude that such divisions are confined to the Labour 'elite' and do not significantly touch on the attitudes of voters. This finding ties in with our analysis in Chapter 4 which shows that Labour has lost electoral support, not because voters disagree with its policy stands, though many of them do, but because of its performance in office. Voters do not have coherent, well-formed sets of opinions regarding policies and given their limited influence on politics there is no reason why they should. This means that they are not strongly influenced by policy proposals, but are much more influenced by performance. The only effect of the ideological divisions within the Labour elite on the electorate, comes through the loss of confidence engendered by the public faction fighting. In this sense the Conservatives, with their long tradition of faction fighting in private behind a façade of unity in public, have a distinct advantage.

In examining the causes of the ideological disputes within the Labour Party in recent years, we show in Chapter 2 that there are two broad classes of factors at work. Firstly, there are differences in the social background and political experience of activists which partly explain the divisions. Thus young working-class activists without any experience as elected representatives are more left-wing than older, middle-class activists who have such experience. The surprising thing about this finding however, is not that it exists, but that it appears to be relatively weak, and certainly cannot explain the ideological divisions of recent years on its own. Instead these are explained primarily as a result of the enormous gap between the policy aspirations of the Labour elite as a whole, and the performance of the party in implementing those policy objectives. One illustrative example of this is given by the fact that approximately 83 per cent of the Labour elite favoured a policy of nationalizing profitable industries, and during the two Labour governments after 1964 this occurred in only one instance, involving the establishment of the British National Oil Corporation. Even then it is arguable that special circumstances surrounded that decision, given that oil is such a key strategic commodity. We show in Chapter 2 that Labour governments have routinely ignored or opposed the preferences of their own supporters at the elite level, in a wide variety of policy areas. Moreover, in doing this Labour governments have been generally unsuccessful and this has triggered the ideological disputes of recent years.

There are similar processes at work in explaining the decline in the individual membership of the party, which is discussed in Chapter 3. In this case, however, the picture is more complex, since the decline in membership is disproportionately a working-class phenomenon. Working-class activists are more likely to leave the party than middle-class activists at a time of failing policy performance for a number of separate reasons. Firstly, they are more 'instrumental' in their approach to politics than the middle class; that is, they are more concerned with achieving concrete material benefits from policies than are middle-class activists, who are more concerned with idealistic and symbolic questions. This makes working-class activists more likely to defect than the middle class, when material benefits are not forthcoming. Secondly, middle-class activists tend to have more coherent ideological attitude structures than the working class, and this serves to protect them from disillusionment engendered by policy failure. In this sense, ideology acts as a mechanism for insulating them, making it easier to retain their attachment at a time when activists with weak attitude structures are defecting. Finally, the language of contemporary politics favours the middle class rather than the working class. This makes it easier for the middle class to compete as activists at the local level in discussions of policy and politics, and this again serves to strengthen their attachment to the party in comparison with the working class. Thus there are a number of separate reasons why the working class should defect from the party at a faster rate than the middle class.

In Chapter 4 we examine the performance hypothesis in relation to voting behaviour. In this chapter it is necessary to develop quite a complex multivariate model to do justice to the separate factors which explain voting behaviour. In this model, voting is explained as a product of two groups of factors. Firstly, there are the objective social circumstances of individuals which refer to their relationship to the means of production and consumption in society. The traditional measure of social class, occupational status, is one of the key relationships of an individual to the means of production. However, there is also the sector of the economy in which the individual works whether it is the public sector, the corporate sector (large scale capital), or the market sector (small scale capital). Relationships to the means of consumption are defined by whether or not the individual depends on collective modes of consumption, such as public transport and council housing, or private modes, such as a car and owner-occupied housing. These modes of consumption have an influence on voting behaviour independent of social class and attitudes.

The second class of factors which explain voting are subjective or attitudinal factors. These are associated with objective social status, but are for a variety of reasons not the same thing. It appears from the analysis in Chapter 4 that subjective factors, principally voters' evaluations of the performance of Labour in office and affective attachments to the party, are more important than objective factors in explaining voting behaviour. Taken together, voting behaviour is explained by the different production and consumption locations of individuals which give rise to different objective and subjective needs and attitudes, and these are translated, albeit imperfectly, into policy outputs by the party system. The decline in support for the Labour Party is explained partly as a product of changes in the social structure, such as the rise in home ownership, which gives rise to changes in objective needs, but also, in terms of the failure of the party to meet the objective and subjective needs of its supporters.

The general conclusion from Part I of this study is that the performance hypothesis is confirmed as a major factor in explaining all three crises facing the Labour Party. In the second part of this book we go on to examine the nature and origins of this policy failure in two key areas: economic policy and social security policy. This is done after examining Labour's policy objectives as they have evolved over the years since 1918, when the party published its first comprehensive statement of policy goals. Unlike the first part, the second section of the book is inherently evaluative, so that we examine whether policies succeeded or failed in relation to objectives, not merely what was actually done. This means that we make a number of normative judgements since it is impossible to evaluate policy without doing this. However, these judgements are not made in a vacuum but are set in the context of the empirical evidence of Labour's performance in economic and social security policy. Usually this involves examining performance in relation to pre-defined objectives, or in relation to the performance of the Conservatives.

In Chapter 5 we observe great continuities in the articulation of Labour's policy objectives over time. Key objectives like full employment and social insurance were first clearly set out in 1918 and have been retained in modified forms over the years. The party is much better at articulating broad objectives than it is about specifying the means to fulfil these objectives. This is seen most clearly in the case of economic policy. From 1918 onwards the party was committed to full employment, to the democratic control of industry, to minimum standards of living for all and to the stimulation of investment and growth. Before 1933 it lacked any coherent strategy for achieving these goals, and as a result the Labour governments of 1924 and 1929 were largely unsuccessful in achieving any of these objectives. The government of 1929 to 1931 was particularly disastrous in this regard.

The party first developed a coherent 'Keynesian' economic strategy in 1933 which was set out in *Socialism and the Condition of the People* (Labour Party, 1933). This presented the main features of an economic strategy of demand management which, with some exceptions, was successfully applied between 1945 and 1951. Unfortunately this Keynesian strategy contained the seeds of its own long term failure as we see in Chapter 6. The key problems of the Keynesian approach were twofold. Firstly, it routinely ignored the long term consequences of short term stabilization policies, and ultimately as time went on these policies became increasingly self-defeating. Secondly, it ignored the problems of technological innovation and industrial policy or as they later became known 'supply side' questions, and focused solely on demand management. Largely because of these weaknesses, and because Keynes' theories tended to be misinterpreted and misapplied by his followers, it became increasingly apparent by the late 1950s that demand management was inadequate. The Labour Party recognized this and included a radical set of proposals in the 1964 Manifesto for a national plan designed to promote investment and growth. These plans were not, however, properly worked out with regard to their implementation and they were quickly abandoned in favour of orthodox fiscal conservatism as a means of dealing with inflation. Ultimately all the economic objectives of this government were abandoned in favour of the single overriding aim of maintaining the dollar parity of the pound, and even this had to be abandoned in 1967. The Labour government of 1974 to 1979 followed a similar pattern. It fought the election on a radical interventionist programme, which was more comprehensive than the proposals made in 1964; but it rapidly abandoned these proposals within months of taking office.

In evaluating Labour's economic record it is possible to point to specific decisions, such as the failure to devalue before 1967 and the acceptance of a quasi-monetarist strategy after 1976, which in retrospect were mistakes. But ultimately the failure was one of a confused and inconsistent economic strategy which represented no alternative to financial orthodoxy which was one of the primary causes of the problems in the first place.

In the case of social security policy, the key instrument of anti-poverty policy, there is again a process of ambitious plans being made in opposition and being modified or abandoned in office. This was particularly true of the Wilson government of 1964 to 1970. In some areas, notably unemployment insurance, Labour did much better than the Conservatives, although in others, notably family support, it did worse. But overall in terms of the ultimate objective of abolishing poverty and providing universal benefits at adequate levels in accordance with the Beveridge principles, Labour clearly failed. It did little to prevent the secular trend increase in the numbers of people dependent on means-tested benefits, something directly contrary to the principles of the Beveridge Report (HMSO, 1942), implemented by Labour between 1945 and 1948. It allowed tax thresholds to fall to lower and lower levels, so that by the late 1970s individuals with incomes well below the poverty line were paying income tax. At the same time it reduced corporate taxation and left the burgeoning system of tax allowances (which disproportionately benefited the affluent) largely untouched. By the end of the 1970s large tax transfers were being made to industry and to the affluent, and a significant amount of this was being paid for by the poor. Finally, it failed to ensure that benefits were adequate in relation to means, so that as time went on increasing numbers of people were dependent on means-tested benefits, and pensioners in particular became increasingly reliant on a variety of exceptional needs payments made at the discretion of officials.

Overall our evaluation of the record in economic and social security policy is that objectives were often clear but that the means of implementation were badly thought out or ignored, so that plans worked out in opposition were often abandoned in office. In the case of economic policy, which is the centrepiece of any government's strategy, no workable alternative strategy which the leadership in power intended to implement was developed to fill the vacuum created by the demise of Keynesianism in the early 1970s. The industrial strategy worked out in *Labour's Programme for Britain, 1973* (Labour Party, 1973), and included in the 1974 Manifesto, was abandoned so quickly in office that one can only conclude that the Wilson government never intended to implement it in the first place. These events, which are discussed in more detail in Part II, laid the basis for the problems discussed in Part I; policy failure preceded and produced the political crises.

We conclude in Chapter 8 on a cautiously optimistic note. The party has evolved the elements of an alternative economic strategy set out in *Labour's Programme 1982* (Labour Party, 1982b), which give it the chance of breaking out of the long years of economic decline. The disaster of monetarism has opened up the political agenda for new approaches which present the party with a new opportunity. However, there are major flaws in this strategy as it stands, and these will have to be remedied if success is to be achieved. It may take a number of years for this strategy to evolve, so that it will create the possibility of turning round the economy and the fortunes of the party at the same time. In the meantime the party will have to work out the strategy in more detail, paying particular attention to questions of implementation, if it is not to repeat the same mistakes again in the future. Whether or not this will be done remains to be seen.

I
The political sociology
of the crisis

2

The ideological crisis

There have been ideological divisions in the Labour Party since its foundation as the Labour Representation Committee in 1900. This committee was an amalgamation of four different organizations; three of them were socialist societies and the fourth was the trade union movement (Pelling, 1965). They were united in the common aim of increasing working-class representation in Parliament, and in certain political aims such as the establishment of legal immunities for trade unions, but they were also very divided about the best strategy in representing the interests of the working class, and also about the nature and even desirability of socialism.

The three socialist societies were the Marxist Social Democratic Federation, the Fabian Society and the Independent Labour Party. These groups differed widely in their analysis of capitalism and in their aims with regard to socialism. The Social Democratic Federation had been established by Hyndeman in 1881; its ideas had been greatly influenced by Marx and Engels and essentially it advocated revolution. The Fabian Society explicitly rejected the revolutionary road. The most influential Fabians of that period were, of course, Beatrice and Sidney Webb and George Bernard Shaw. Thirdly, there was the Independent Labour Party founded by Keir Hardie, working class in its social composition and utopian socialist in its outlook. Each of these groups brought their own distinctive view of the Labour Party and the strategy for building socialism (Bealey, 1970).

The strands of thought represented by these various different groups in the Labour Representation Committee are still present in the party today. There are revolutionaries, evolutionaries and for that matter non-socialists in the party, and faction fighting between these groups is nothing new. At the same time, the split with the Social Democrats and the major constitutional upheavals discussed in Chapter 1 indicate that the level of ideological conflict in the party in recent years has been greater than any time since the war, including the period of the Bevanite split in the 1950s.

The purpose of this chapter is to examine the causes of the ideological crisis in the Labour Party at the present time. This will not be done by an historical analysis of the main phases of the constitutional struggle, which has been done elsewhere (Coates, 1975; Howell, 1976; Kogan and Kogan, 1982) but by looking at the attitudes and beliefs of participants in the Labour Party at all levels from voters to Members of Parliament. We shall examine three broad questions. Firstly, what is the scope of the ideological divisions within the party? Do they concern only the Labour elite, or are they a division between voters and the elite, as well as a division within the elite? Secondly, we shall examine the nature of the ideological division, analysing which issues are salient and which are not. Finally, we shall give an account of the causes of the present ideological divisions in terms of the experience of Labour in office since 1964.

Discussion of socialist ideology, like ideology in general, is plagued by the vague and imprecise meaning of the concept of ideology. Thus it is necessary to attempt to clarify the concept before discussing it further.

The meaning of ideology

Ideology is a key concept in politics and it has attracted the attention of many writers. It is however an elusive and confusing concept. Ideology has been defined as a 'rigid and doctrinaire set of ideas' (Adorno *et al.*, 1964); a distorted set of ideas related to the social status of the individual (Mannheim, 1936); to any ideas of a moral or ethical nature held by an individual or group (Lane, 1962); to a pattern of beliefs organized to simplify and direct political choices (Gould and Kolb, 1962); and to a particular way of understanding political events, in terms of general principles (Putnam, 1973).

These examples merely illustrate the great variety of meanings which have been attached to the concept by different writers. Putnam (1971, p. 655) facetiously invites the reader to construct his own definition of ideology by choosing at random a combination of concepts from a list associated with ideology. Obviously any discussion of democratic socialist ideology has to begin by clarifying the meaning of the concept in the context of contemporary Labour Party politics. We shall do this by focusing on one approach to the analysis of political ideology which has been particularly influential in political science. This is Converse's notion of ideology (1964).

For Converse an ideology is a set of beliefs which cover a wide variety of issues, and which are functionally interrelated, or in his terminology 'constrained'. Converse defines constraint as follows: '"Constraint" may be taken to mean the success we would have in predicting, given initial knowledge that an individual holds a specified attitude, that he holds certain further ideas and attitudes' (p. 207).

If a set of attitudes is highly interrelated, so that one belief can be predicted from another, then those attitudes constitute an ideology. Converse was particularly interested in comparing the attitudes of elite political actors with those of the mass public, in order to assess the scope of ideological constraint in the American electorate. With evidence from voting surveys he showed that attitude constraint in the mass public in the US was rather low, and thus it was difficult to predict the attitudes of the average voter from knowledge of some of his or her attitudes. From this he argued that political ideology is purely an elite phenomenon. As we shall see below, this finding is relevant for the understanding of ideological divisions within the Labour Party.

Converse focused primarily on the cognitive and perceptual aspects of ideology; or the way in which individuals perceive the world. However, ideology has an affective as well as a cognitive dimension (Merelman, 1969); that is it influences how individuals feel about the world, and the moral positions they take up on issues. Accordingly, since ideology has both cognitive and affective components, we shall define it as an 'interrelated or constrained set of attitudes which constitute a cognitive and an affective system'.

At some time everyone makes moral judgements about the political world, but the ideologue is distinguished from other people by the scope and range of his or her beliefs and the structuring of their component attitudes. If ideas are structured this implies that they are arranged in some sort of hierarchy from the general to the specific. The link between general principles and specific attitudes need not be a neat deductive chain, and not all attitudes are necessarily incorporated into the structure, but in general the ideologue can be distinguished from the non-ideologue by the extent to which his political attitudes are structured and constrained.

The structure of his attitudes enables the ideologue to evaluate political events in terms of an overall world view, and he can 'explain' the links between political events which would seem unrelated or inexplicable to the non-ideologue. He can develop a 'predictive' theory of politics which accounts for the causes of certain political events. It also seems likely that the ideologue would have greater knowledge than the non-ideologue, who may often be very ignorant of political events. The ideologue is much more likely to be consistent than the non-ideologue, because the general principles which underline his beliefs tend to root out inconsistencies. The non-ideologue may be quite capable of believing inconsistent propositions to be true, because there is no strain produced in his attitudes derived from a set of underlying propositions. It also seems likely that the ideologue is much more likely to be a political activist than the non-ideologue, his or her level of interest is likely to be higher and this makes for involvement.

Essentially the ideologue has an underlying 'theory' of the political system, about who gets what, why and how. Of course the validity or objective accuracy of this theory in terms of the external world is a separate and distinct question; the theory may be wholly mistaken. But he will be able to 'explain' political phenomena to his own satisfaction in a way in which the non-ideologue cannot.

We can see that a number of things follow from this conception of ideology. One of the most important points, however, is that our conception of ideology is testable, so that we can examine the attitudes and opinions of Labour Party supporters and activists to see whether or not such ideological structuring exists. We need to examine this question at all levels of the party.

The scope of ideological structuring in the party

Ideology and Labour voters

To consider Labour voters first, we have seen that Converse argued that no significant ideological constraint exists at the level of the mass public. This argument is supported in the case of the British electorate by Butler and Stokes (1974, pp. 316–37) who showed that only 25 per cent of the electorate think in left–right terms about party politics, and even the ones who do think in these terms do not have highly constrained attitudes. Their most telling evidence about mass attitudes related to the low level of consistency in opinions over time. They used panel data to examine the stability of opinions about the issue of nationalization between 1963 and 1970. During this period only 43 per cent of respondents consistently supported or opposed nationalization in four successive interviews (Butler and Stokes, 1974, p. 281) and fully 26 per cent said they had no opinion on the subject, in at least one of the interviews.

However, further research with more sophisticated techniques has shown that attitude constraint may be rather higher in the electorate than Butler and Stokes thought, although even then it is relatively modest. For example, Alt (1979, pp. 249–62), using cross sectional survey data from 1974, found three separate attitude dimensions underlying the opinions of the electorate on a variety of political issues. He called these 'socio-economic radicalism' which included issues like attitudes to comprehensive education, the redistribution of wealth and spending on poverty; 'permissiveness' which included attitudes to abortion, nudity and sex in the media, and curbing communism; and 'racial nationalism', which included issues like the repatriation of immigrants and the equality of black people. Crewe and Särlvik (1980) found rather similar dimensions or groupings of attitudes which they labelled 'left–right socio-economic', 'populist authoritarian' and 'racial'. Himmelweit *et al.* (1981, pp. 130–56) argued that attitudes to issues among voters in their panel sample were quite highly structured into what they describe as 'supra families' of issues. They found two clusters of issues, one relating to public owner-ship, attitudes to education, and rich–poor relations, and a second relating to law and order, and abuse of the Welfare State. However, their results relate to a highly select sample which is not at all representative of the electorate as a whole, so we cannot draw any significant conclusions from their research for voters in general.

None of these studies examine attitude constraint amongst Labour voters as a separate group, and so we need to examine this before making any inferences about the scope of ideological divisions within the party as a whole.

The British Election Study cross section survey of voters at the time of the 1979 General Election contains a large number of attitude indi-cators of political issues. Some are 'valence' issues (Butler and Stokes, 1974, p. 292) on which there is essentially a consensus of opinion about the goal or value. Thus everyone favours a policy of reducing inflation and unemployment, but they disagree about the means for achieving these goals or about the success of the different political parties in pursu-ing such policies. However, there are no ideological differences in the electorate about the goals themselves. This is not the case with 'position' issues such as attitudes to comprehensive education or welfare spending where there are wide differences of opinion over goals or values. For this reason we examine the attitude constraint in the electorate over position issues, but not valence issues. If we define position issues broadly there are no less than forty-one attitude indicators of this type in the British Election Study Survey of 1979; they cover everything from attitudes to public ownership, to comprehensive education, the redistribution of wealth, trade union power, abortion, immigration and many others. A number of different measurement scales were used to examine attitudes to these issues varying from 4 point to 7 point scales, each scale represent-ing an ordering or ordinal scale. To illustrate this respondents were asked their views on nationalization varying from 'a lot more industries should be nationalized', 'a few more industries', 'no more industries' to 'some nationalized industries should become private companies'.

Respondents were also asked 'Generally speaking, do you think of yourself as Conservative, Labour, Liberal or what?' Some 680 individuals or 37.5 per cent of the respondents to this question described themselves as Labour. We extracted this group and analysed their attitude structur-ing on the position issues in the survey.

To assess the level of attitude structuring we used a multivariate statistical technique known as factor analysis. This is described in detail for the interested reader in Appendix I, but the main idea behind it can be described easily. Factor analysis starts with a set of correlations[1] between issue indicators calculated for the sample of Labour identifiers (Harman, 1976). If Labour voters possess an attitude structure this means that they link together different issues in their minds, and so those issue indicators should be correlated with one another. Unfortunately, we cannot determine whether or not such a structure exists by examining a set of correlations between indicators, because correlations refer only to issues taken two at a time; we need to examine the simultaneous links between many issues taken altogether. This can be done by factor analysis. The analysis transforms the set of correlations so as to express them in terms of a few broad factors underlying the data. We then interpret these broad factors by looking at the correlations between them and the issue indicators. If there is structure or constraint in the data, the analysis should produce a few factors which demonstrate the relationship between different issues.

To give ourselves the best chance of finding an attitude structure for Labour voters, we did the analysis twice. The first analysis used all forty-one position issues. We then deleted those variables which appeared to be unrelated to the factors produced by the analysis, and then repeated the exercise for the remaining twenty-seven indicators.

The factor analysis of the twenty-seven position issues produced eight significant factors which altogether explained 53 per cent of the variance in the data (see Appendix I). This is a relatively modest percentage of variance explained for eight factors, which suggests that the attitude structuring is not high. However, we have expressed half of the 'information' in twenty-seven variables by means of eight new variables or factors, and this is quite a significant reduction. We can interpret the meaning of the extracted factors by examining the correlations between the factors and variables. This is done in Table 2.1 which includes all correlations between factors and variables which exceed ±0.30. The percentage of the total variance explained by each factor is also included in Table 2.1.

Factor 1, which explains most variance of any factor, is described as a 'nationalization, education and redistribution' factor because it is significantly related to all these issues. The pattern of correlations on this factor means that respondents who favour nationalization also tend to favour comprehensive education, the control of building land and the redistribution of wealth. The same respondents tend to disagree that teaching methods have gone too far. Clearly this factor provides evidence of a certain amount of interrelationship between different issues in the minds of Labour voters.

Factors 2 and 3 are essentially single issue factors concerned with immigration and race relations, and devolution respectively. Obviously the racial factor identified by Crewe, Särlvik and Alt (1977) also exists in the minds of Labour voters. An individual who believes that racial equality has gone too far is also likely to favour the repatriation of immigrants, and is likely to be against overseas aid.

Table 2.1 The factor analysis of the issue indicators for Labour identifiers in 1979

Factor	Correlation with factor	Variance explained
1 *Nationalization, education and redistribution*		
Attitude to nationalization	−0.37	
Teaching methods gone too far	0.62	
Comprehensive education should be established	−0.63	
Control of building land by government	−0.61	
Redistribution of wealth	−0.34	14.0
2 *Immigration and race relations*		
Race equality gone too far	0.62	
Too many immigrants have been let in	0.73	
Stop immigration to improve race relations	0.76	
Send immigrants back	0.74	
Give more overseas aid	−0.60	7.9
3 *Devolution*		
Attitude to a Scottish assembly	0.85	
Attitude to a Welsh assembly	0.88	
Attitude to regional assemblies	0.59	7.3
4 *Abortion, pornography and authority*		
Pornography has gone too far	0.75	
Challenging authority has gone too far	0.44	
Abortion has gone too far	0.68	
Military cuts have gone too far	0.32	5.6
5 *Trade unions*		
Trade unions have too much power	−0.71	
Trade unions do a good job for the country	0.70	
Government should set guidelines for incomes	−0.36	
Stricter laws for regulating unions are needed	−0.74	5.4
6 *Social welfare*		
Social benefits are needed	0.84	
Welfare benefits have not gone far enough	0.83	4.7
7 *Job creation, education and redistribution*		
Attitude to nationalization	−0.34	
Government should create jobs	0.47	
Teaching methods gone too far	−0.49	
Redistribution of wealth	−0.38	
Withdraw troops from Ulster	−0.35	
Reduce the power of the Lords	−0.58	4.3
8 *Pay differentials, authority and Ulster*		
Challenging authority gone too far	−0.35	
Military cuts gone too far	−0.39	
Withdraw troops from Ulster	0.55	
Increase differentials for skilled workers	−0.64	3.8

Source: British Election Study, University of Essex.

Factor 4 links the questions of abortion, pornography, attitudes to authority, and to a limited extent attitudes to military cuts. Apart from the last issue these are libertarian issues, and it is interesting to see that they are linked in the minds of Labour voters. Factor 5 is primarily about trade unions, but is also related to the issue of incomes policy. Respondents who favour government guidelines for incomes tend to support stricter laws for regulating unions. Factor 6 is concerned with social welfare and is a single issue factor. Factor 7 is rather similar to factor 1, except the correlations with the variables are rather weaker. Finally, factor 8 links the disparate issues of Ulster, military costs and pay differentials.

We can also investigate the correlations between factors to see the extent to which the issues are grouped into clusters of factors. However, these correlations turned out to be rather weak. The largest correlation was between factor 1 and factor 6 which was 0.18, followed by factor 1 and factor 7 at 0.17. It is clear that there are no 'superclusters' of issues which link together different factors.

Taken as a whole these results indicate a modest amount of attitude structuring with respect to a limited number of issues in the minds of Labour voters. They do link issues like nationalization, comprehensive education, and the redistribution of wealth. Issues like race relations and immigration also figure in their attitudes, although they are not significantly related to the other issues we have mentioned. However, the relationships are not strong enough or comprehensive enough to constitute an ideology. An ideologue who takes a strong line on an issue like, say, wealth redistribution is likely to be significantly influenced in his political behaviour if the party adopts a new policy on this issue. The relationships are not strong enough to suggest that this is true of voters.

We can conclude by inferring that the ideological crisis in the Labour Party does not directly touch on Labour voters to any significant extent. Undoubtedly faction fighting within the party at the elite level discourages Labour supporters but it does this because of the disunity it creates, not because voters strongly agree or disagree with one or other of the protagonists.

Ideology and party members

In discussing Labour Party members we have to distinguish between the ordinary grassroots party member and the local party activists, and the Labour elite of elected representatives and party notables. We shall discuss the numbers involved in these groups in Chapter 3, but for the moment we shall focus on the question of ideology and grassroots party members.

There are perhaps three broad points to be made about ideology and Labour Party members from existing studies. Firstly, the empirical evidence shows that the level of political knowledge amongst the grass-roots does not appear to be particularly high. Bealey *et al.* (1965) found this to be the case in a study of the Newcastle-under-Lyme constituency party. They questioned party members about controversial aspects of Labour policy and concluded that 'Just over a quarter of the Party can be considered to have sound political knowledge on this evidence' (p. 285).

In a study of the City Labour Party in Liverpool, Hindess (1971, pp. 70–1) examined policy discussions at the ward level. His methodology was unusual in that he did not ask questions of party members, arguing that this would involve imposing prior preconceptions on the analysis; instead he observed ward party meetings and analysed the topics dis-cussed. He found that local ward parties spent only about 30 per cent of the time at meetings discussing policy, as opposed to matters of organiz-ation and procedure. Moreover, out of the time spent discussing policy, working-class wards spent only 11 per cent on national issues, compared with 51 per cent in middle-class wards. If political knowledge and the time spent discussing national political issues are rough indicators of ideological sophistication, it does not appear to be very high, particularly in working-class wards.

It could be argued that time spent on policy discussions is a poor measure of ideological sophistication. But this evidence does accord with the second broad finding, which is that the level of consensus on policy among grassroots members is rather low. This inference is supported by findings from Donnison, Plowman, Birch and Berry. Donnison and Plow-man analysed party meetings in a Manchester constituency and con-cluded that: 'Analysis of opinions about four political issues gave no evidence that members support the "party line". The consensus was greater than due to chance, but not large enough to suggest a firm body of opinion within the party' (1954, p. 167). A related finding came from Berry's (1970) study of Walton constituency party. He obtained responses from grassroots Labour and Conservative Party members, to a set of six attitude indicators. From these he found a substantial degree of agree-ment between grassroots Conservatives and Labour Party members. This hardly suggests the existence of a distinct socialist ideology at the grass-roots level. Birch (1959) obtained similar findings in his study of Glossop. He compared the opinions of Labour, Conservative and Liberal Party members on six political issues including the sale of council houses, rais-ing of the school leaving age and nationalization. There were some differ-ences between the parties, but only in the case of nationalization did a majority of Labour Party members oppose a majority of Conservatives, and even then only on four out of ten possible candidate industries.

A third broad finding consistent with these others concerns the political opinions of party activists as expressed in resolutions to party conference. It has often been argued that the Labour Party Conference is 'extreme' compared with the parliamentary party, and Labour voters. Rose (1962) examined conference resolutions over a six year period and found that some 46 per cent of resolutions were essentially non-partisan, only 17 per cent of resolutions in Rose's sample were both left-wing and controversial in the party.

Taken together these results seem to indicate that grassroots party members as a whole are not strong ideologues. Of course there are ideologues in the ranks of the party members and activists, but they probably constitute only a relatively small minority. There are of course differences between activists and ordinary members; simply being a party member might not even guarantee that an individual will vote in an election. Activists are likely to be different because their political involvement implies a degree of socialization into the attitudes, beliefs and the ethos of the Labour Party (Drucker, 1979). But even this can be exaggerated since an activist could be someone who attends the occasional meeting and perhaps helps out a bit at election time. This hardly constitutes a very extensive political socialization.

There is no survey evidence on party members throughout the country as a whole available to examine this question of ideological structuring. As a second-best substitute for such evidence we can select those respondents from the British election study who described themselves as 'very strong' Labour identifiers. If this is done and the factor analysis repeated, then no significant differences appear to exist between this group and Labour voters as a whole. Their attitudes do not appear to be more highly structured than voters, nor do they appear to be more left-wing in their responses. From this evidence we can argue that Labour members taken as a whole are very similar to Labour voters in their ideological characteristics. Clearly we are more likely to find evidence of ideological structuring amongst the Labour elite, so we turn to them next.

Ideology and the Labour elite

The definition of the Labour elite is to some degree arbitrary, but we shall take it to mean elected representatives at the parliamentary or local level and party notables such as parliamentary candidates and constituency party officers. There are a number of studies which have been carried out at this level which are relevant to the present discussion; they may be conveniently divided into studies which have used survey methods, and those which have used other methods.

To focus specifically on the question of analysing ideology the survey based studies have one major defect in common: they do not use sufficient attitudinal indicators to measure adequately the range of issues encompassed by democratic socialism. Thus it is not possible to infer any overall ideological structure from the attitude data used. This is true of

Janosik (1968), Kornberg and Frasure (1971) and Putnam (1971, 1973). For example, Janosik in his study of MPs, parliamentary candidates, constituency chairmen, secretary-agents and conference delegates uses five issues to explore political attitudes: membership of the EEC, defence policy, the Cuba crisis of 1962, the Sino–Indian border war of 1962 and the comparative status of the United States and Soviet Union. Kornberg and Frasure in their study of backbench Members of Parliament used ten issues altogether in an attempt to measure differences between the parties, as well as differences within the parties in the House of Commons. Only five issues significantly discriminated between Labour and Conservative backbenchers; they were comprehensive education, prices and incomes policy, trade union reform, Rhodesia and defence east of Suez. It may be argued that some of these issues are related to socialist ideology but there are clearly not enough indicators to measure any overall ideological structure.

Putnam (1971, 1973) compared backbench MPs with Italian deputies, using an open-ended interview approach. He was not so much concerned with the characteristics of a particular ideology, but whether or not politicians perceive politics in terms of general principles or in terms of specific cases. He argues, 'it is not the what, but the how of political thought which makes it ideological' (1971, p. 657). Thus he does not really attempt to map out the content of ideology so much as to investigate the political styles of elected representatives. His approach, though interesting, faces the problem that ideology need not be articulated in general principles for it to be potent and important to the individual.

One of the most fruitful lines of research into the political attitudes of the Labour elite does not use a survey approach at all, but uses Early Day Motions signed by backbench MPs (Finer *et al.*, 1961; Berrington, 1973; Berrington and Leece, 1977). Early Day Motions are resolutions tabled by backbench MPs to express their views about topical issues, without interference from the Front Bench or the Whips. In the two volumes Berrington and his associates examined the attitudes of Labour MPs between 1945 and 1958 over a wide variety of issues. On the basis of their analysis the authors concluded:

> There are then, some basic attitudes which, in some degree or other must be held simultaneously to constitute British Socialism; pacifism, anti-colonialism, humanitarianism, zeal for the welfare services, libertarianism, a belief in the need for public enterprise and the control of the economy; and a desire for social equality. These held concurrently, make up Socialism.
> (Finer *et al.*, 1961, pp. 49–50)

Apart from egalitarianism and public ownership the Early Day Motions provided information on all these issue areas. From the point of view of measuring socialist ideology this approach is one of the most sophisticated yet. However, it does face certain problems; Early Day Motions have been criticized because of the fortuitous way in which signatures are often obtained. Fellowes (1961–2) cited a report in *The Times* that only 26 Labour MPs supported a motion at a meeting of the Parliamentary Labour Party, when 54 had signed an EDM on the same issue. Moreover, there is the problem that the attitudes measured by an EDM are all in favour of the motion, and we have no measures of the numbers of MPs who are against that motion. This makes the data rather skewed in terms of measuring attitudes.

We shall investigate the ideological variations within the Labour elite using data from a series of surveys carried out by the author and others between 1975 and 1978. These surveys provided information about the backgrounds, political experiences and attitudes of a cross section of the Labour elite including Members of Parliament, parliamentary candidates, councillors and party conference delegates. The details of these samples are given in Appendix II. Some of the results of analysis from these data have already been published (Gordon and Whiteley, 1977, 1979; Whiteley, 1978, 1980; Whiteley and Gordon, 1980), but the data have not been analysed as a whole. Altogether there are 554 respondents in our survey consisting of 51 MPs, 160 parliamentary candidates, 89 councillors and 254 conference delegates.

To measure ideological structuring we use 25 Likert scaled[2] statements relating to all the major controversial political issues within the Labour Party. The statements were derived from a literature search of party conference documents, pamphlets and publications of affiliated organizations over a ten year period. The statements were phrased so as to emulate the style of the original resolution or document from which they were taken. This is because many of the controversies within the party are matters of recurring dispute. After a period the language and phraseology of participants take on the catalytic character of a slogan, i.e. they provoke a series of ideas and associations either for or against depending on the respondent.

There has been some discussion in the psychological literature on the processes which occur when individuals respond to attitudinal indicators of this type. Wilson (1973, p. 49) has argued that responses can be analysed into two sequential stages. Firstly, there is an immediate emotional response to the central idea expressed in the statement which is followed, secondly, by qualifications and justifications while the details of the statement are examined. The Likert scale technique is designed to elicit the first of these, since it is the emotional content which gives the attitude its significance.

The responses of the pooled sample of MPs, candidates, councillors and delegates to the attitude indicators appear in Table 2.2. The

Table 2.2 Responses of pooled sample to attitudinal indicators, percentages (N = 554)

Attitude indicators	Strongly agree	Agree	Neither	Disagree	Strongly disagree
1 Central question of British politics is the class struggle between labour and capital	38.9	33.1	14.0	11.7	2.2
2 The Labour Party should adjust its policies to capture the middle ground	10.2	24.0	12.2	35.1	18.5
3 Moderates in the Labour Party should speak out against extremism	17.6	23.3	24.1	21.3	13.7
4 Labour should nationalize profitable industries when it is in power	51.3	31.5	10.1	5.7	1.3
5 The implementation of Clause 4 should be the central concern of a Labour government	34.5	27.8	14.8	16.3	6.5
6 Labour should condemn political activists and councillors who break the law	21.6	26.2	20.1	22.1	10.0
7 Labour is often concerned with ameliorating inequality rather than attacking the causes	35.1	49.9	7.6	6.7	0.7
8 A Labour government should not interfere with free collective bargaining	19.4	23.3	11.6	36.6	9.1
9 A Labour government should establish an incomes policy backed by law	8.9	24.0	11.2	34.5	21.4
10 The Labour Party should withdraw Britain from the Common Market	33.3	19.5	11.0	23.0	13.2
11 Labour should boycott the European Parliament	20.7	20.2	6.9	29.8	22.2
12 The parliamentary party must accept conference decisions as party policy	30.6	21.5	10.2	30.6	7.0
13 Public industries hived off by the Tories should be nationalized without compensation	46.8	31.4	7.9	12.4	1.5
14 The trade union movement has too much power over a Labour government	4.2	16.3	11.4	44.4	23.7
15 Labour should take over the freeholds of all land, making it leasehold land	36.0	34.0	9.6	15.5	4.8
16 A Labour government should support liberation movements in Africa	34.8	40.9	14.2	8.4	1.7
17 The Labour Party should give unequivocal support to Israel	4.5	9.9	21.2	36.8	27.7
18 A Labour government should withdraw from NATO and similar alliances	18.5	19.6	14.8	36.6	10.5
19 Britain should retain possession of thermonuclear weapons	4.8	20.6	12.1	30.1	32.3
20 A Labour government should abolish private education entirely	56.9	27.5	5.5	8.6	1.5
21 Britain should reduce military spending substantially	41.6	27.7	13.1	13.7	3.9
22 It is desirable to retain private health care	5.7	12.2	6.6	28.4	47.1
23 A Labour government should nationalize Rolls-Royce without compensation	27.7	28.8	20.3	20.5	2.7
24 In the long run it would be a good thing to abolish the Monarchy	23.4	28.8	22.9	19.9	5.0
25 There are not enough working-class MPs in the parliamentary party	28.3	35.4	20.6	14.4	1.3

distribution of opinions along the five point Likert scale differs markedly between the indicators. On some there is a high level of consensus, with a large majority of respondents agreeing or disagreeing with the statement. On other indicators there is no consensus at all. To clarify this point we can describe those items having 75 per cent of the respondents agreeing or disagreeing as 'high consensus' items; those having 60 to 74 per cent in this as 'moderate consensus'; those having 50 to 59 per cent as 'low consensus'; and finally, those with less than 50 per cent as 'no consensus' items.

If we examine the high consensus items first, there are seven indicators which fall into this category. They are items 4, 7, 13, 16, 20, 22 and 25. No less than four of these (4, 13, 20 and 22) are concerned with the relationship between the state and private sectors of the economy, i.e. public ownership, private education and health care. There is strong agreement within the sample that the public sector should be extended at the expense of the private sector in these areas.

If we examine the 'moderate consensus' items there are seven indicators which fall into this category (1, 5, 14, 15, 17, 19 and 21). Two of these are concerned with Labour's broad strategic approach to politics (1 and 5), three are concerned with foreign and defence policy questions (17, 19 and 21), one is a general comment on the relationship between the party and the trade unions (14) and the other remaining indicator is concerned specifically with policy (15).

In the low consensus group again there are seven items (2, 9, 10, 11, 12, 23 and 24) which make up a fairly heterogeneous group of issues. They are concerned with broad questions of philosophy (2, 12), specific questions of domestic and foreign policy (9, 10, 11, 23), and an indicator about long run attitudes to the monarchy (24).

Finally, there are four no consensus items (3, 6, 8, 18). These are highly radical policy proposals such as withdrawal from NATO or extremely sensitive political questions like interference in collective bargaining (8) or condemning activists and elected representatives who might break the law (6) and condemning extremism (3).

In order to examine the attitude structuring which underlies these indicators we use factor analysis, as in the case of voters. The results of this appear in Table 2.3 which includes the correlations between factors and indicators, and the percentage variance explained by each factor. There were five significant factors extracted which altogether explained 54 per cent of the variance in the data. Clearly the level of attitude structuring in these data is much greater than it is for voters. It will be recalled that in the case of voters the analysis reduced twenty-seven variables down to the eight factors, whereas this reduces twenty-five variables down to five factors. Perhaps more importantly though, there are many more separate issue indicators related to the individual factors. The first factor is the most general in this respect and is dubbed 'Socialism versus Social Democracy' because it includes most of the issues which distinguish democratic socialists from social democrats. These are questions of political strategy such as 'capturing the middle ground' and 'condemning extremists' and 'condemning political activities against the law'; but they are also particular policy questions, such as withdrawal from the EEC and from NATO and retaining nuclear weapons. All these issues group together so that individuals who favour unilateral nuclear disarmament tend to favour withdrawal from NATO and reduced military spending; they also disagree that Labour should seek the middle ground of politics, should support Israel and should speak against extremism.

In addition to factor 1, there are two more or less single issue factors, namely factor 3 which relates to the Common Market and factor 4 which relates to attitudes to trade unions. Factors 2 and 5 are both concerned with nationalization, but both linking it with other issues. Factor 2 contains rather specific proposals for the nationalization of land, Rolls-Royce, and industries which have been hived off by the Conservatives. Factor 5 contains more general proposals such as nationalizing profitable industries, implementing Clause 4 of the party constitution and the abolition or retention of private health care.

If we examine the correlations between factors there is quite strong evidence of attitude constraint. The highest correlation between factor 1 and factor 5 is 0.69; factor 1 which is a general 'left–right' factor is relatively highly correlated with all the other factors except factor 3 (Common Market) and since the Common Market already figures in factor 1, this suggests that the issue is an integral part of the attitude structure in any case. Clearly these issues can be grouped together into a supercluster of issues. In the light of these results it seems likely that all twenty-five issues could be combined into an overall left–right dimension which can summarize all the indicators by a single factor.

To investigate whether or not a single left–right dimension underlies the data we carried out a principal components analysis, which is a type of factor analysis in which the first factor or principal component explains the maximum amount of variance possible in the data, the second principal component explains the maximum amount of variance not explained by the first component, and so on. Principal components analysis provides an ideal measure of the extent to which a single dimension underlies the data. The results of this analysis appear in Table 2.4, which contains the correlations between the variables and the first principal component together with the variance explained in each variable by this component. Without exception all variables are correlated with the first principal component with a coefficient greater than ±0.30, which entitles us to describe it as a left–right ideology continuum. Indicators of a left-wing orientation are positively correlated with it, and indicators of a

Table 2.3 The factor analysis for the Labour elite, and correlations between factors

Factor	Correlation with factor	Variance explained
1 *Socialism versus social democracy*		
Adjust policies to capture middle ground of politics	−0.86	
Moderates speak against extremism	−0.72	
Condemn political activities against the law	−0.75	
Withdraw from the Common Market	0.48	
Support Israel	−0.57	
Withdraw from NATO	0.81	
Retain nuclear weapons	−0.95	
Reduce military spending	0.50	29.8
2 *Nationalization and conference sovereignty*		
No interference in free collective bargaining	0.49	
The parliamentary party must accept conference decisions	0.52	
Renationalize hived-off industry without compensation	0.73	
Take over the freeholds of all land	0.85	
Nationalize Rolls-Royce without compensation	0.65	8.5
3 *Common Market*		
Withdraw from the Common Market	−0.58	
Boycott the European Parliament	−0.60	
Abolish private education	0.53	6.6
4 *Trade unions*		
No interference in free collective bargaining	−0.59	
Incomes policy backed by law	0.78	
The trade union movement has too much power	0.71	4.7
5 *Nationalization and perceptions of class*		
Central questions of politics in class struggle	0.77	
Nationalize profitable industries	0.86	
Implement Clause 4 of the party constitution	0.68	
Labour ameliorates rather than attacks on inequality	0.76	
Retain private health care	−0.47	4.2

Correlation between factors

	1	2	3	4	5
1	1.0				
2	0.43	1.0			
3	0.14	−0.10	1.0		
4	−0.42	−0.33	0.12	1.0	
5	0.69	0.57	−0.05	−0.44	1.0

right-wing orientation negatively correlated. Thus respondents who tend to agree that 'the central question of British politics is the class struggle', also tend to agree that the 'Parliamentary Labour Party should accept conference decisions', and they tend to disagree that 'Labour should capture the middle ground' and 'moderates should speak against extremism'. Moreover, the highest correlations in Table 2.4 are with variables that are central to the present ideological disputes in the party, such as condemning extremism (e.g. the Militant Tendency), withdrawing from the Common Market, conference sovereignty and nationalization. The

Table 2.4 The relationship between attitudinal indicators and the first principal component

Indicator	*Correlation with principal component*	*Variance explained by first principal component*
1 Central question of politics is class	0.63	0.40
2 Adjust policies to capture middle ground	−0.65	0.42
3 Moderates speak against extremism	−0.72	0.51
4 Nationalize profitable industry	0.62	0.38
5 Implement Clause 4 in office	0.52	0.28
6 Condemn political activities against law	−0.63	0.39
7 Labour ameliorates not attacks inequality	0.40	0.16
8 No interference in collective bargaining	0.32	0.10
9 Establish legally backed incomes policy	−0.51	0.26
10 Withdraw from Common Market	0.60	0.36
11 Boycott the European Parliament	0.55	0.30
12 PLP should accept conference decisions	0.65	0.42
13 Renationalize hived-off industry	0.54	0.29
14 Trade unions have too much power	−0.40	0.16
15 Labour should take over freeholds	0.40	0.16
16 Support African liberation movements	0.53	0.28
17 Give unequivocal support to Israel	−0.31	0.10
18 Withdraw from NATO	0.70	0.49
19 Retain thermonuclear weapons	−0.51	0.26
20 Abolish private education	0.49	0.24
21 Reduce military spending substantially	0.60	0.36
22 Retain private health care	−0.43	0.19
23 Nationalize Rolls-Royce	0.61	0.38
24 Abolish the monarchy in the long run	0.56	0.32
25 Not enough working-class MPs	0.47	0.22

% total variance explained by first component = 29.8
% common variance explained by first component = 55.5

larger the correlation between the indicator and the left–right dimension, the more central that indicator is to the present ideological divisions within the party, and the more variance explained in the variable by the left–right dimension.

We can utilize the left–right dimension to calculate ideology scores for each of the respondents in the pooled sample. This can be done by weighting each respondent's reply to a particular indicator by the correlation of that indicator with the left–right dimension and then aggregating these scores for each of the twenty-five indicators. In other words we weight each respondent's answer to the individual indicators by the importance of that indicator in the overall left–right dimension. The resulting scores when rounded to the nearest integer vary from –12, the far left to +30, the far right. The distribution of respondents along the left–right continuum appears in Figure 2.1. This distribution has a mean score of 7.3 and a standard deviation of 8.9. If we define the 'Left' as those respondents with a score less than –1.6, i.e. one standard deviation below the mean there are 19.1 per cent of the total sample in this group. If we define the 'Right' as those respondents with a score greater than +16.2,

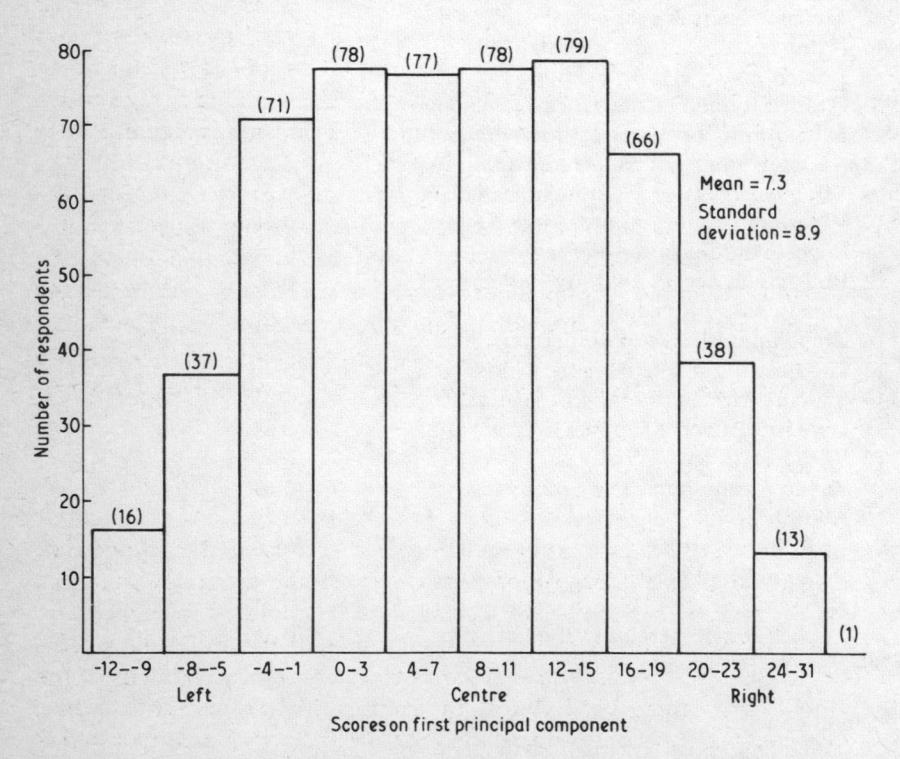

Figure 2.1   Distribution of respondents along the left–right ideology scale

i.e. one standard deviation above the mean there are 17.7 per cent of the total sample in this group. Thus the overall distribution is skewed slightly to the Left. Apart from this the distribution is almost a bell-shaped 'normal' distribution, which in a way is a good thing for the Labour Party, since 65 per cent of respondents are within one standard deviation either side of the mean.[3] Although large ideological differences exist in the party there are no distinct groupings which are clearly separate from the rest of the sample. If for example the distribution contained two modes, one far to the Left of the other, it would imply a much greater potentiality for a split in the party than is true with the distribution in Figure 2.1.

We have examined the pattern of ideological variation within the Labour elite; we now turn to the question of explaining the sources of such variations and relating this to the ideological crisis.

The sources of ideological variations

We shall look for the sources of ideological variation in the elite samples in terms of three broad classes of factors. Firstly, there are social background characteristics such as education, occupational status, age, sex and so on. These are relatively permanent attributes of an individual and as such might be expected to influence his or her attitudes. Secondly, there is the political experience of the individual, and in particular his or her current political status; again if an individual is a young party conference delegate it seems likely that he will have a different set of attitudes than an individual who is a middle-aged Member of Parliament, simply as a result of a different experience of politics. Finally, there is the ideological coherence of the individual; our factor analysis tells us that a significant level of attitude structuring exists in the sample as a whole, but it does not identify the degree of structuring or ideological coherence for particular individuals. It seems plausible that individuals who are highly coherent or consistent in their beliefs will differ from individuals who are less coherent, in terms of the left–right dimension, and we shall investigate this possibility.

Social background

To consider social background characteristics first, it can be argued that because ideology is a fairly fundamental part of an individual's personality when he or she is politically active, then it should be influenced by all the major social background characteristics of the individual. This would include factors like the social and economic circumstances of the individual when they were young, their educational experiences, their occupational status, age, sex and so on. There is, however, a danger in this argument of a crude social determinism; ideology is very much an intellectual phenomenon developed over many years and it is influenced by many individual experiences not captured by the categorization of individuals into various social groups. It is not social background but political consciousness which determines whether or not one is a Socialist. For this reason we are unlikely to see any neat one-to-one relationship between a particular social attribute and ideological radicalism. However, it is important to investigate the links between social background characteristics and ideology.

We can use the left–right ideology score derived earlier to examine the influence of social background characteristics on ideology. We investigated the relationship between many such characteristics including educational experience, social class, age, sex and income. Many interesting relationships appear if one compares a given social attribute with ideology without controlling for the influence of other attributes. For example, there is a statistically significant correlation between the type of school attended and a respondent's ideology score; ex-comprehensive schools pupils appeared to be more left-wing than ex-grammar school pupils. However, this tantalizing result promptly disappeared when we controlled for current occupational status. In other words the apparent bivariate link between education and ideology is really measuring something else, i.e. occupational status. This is of course a general problem with all types of bivariate analysis where significant relationships can disappear when proper controls are introduced. For this reason we must use another multivariate technique known as multiple regression analysis. This is discussed in detail in Appendix I, but the basic idea is easy to grasp. Essentially multiple regression analysis enables us to calculate the extent to which one variable can be used to predict the behaviour of another, controlling for the influence of a third, fourth or more variables. Thus we can investigate the relationship between, say, occupational status and ideology controlling for age, sex, education and so on. Such an approach is essential if we are to get a true picture of the influences of social background on ideology.

After an extensive multivariate analysis of the relationship between social background and ideology only two relatively robust and statistically significant relationships were found. Firstly, there was a significant relationship between ideology and age; younger respondents were more left-wing than older respondents. Secondly, there was a significant relationship between ideology and occupational status, with working-class respondents being more left-wing than middle-class respondents. However, both relationships were rather weak, especially the latter; the correlation between ideology and age was +0.25 and between ideology and occupational status +0.15, which indicates that social background characteristics are very poor predictors of ideological variations.

The relationship between ideology and age appeared in our earlier analysis of the samples of MPs and parliamentary candidates (Whiteley, 1978). In this analysis we argued that if ideology was influenced both by contemporary events and events in the earlier life of the individual then we might expect to see a relationship between ideology and age. There is evidence to suggest that individuals acquire their basic political orientations at an early age, and these orientations tend to persist over time (Greenstein, 1968; Weissberg, 1974; Searing, Wright and Rabinowitz 1976). The older respondents in our sample will have acquired their first political experiences in circumstances very different from the younger respondents. Those whose first political experiences date from the 1930s would have acquired them at a time of political defeat and demoralization for the Labour Party. On the other hand individuals who acquired their first experiences in the postwar years, particularly 1945–50, were in a very different era. This was a time of radical political change and electoral success for the Labour Party. This period has been referred to as Labour's 'golden age' (Forrester, 1976). Even respondents whose first political memories go back only to the 1950s and early 1960s were in a period of comparative optimism for the future of the Labour Party, when things were much better than in the 1930s. We have to be very careful about making inferences about contemporary attitudes from early political experiences (Marsh, 1971) but it seems plausible that the individual's general outlook on politics can be influenced by the political environment of their youth.

Ideology is also influenced by current events, and the experiences of the Labour governments of 1964–70 and 1974–9 are likely to have influenced the attitudes of Labour activists. The performance of these governments have given rise to widespread disillusionment and discontent within the party (Coates, 1979, 1980; Bosanquet and Townsend, 1980; Holland, 1975). After the defeat of 1970 a determination grew within the party to steer a subsequent Labour government in the direction of more socialist policies as we have seen in Chapter 1. A similar thing happened again after the General Election of 1979. Unlike the 1930s when the party was massively defeated at the polls as well as being betrayed by its leadership, the experience of the 1960s and 1970s was for many activists one of lost opportunities and wasted hopes. This tended to radicalize rather than demoralize.

Thus both early political experiences and contemporary political events can be used to explain why the young are more radical than the old. The defeats of the 1930s engendered a cautious attitude to policy in the face of the overwhelming conservative hegemony of those years; whereas the successes of 1945–50 and the promise of future success in the 1950s and 1960s engendered a more radical perspective.

On the relationship between ideology and occupational status there has been something of a controversy in the literature over differences between middle-class and working-class activists in the party (Hindess, 1971; Beackon, 1976; Forrester, 1976). An earlier analysis of the councillors sample revealed no significant differences between ideological radicalism and occupational status (Gordon and Whiteley, 1979). However, this sample was rather small. It is evident that there is such a relationship in the pooled sample as a whole, albeit a weak relationship. To investigate this further we coded the ideology scale into four categories, and cross-tabulated the scale with occupational status measured by the Registrar General's scale. The results appear in Table 2.5.

The strength of the relationship between ideology and occupational status can be seen in the first column of Table 2.5. Some 16 per cent of the professional and higher management group are in the left-wing category, compared with 22 per cent of this group in the overall sample; some 6.2 per cent of skilled manual workers are in the left-wing group compared with 2.6 per cent in the sample overall. The relationship is rather weak, but statistically significant.

Table 2.5 Occupational status by ideology for the pooled sample (for each category the score and percentage are recorded)

	Recoded ideology scale				
	Left (−12 to 0)	Centre-Left (1 to 9)	Centre-Right (10 to 19)	Right (20 to 30)	Marginal totals
Professional/high management	21 16.2	32 21.9	45 26.3	13 26.5	111 22.4
Mid-management/ teachers	53 40.8	76 52.1	78 45.6	26 53.1	233 47.0
Intermediate supervisory	21 16.2	18 12.3	20 11.7	7 14.3	66 13.3
Skilled non-manual	20 15.4	17 11.6	16 9.4	2 4.1	55 11.1
Skilled manual	8 6.2	1 0.7	4 2.3	0 0.0	13 2.6
Semi and unskilled manual	7 5.4	2 1.4	8 4.7	1 2.0	18 3.6
Marginal totals	130 26.2	146 29.4	171 34.5	49 9.9	496

$\chi^2 = 25.89$ (significant at 0.05 level)
$\gamma = -0.18$
Pearson $r = -0.15$

Occupational status is a proxy measure of social class and in view of our earlier discussion about the complexities of ideology, it is unlikely that any one single factor accounts for the relationship in Table 2.5. However, we might tentatively explain this in terms of the work experience and life chances of the individual. The people who bear the brunt of the inequalities generated by capitalism are in low status, low paid jobs, or are unemployed. For many in work their experience is one of boring, often dirty and unrewarding jobs, which is often coupled with low income and lack of job security. Such conditions do not of course necessarily turn people into socialists, but we can argue that when they are socialists their life experience tends to make them radicals. We controlled for trade union membership to see if this explained the pattern in this table, but it did not. Clearly we are measuring something which influences the life chances and experiences of the individual, quite separately from political activism in the trade union movement.

Political experience and ideological coherence

If we turn to the political experience of the sample we can examine the relationship between political status and ideology again categorized into four groups, in Table 2.6. Once again we can assess the pattern of variation by looking at the left column in this table. Some 17.6 per cent of Members of Parliament are in the left-wing category, 25.6 per cent of parliamentary candidates, 11.2 per cent of councillors and 33.1 per cent of conference delegates. Looking at the table as a whole the real distinction is between conference delegates and parliamentary candidates on the one hand, and councillors and Members of Parliament on the other; some 61.8 per cent of delegates and 65.6 per cent of candidates are in the left-wing or centre-left categories of Table 2.6, compared with 37 per cent of councillors and 43.1 per cent of MPs.

These figures suggest a reason for ideological differences between these groups. It is only amongst the candidates and delegates that there are respondents who have no experience at all as elected representatives. Some 57 per cent of delegates and 49 per cent of candidates had no experience of this kind, and within these groups respondents without such experience tended to be more left-wing than respondents with such experience. Thus 67 per cent of delegates in the left-wing category had no experience as an elected representative, and 51 per cent in the right-wing category had such experience. For candidates those with such experience constituted 58 per cent of the right-wing category, although they were not underrepresented in the left-wing category. Therefore it is clear that experience as a local councillor explains much of the differences between the subsamples which we observe in Table 2.6.

Much of local council work is often mundane and routine with little

Table 2.6 The relationship between ideology and political status in the Labour elite (for each category the score and percentage are recorded)

	Left (−12 to 0)	Centre-Left (1 to 9)	Centre-Right (10 to 19)	Right (20 to 30)	Marginal totals
Member of Parliament	9	13	21	8	51
	17.6	25.5	41.2	15.7	9.2
Parliamentary candidate	41	64	46	9	160
	25.6	40.0	28.7	5.6	28.9
Councillor	10	23	41	15	89
	11.2	25.8	46.1	16.9	16.1
Conference delegate	84	73	77	20	254
	33.1	28.7	30.3	7.9	45.8
Marginal totals	144	173	185	52	554
	26.0	31.2	33.4	9.4	

$\chi^2 = 36.9$ with 9 DF significant at 0.001 level
$\gamma = -0.10$
Pearson $r = -0.08$

partisan content. The detail often obscures everything else and councillors become preoccupied with questions like: should this road improvement scheme go through? Or should this planning application be accepted? The big issues of politics do of course intrude on council business in the course of the council year; questions of rating levels, council house rents and budget cuts are the very stuff of politics. But these issues probably occupy a local councillor for a relatively small proportion of his or her time. A long exposure to the minutiae of local council business will blunt ideological radicalism, and induce a more 'pragmatic' concern with the small but important issues of politics rather than the large issues which divide the parties.

It is also true that a young conference delegate, for example, with no significant political experiences outside the Labour Party, will tend to be insulated from the dominant value system of British politics. Parkin (1971) refers to this as the 'dominant ideology', which is concerned with legitimizing inequality, supporting the monarchy, reinforcing the private market and so on. One could argue that a radical political culture thrives best when it is insulated from these dominant values, much as the old mining communities maintain their radical tradition by being separate from mainstream culture. If we apply this to the sample, respondents who operate solely within the party are more insulated from the dominant ideology than those who work as elected representatives in the wider political culture.

A final factor we shall consider in explaining variations in the ideology scores of individuals is individual attitude coherence. As we have seen, the factor analysis demonstrates that there is a coherent structure in the attitudes of the sample as a whole, but obviously individuals will differ in their own level of coherence. Moreover, different individuals can achieve a similar score on the ideology scale in a variety of different ways; one individual may be consistently left-wing on a few issues, but be more or less indifferent on others, whereas another individual might be consistently moderately left-wing throughout and achieve the same score as the first. To measure ideological coherence we might pick out the perfect case of a left-wing ideologue. He will reply consistently in agreement with those indicators which correlate positively with the ideology scale, and consistently in disagreement with those indicators correlating negatively with this scale. A right-wing ideologue would do the exact opposite, and a non-ideologue would be equally likely to agree or disagree with both types of indicator. Thus a measure of ideological coherence for individuals is provided by the number of times an individual agrees with the 17 left-wing indicators on the left–right ideology scale, i.e. the indicators positively correlated with the first principal component in Table 2.4. Respondents who agree with all of them, or none of them, are coded 1 (i.e. the consistent left and right-wingers), respondents who agreed with all but one, or disagreed with all but one, are coded 2, and so on, up to those who agree with nine and disagree with eight who are coded 9.

The correlation between ideological coherence and the ideology scale is a highly significant 0.48, which indicates that left-wingers are much more ideologically coherent than right-wingers. Once again we can interpret this in terms of the dominant ideology thesis. A more coherent attitude structure is more likely to be sustained in the face of the dominant political culture. Therefore the coherence protects the attitudes of the left-wing ideologue in comparison with the right-winger.

We bring together the social background, political experience and attitude coherence variables as predictors of ideology in a multiple regression model in Table 2.7. Each of the political status categories is recoded into a dummy variable (e.g. delegate = 1, non-delegate = 0) and these are included as separate predictors of ideology. For statistical reasons we cannot put them all into a model at the same time, and so there are four different models in this table, each omitting one of the categories of political status in turn. Each of the standardized regression coefficients can be interpreted in the same way as a correlation coefficient, except they measure the relationship between a variable and ideology controlling for the influence of other variables. In effect we are holding other variables statistically constant. It can be seen that the strongest relationship is between ideology and attitude coherence, and is twice as strong as the next most significant predictor, age. Occupational status remains a

Table 2.7   Social background, political status and attitude saliency as predictors of ideology (the dependent variable is the ideology index)

Predictor variables	Correlations	Standardized regression coefficients			
Attitude coherence	0.48	0.45[a]	0.45[a]	0.45[a]	0.45[a]
Age	0.25	0.20[a]	0.20[a]	0.20[a]	0.20[a]
Occupational status	0.16	0.12[a]	0.12[a]	0.12[a]	0.12[a]
Member of Parliament	0.08	0.05	−0.04	0.06	—
Parliamentary candidate	−0.08	−0.01	−0.17[a]	—	−0.10[b]
Councillor	0.20	0.12[a]	—	0.13[a]	0.05
Conference delegate	−0.12	—	−0.16[a]	0.02	−0.09
R^2		0.32	0.32	0.32	0.32

[a] Significant at 0.01 level
[b] Significant at 0.05 level

weak though statistically significant predictor of ideology. Finally, we have to interpret the political status variables in the different models; the effects of being a parliamentary candidate and being a delegate are about the same, and they make the respondent more left-wing than the others in the sample. The effect of being a councillor makes the respondent marginally more right-wing and being an MP has no statistically significant effect on the respondent's ideology score.

The sources of the ideological schism with the party

The relationships between social background, political experience, attitude coherence and ideology explain to some extent the ideological conflicts in the party in recent years. Thus the conflicts between Left and Right are partly a product of age, social class and differences in political experience between individuals. But these are not the whole story. This is partly because the variables we have examined only explain about a third of the variation in the ideology scale (see Appendix I) which means that other factors exist which are important and are not included in the model. However, it is also because ideological schisms tend to occur to a much greater extent when Labour is in opposition than when it is in power. Clearly, social background cannot explain this.

We shall argue that the main source of ideological conflict in the party in recent years is the large discrepancy between the policy preferences of the great majority of the Labour elite, and the performance of the party in power. Loyalty to a Labour government and a reluctance to damage the party's electoral chances keep the criticisms muted when Labour is in office. But when Labour is out of office the resentments build up within the Labour elite and break out into the open as the party holds a postmortem on its period of office. To examine the size of the discrepancy between the preferences of the elite and the performance of the party we can summarize the responses of our sample to the specific policy statements in our set of attitude indicators and compare them with the actual policy outcomes implemented by the Labour governments from 1964 to 1979. The results appear in Table 2.8. With very few exceptions there are glaring discrepancies between the preferences of the elite and the policy outcomes.

The biggest discrepancies in Table 2.8 relate to the abolition of fee paying education, unilateral nuclear disarmament, private health care, withdrawal from the EEC and the nationalization of profitable industries. There are only two policies in which a Labour government received the support of a plurality of the Labour elite for the policies implemented; those were incomes policy, where a plurality disagreed with free collective bargaining, and cuts in defence spending, where Labour governments reduced the percentage of gross national product allocated to defence. This table summarizes in a nutshell the main causes of the ideological schisms of recent years. In opposition the Left attack the record of the Labour Party in power, and many of the Centre and Right either agree with them or have to resort to apologetics which they are not really convinced of themselves. Ken Livingstone, the Labour leader of the Greater London Council, summarizes the whole question as follows:

> People like myself have shifted to the Left not on any theoretical basis but because we have seen two Labour governments in the 1960s and 1970s fail to deliver. We have seen the Social Democrats abysmally fail to produce the reforms that didn't even cost money but simply required a bit of courage, like not expelling Agee and Hosenball, and not having racist immigration legislation.
> (Kogan and Kogan, 1982, p. 122)

This analysis is reinforced by an examination of opinions in the touchstone area of attitudes to nationalization. Apart from the delegates, the respondents in the sample were asked to indicate the level of public ownership which they would like to see in a set of fifteen industries and services in the long run. The results appear in Table 2.9. The responses in this table should be viewed with the fact in mind that during the eleven years of Labour government between 1964 and 1979 there were no examples of entire industries being nationalized; there were three industries – steel, shipbuilding and aerospace – in which most of the industry was taken into public ownership. In addition to this the government established the British National Oil Corporation and acquired the majority shareholding in British Leyland in 1975, both of which would come into the category of the nationalization of some of an industry. The only other initiative in this area was the setting up of the National Enterprise Board in 1975, but this

Table 2.8 The discrepancy between the attitudes of the Labour elite and the Labour government's performance in office

Policy statement	Percentage of respondents who		Action taken by Labour in office
	strongly agree/ agree	*strongly disagree/ disagree*	
Nationalize profitable industry	82.8	7.0	Establishment of British National Oil Corporation, British Aerospace and National Enterprise Board
No interference in free collective bargaining	42.7	45.7	Incomes policies 1966–9, 1975–9
Withdraw from the EEC	52.8	36.2	Labour government recommended staying in at the time of the referendum of 1975
Return hived-off industry to public ownership without compensation	78.2	13.9	Steel renationalized in 1967 with compensation
Take over the freeholds of all land	70.0	20.3	No action
Support African liberation movements	75.7	10.1	Policy of 'neutrality' between both sides in Zimbabwe war
Withdraw from NATO	38.1	47.1	Strong reaffirmation of support for NATO by successive Labour governments
Abolish fee-paying education	84.4	10.1	No action
Reduce defence spending	69.3	17.6	Spending reduced as a percent of GNP
Nationalize Rolls-Royce	56.5	23.2	No action
Unequivocal support for Israel	14.4	64.5	Qualified support for Israel
Retain nuclear weapons	25.4	62.4	Polaris retained by 1964–70 government. Chevaline nuclear warhead programme initiated by Labour in 1974–9
Retain private health care	17.9	75.5	Private health care retained. Pay beds removed from NHS hospitals

became merely a public sector merchant bank and a prop for the ailing parts of the private sector.

This performance contrasts sharply with the policy preferences expressed in Table 2.9; in eight of the fifteen industries a majority of respondents wanted the entire industry to be taken into public ownership, and a plurality wanted this for three of the remaining industries. If we combine the first two categories in the table, then without any exceptions a plurality of respondents wanted all or most of the industry to be taken into public ownership. There is very strong support for extensions of public ownership on a scale which would transform British capitalism. The performance of Labour in office in achieving these aims in the eleven years of office after 1964 was modest to say the least. This above all explains the origins of the ideological crisis in the Labour Party.

This gap between aspirations and achievement must be set against a background of endemic economic failure which has served to discredit the Social Democratic analysis within the party. Their case was put most thoroughly by Crosland (1956), although it has been restated more recently by others (Jenkins, 1972; Williams, 1981). The central concern of this analysis is equality, and equality of opportunity. But it was to be an equality based on redistribution out of growth, not out of redistribution

Table 2.9 Attitudes of the Labour elite (Members of Parliament, parliamentary candidates and councillors) to the public ownership of industries and services in the long run (N = 300)

Industry or Service	Degree of public ownership (%)			
	Entire industry	Most of industry	Some of industry	None of industry
Pharmaceuticals	58.2	28.6	11.8	1.4
Building societies	72.3	11.9	11.1	4.7
Banks	63.8	16.5	14.7	5.0
Insurance	60.9	18.6	16.1	4.3
Aircraft construction	69.4	18.7	9.7	2.2
Shipbuilding	66.8	21.1	10.0	2.1
Engineering	29.6	23.0	43.3	4.1
Petrochemicals	60.9	24.9	13.5	0.7
Chemicals	41.2	29.6	24.4	4.7
Computers	43.1	21.3	26.6	9.0
Road transport	56.7	28.0	12.1	3.2
Electronics	31.8	21.6	38.6	8.0
Cars	35.5	17.6	33.7	13.2
Textiles	23.4	20.1	33.8	22.7
Plastics	28.4	19.7	33.0	18.9

ocial classes. To be effective it required successful Key-
nic management to underpin social welfare policies. The
eynesianism will be discussed more fully in a later chapter,
elopment removed a key cornerstone of the Social Demo-
The founders of the Social Democratic Party were essentially
f the Gaitskellite revisionist group within the party who had
seen u.. position being eroded from one of intellectual and political
dominance in the early 1960s to political isolation in the late 1970s. The
collapse of the revisionist case led to an intellectual and political vacuum
being created which further exacerbated the discontent over policy performance, which we have described. This also gave a new lease of life to
the revolutionary Marxist tradition within the party which was dormant
during the postwar years, but reawakened during the 1960s. The social
democratic grassroots Campaign for Democratic Socialism was very
successful in the early 1960s in reversing the commitment to unilateralism made at the party conference, but when an attempt was made to
rerun history by establishing the Campaign for Labour Victory in 1977, in
order to counter the grassroots influence of the Left, the campaign failed
ignominiously. This was because there was no politically significant
social democratic group to be found any longer in the Labour grassroots
by 1977, and this represented an important development as far as Labour's
ideological crisis was concerned. It paved the way for revolutionary
entryism at the grassroots, and it increasingly isolated the beleaguered
Social Democrats in the parliamentary party. This isolation eventually
pushed them into an open breach with the party and the establishment of
the Social Democratic Party. The *coup de grâce* to the revisionist analysis
was perhaps delivered by the arrival of Thatcherite Conservatism, and its
proud boast of abandoning consensus politics. Such a development has
polarized British politics in general, not merely the politics of the Labour
Party. It represented the final demise of 'Butskellism'. Ironically, this
development has also polarized the politics of the Conservative Party as
much as it has the Labour Party, but that is another story.

Conclusions

If we examine the attitudes of a cross section of the Labour Party, from
Members of Parliament down to Labour voters, it is clear that the ideological structuring of attitudes only occurs to a significant extent amongst
the Labour elite. In the case of ordinary Labour voters, and even strong
Labour identifiers, there is only a relatively weak level of attitude structuring, and this exists for only a small number of issues. By contrast, for
the Labour elite, attitudes are structured sufficiently to make it possible
to identify a distinct left–right continuum of opinions underlying beliefs.

This left–right continuum can then be used to model the causes of ideological variations within the Labour elite. Social background, as measured by occupational status and age, is weakly but significantly related to ideology, as is political experience. Thus, young working-class activists who lack any experience as elected representatives are significantly more left-wing than old, middle-class Members of Parliament. Such differences may have contributed to the ideological dissensions in the Labour Party in recent years, but they are not the main cause. The underlying cause of the ideological crisis in the party is the enormous gap between the policy aspirations of the Labour elite, particularly with regard to nationalization, and the poor performance of the party in power, in achieving those policy goals.

These findings imply that the present conflicts over policy and the constitution are likely to continue until there is a decisive outcome in favour of one side or the other. The advances achieved by the Left in changing the party constitution were brought to an end at the 1982 conference, when the Right gained control of the National Executive Committee. This, however, could be only a temporary success for the Right, since it was very largely based on the fears of the leading trade unionists that the party would destroy its electoral chances if the wrangling continued. It was not based on any coherent and credible alternative strategy, unlike the revisionist strategy of the Gaitskell years. This is the Achilles heel of the Right; they possess power in the form of the bloc vote at conference but they lack the legitimacy of a coherent alternative strategy. Once the election had taken place the immediate reason for closing ranks and imposing discipline disappeared, and the disputes could resurface. The long term prospects for the Right are bleak anyway, since their base, the parliamentary Labour party, is being eroded by retirement and reselections. The great majority of candidates selected under the new procedures are left-wingers. So it seems evident in the long run that the conflicts over policy will be resolved in favour of the Left. Of course the Left is not homogeneous, and it is certain that a victory for the Left will not turn Labour into an overtly anti-system Marxist party. But it will mean a reassertion of socialist principles, both in programmatic and in policy terms. Nationalization will again become a central focus of policy, as will industrial democracy and intervention in the economy. Moreover, it will be a socialist resurgence which stresses the importance of policy implementation, as well as developing the party programme. This is the lesson of the conflicts over the constitution, in which the Left recognized that it was not sufficient to change the party programme in order to change the behaviour of Labour in power. If, on the other hand, there is no clear victory for the Left and the two wings of the party stalemate each other's attempts to gain control, the ideological disputes will probably continue indefinitely.

Notes

1 The correlations used in this book unless otherwise defined are Pearson product moment correlation coefficients which vary from +1.0 to −1.0. The correlation coefficient is a numerical measure of the extent to which variables are associated with each other, i.e. the extent to which high values of one variable coincide with high (or low when the correlation is negative) values of another. Thus a correlation of between 0.60 and 0.90 is strong, between 0.30 and 0.60 moderate, and between 0.10 and 0.30 weak.

2 A Likert scale is a five point attitude scale denoting the respondents' agreement or disagreement with a given statement. For example our first statement was: 'The central question of British politics is the class struggle between Labour and capital.'

The possible responses are:

1 strongly agree
2 agree
3 neither agree nor disagree
4 disagree
5 strongly disagree

3 The standard deviation (SD) is the most commonly used measure of dispersion, and it may be thought of as measuring the dispersion of a set of numbers relative to their mean. It is defined by the following formula:

$$SD = \sqrt{\left(\sum_{i=1}^{N} (x_i - \bar{x})^2 / N \right)}$$

where x_i is the value of the ith number in the set, $\bar{x}$ is the mean of the set of numbers, and N is the number of scores in the set.

To illustrate, consider the following set of five numbers: 5, 6, 7, 8, 9. The mean $\bar{x}$ of this set is 7. The standard deviation is calculated as follows:

$x_i - \bar{x}$	$(x_i - \bar{x})^2$
5 − 7 = −2	4
6 − 7 = −1	1
7 − 7 = 0	0
8 − 7 = 1	1
9 − 7 = 2	4

$$\sum_{i=1}^{5} = 10$$

Thus

$$SD = \sqrt{\left(\sum_{i=1}^{5} (x_i - \bar{x})^2 / N \right)}$$

$$= \sqrt{(10/5)} = 1.4 \text{ (approximately)}$$

3

The membership crisis

No discussion of contemporary Labour Party politics is complete without an analysis of one of the major problems facing the party today, the decline of the grassroots membership. The dimensions of this decline can be seen in the published figures for individual membership, the component of the total not tied to trade union affiliations. The decline in Labour's published individual membership, which as is well known exaggerates the true levels of membership, can be seen in Figure 3.1. On the published figures the party has been losing on average more than 11,000 members per year, and the true loss might well be higher than this.

In this chapter we attempt to explain why this decline in membership has taken place, but before discussing the membership figures over time, it is useful to try and estimate more accurate figures of individual membership than those published by the party.

Individual membership and activism in 1979

There are no accurate estimates of the true levels of membership of the Labour Party held in the party headquarters. Equally the accuracy of local membership figures will vary depending on the efficiency of the local party organization. The party had a rule that constituency parties must affiliate with at least 1000 members which operated since 1963 and was abolished at the 1979 party conference. So the affiliation membership figures since then may be more accurate than in the past. The only way to obtain really accurate estimates of the individual membership of the party is to survey key members of the local constituency parties.

Accordingly, estimates of Labour's membership figures were obtained from the random sample of delegates to the 1978 party conference. Delegates were asked to provide information about levels of membership and activism in constituency parties. There are of course

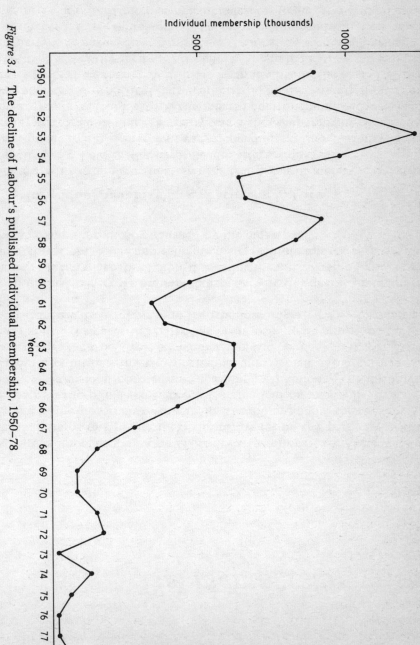

Figure 3.1 The decline of Labour's published individual membership, 1950–78

Source: Butler and Sloman (1980, p. 143) and Labour Party headquarters.

difficulties in obtaining accurate figures from delegates, and it is not easy to verify them. But conference delegates are for the most part prominent activists in their constituency parties, and as such are likely to be at least as well informed about the state of the membership as anyone in the local parties. Thus their responses are taken as accurate measures of the state of the membership.

The responses of constituency party delegates to the questions relating to membership are set out in Table 3.1. They were asked to provide an estimate of the total membership, the number of male activists, and the percentage of active wards in a constituency. It can be seen from Table 3.1 that more than 50 per cent of constituency parties had less than 500 members, and only 13 per cent reported more than 1000 members, the minimum for affiliation. This last figure provides an independent check on the accuracy of the survey, since it is possible to calculate the percentage of constituencies which affiliated with more than 1000 members in 1978. This turned out to be 14 per cent of constituency parties, and thus the sample and the population of all constituency parties are roughly the same. This suggests that the sample is representative of the population.

The median number of members of constituency parties in the sample was 400, and median number of activists was 90. Thus approximately 23 per cent of the total membership was reported as active. However, wide variations existed across constituencies in the proportion of total members reported as active. Some 17 per cent of parties who reported less than 50 activists said they had less than 100 members; whereas 28 per cent of those who reported less than 50 activists claimed to have more than 500 members. This highlights the variation in the ratio of activists to members across constituencies. To some extent this variation reflects the recruitment policies of local parties, with some parties seeking to maximize membership, and others not wanting a large passive membership which has to be serviced. Another factor is the proportion of wards which are active in constituencies. When all wards are active this produces a larger total membership than when only some wards are active which in turn influences the ratio of the active to total membership.

Given these figures we can extrapolate the same results to the country as a whole. Taking the median number of members and activists as representative of the average constituency there must have been around 250,000 individual members, and 55,000 activists in 1978. This contrasts sharply with the published figure for affiliated membership in 1978 of 675,000.

It is interesting to compare these estimates with the only other national sample survey of local party membership available, which was carried out by the Houghton Commission on financial aid to political parties. Using a sophisticated multi-stage random sample of 100 constituencies Houghton estimated that constituency Labour parties had an

Table 3.1   Membership and activism in constituency Labour parties, 1978

	Percentage of constituency parties
1 Total membership	
under 100	7
100–499	47
500–999	33
1000 plus	13
2 Male activists (number)	
under 25	21
26–50	42
50–100	23
100 plus	14
3 Female activists (number)	
under 25	52
26–50	28
50–100	13
100 plus	7
4 Percentage of wards which are active	
all	47.8
three-quarters	25.4
half	17.2
quarter	6.5
none	1.3
other	1.7

arithmetic mean number of 500 members (HMSO, 1976b, pp. 30–9). An extrapolation of this to all constituency parties would give a total membership of around 317,000.

However, the Houghton estimates are likely to be overestimates of the true state of Labour's membership, for two reasons. Firstly, the arithmetic mean (or the average) is not an appropriate measure of the representative number of members in constituency parties because the distribution of members across all constituencies is markedly skewed. There are a few constituencies with large memberships and a simple arithmetic mean will be inflated by these, so estimating the total membership from the mean number of members will be misleading. Accurate estimates of the membership figures should be calculated from the median number of members in constituencies. A second reason derives from the sampling method used by the Houghton Commission. They used a multi-stage random sample with varying sampling proportions in

England, Wales and Scotland. Consequently, their sample is biased in favour of Wales and Scotland compared with England (Houghton, 1967, pp. 153–5). This is perfectly legitimate since they wanted to increase the number of constituencies in their sample which had active Nationalist parties. However, it does bias the estimates of the Labour membership. Labour is markedly more popular in electoral terms in both Scotland and Wales than it is in England. Since party membership and voting support are positively correlated (Whiteley and Gordon, 1980, p. 41), it is clear that the Houghton sample of constituencies has an above average level of Labour membership than is true throughout Great Britain as a whole.

We are of course concerned with the decline of Labour's membership over the years. Seyd and Minkin (1979) have suggested that Labour's true membership has been increasing rather than declining over the last ten years. They argued that membership is recovering from the low ebb of the late 1960s. This is an interesting suggestion but it cannot be verified in the absence of a longitudinal study with a representative sample of constituencies. Their results do, however, highlight the point that the relationship between the affiliated or published and the actual membership of the Labour Party is complex, and one cannot make direct inferences about the latter from the former without taking account of a number of facts which might distort the picture. We shall return to this question later.

If we wish to explain the decline of the party membership over the years, a good way to start is to investigate the reasons which activists give for joining the party. Reasons for joining are of course not the same as reasons for leaving, but it turns out that the former can throw useful light on the latter. Delegates were asked to explain the main reason they had for joining the party originally. The results of this are discussed next.

Why join the Labour Party?

In one sense the problem of membership in the Labour Party is to explain why people wish to join at all. This point is not facetious, but is rather rooted in a theoretical analysis of support for voluntary organizations discussed by Olson (1965). He noted that any organization which seeks to provide public goods will have an acute problem of mobilizing support, unless it could use coercion or supply private benefits to members. A public good is defined as any commodity or service such that if it is provided to anyone it will be available to all. Its characteristics are that no-one can be excluded from consuming it once it is provided. For example, once a lighthouse is provided its use cannot be restricted to those ships who might have contributed towards it. Because of this, individuals will have an incentive to 'free ride', and avoid the costs of contributing to the provision of the good, and this is likely to produce a suboptimal provision of the good from the social point of view. Originally, the theory was worked out to explain the difficulties of allocating what were thought to be a relatively restricted type of good such as defence provision, lighthouses, etc. (Samuelson, 1954). But Olson noted that many types of collective action were concerned with the provision of collective goods, notably interest groups of various kinds.

The relevance of this for the question of Labour's membership is immediately apparent. A political party is a collective goods 'producing' organization *par excellence*. This is because public policies are collective goods (or bads). They seek to implement policy changes at the national level which apply to all. This means that an individual who wants particular Labour policies to be implemented, or wants Conservative policies not to be implemented, has an incentive to 'free ride' and not become a party member. Thus in so far as individual membership of the party is motivated by instrumental aims, that is by a desire to see policies implemented, there will be a free rider problem. If membership of the party was solely a matter of instrumental motivation, then the party would, according to the theory, have a very restricted membership indeed.

In discussing instrumental motives a distinction must be made between private and public instrumental motives. An individual may want to join the party simply because he is interested in politics for its own sake, and enjoys the intrigue of political life. This is an instrumental motive, but it is private rather than public. This distinction is important in connection with the paradox of collective action, since private instrumental motives are not subject to the free rider problem.

There are also other reasons for joining the party which are not instrumental in the sense described. People join because they are idealistic and want to give expression to these ideals, and we can characterize such motives as 'expressive' motives. An individual who joins the party to end unemployment, or to achieve increased welfare spending or better housing, is essentially pursuing instrumental goals of 'public goods'. An individual who joins the party in order to 'build socialism' or achieve 'social justice' is pursuing a private good, or the satisfaction associated with expressing generalized idealistic goals. It goes without saying of course that the distinction between instrumental and expressive is not absolutely clear-cut; people wishing to build socialism are likely to have strong opinions about policy and similarly people wanting to pursue particular objectives are not necessarily lacking in ideals. However, there is an important distinction between the pursuit of particular policy objectives, or benefits for one's social group or class on the one hand, and idealistic motive such as the construction of a 'better world', or 'building socialism' on the other. Given this, the Olson problem of collective action will apply to individuals pursuing instrumental goals rather than those pursuing idealistic goals.

Table 3.2 The relationship between social class and motives for joining the Labour Party

Motives for joining the party	Middle class (%) (N = 131)	Intermediate (%) (N = 37)	Working class (%) (N = 62)
Believes in socialism/Clause 4	35.9	24.3	24.6
Wants a more equal society or social justice	27.5	18.9	21.3
Wants to implement or influence specific policies of the party	12.2	10.8	14.8
Has a generalized loyalty to the Labour Party	3.8	2.7	3.3
Sees Labour as representing and promoting the interests of the working class	3.1	13.5	11.5
Wanted to be involved in politics and is interested in political affairs	3.1	10.8	9.8
Joined because of family background	8.4	5.4	1.6
Involved in local parties or in the social life of the party locally	2.3	5.4	3.3
Joined as a reaction to Tory governments or policies	3.8	5.4	0
Involved as an extension of trade union activity	0	2.7	9.8

Note: Middle class represents those respondents with a Registrar General's occupational status coding of 1 or 2, intermediate is a coding of 3N, and working class is a coding of 3M, 4 or 5.

One of the questions on the survey of conference delegates asked respondents to cite their main reason for joining the Labour Party. The question had an open-ended coding so individuals were not required to answer in terms of a predefined set of categories, which makes the replies particularly valuable in highlighting motives. The responses to this question appear in Table 3.2 and for reasons which should become clear they are categorized by occupational status. To pursue the distinction between instrumental and expressive motives for joining, we might tentatively classify the responses in Table 3.2 as follows:

Instrumental reasons	Expressive reasons	Neither instrumental nor expressive
Wants to implement or influence specific policies	Believes in socialism/ Clause 4	Joined because of family background
Sees Labour as promoting the interests of the working class	Wants a more equal society or greater social justice	
Wants to be involved in politics	Has a generalized loyalty to the party	
Wants to be involved with the local party		
Joined as a reaction to Tory governments or policies		
Joined as an extension of trade union activities		

The responses in Table 3.2 represent the main categories of response with idiosyncratic replies (e.g. 'I joined because of my girl friend') excluded. All the responses classified as instrumental have the characteristic that they are concerned with achieving benefits for the individual or social group. Not all of these are concerned with obtaining public goods; individuals who join for social reasons, or because they simply want to be involved in politics are pursuing private benefits. But those who want to achieve specific policies, want to get benefits for workers, or oppose the Tory government's policies are pursuing collective goods (or avoiding bads in the latter case). We can illustrate these motives with some examples of individual responses:

> 'Unemployment and its effects made me want to join the party; I wanted to do something about it.'

> 'I am committed to the social ownership of the means of production, and to the extension of industrial democracy.'

> 'I joined because I believe Labour is the party which looks after the interests of the working class.'

> 'I joined because of Suez, and because of the Tories' attitudes to nationalization.'

Respondents giving expressive reasons tended to reply in much more generalized idealistic terms, not mentioning policies at all. Whilst these are often collective goals, when they are articulated in such general terms they become private aims of an expressive nature. For example:

'I support socialism.'

'I saw it as the best means of achieving a just society.'

'Clause 4.'[1]

Thus whilst the differences between expressive and instrumental reasons for joining the party are not watertight, there is a clear distinction between these motives, which is readily apparent in the responses of delegates. Moreover, it can be seen in Table 3.2 that respondents were very much more likely to give expressive reasons than instrumental reasons for joining the party. This fits the Olson model, since it implies that individuals tend to join primarily for private reasons rather than for the purpose of producing collective goods.

There is a further characteristic of the distinction between expressive and instrumental motives which is particularly important for explaining the decline of the membership. It is clear that important differences exist between middle-class and working-class conference delegates in their reasons for joining the party. Working-class respondents are much more likely to give instrumental reasons for joining than middle-class respondents, who are clearly more expressive. This can be observed in Table 3.2, particularly with regard to the first motive in the list, which relates to the ideal of building socialism. Nearly 36 per cent of middle-class respondents cited a belief in socialism as a reason for joining the party, compared with 24.6 per cent of the working-class respondents. Using the classification of instrumental and expressive motives described above, some 49.2 per cent of working-class respondents cited instrumental reasons for joining, compared with 24.5 per cent of middle-class respondents. Similarly, the intermediate occupational status group is also more instrumental than the middle class with 45.9 per cent of them in this category.

If working-class delegates are more likely than the middle-class to cite instrumental reasons for joining, particularly the reason that 'Labour stands for the interests of the working class', what implications could this have for the decline in membership? This is discussed next.

The decline in Labour membership

We shall argue that a substantial part of the decline of party membership is due to the decline of working-class involvement in politics, which in turn is related to their instrumental approach to politics. The decline of working-class politics was originally discussed by Hindess (1971) and although the idea has been criticized (Baxter, 1972; Dowse, 1973) it has aroused a lot of interest. Strong evidence of this decline exists at the elite level in Parliament and in the National Executive Committee (Johnson, 1973; Hanby, 1974). The present survey confirms that party conference delegates are predominantly middle class, so it may well have happened at this level too. Labour councillors also appear to be predominantly middle class too, so it may have happened there (Sharpe, 1964; Brand, 1973; Gordon and Whiteley, 1979), and it has definitely happened at the electoral level with an increasing middle-class Labour vote over time (Crewe, Särlvik and Alt, 1977).

At the level of constituency parties the evidence concerning the changing class composition of the membership is much less clear-cut than at the elite level. Forrester summarized a number of empirical studies of local Labour parties, and also carried out a detailed study of one constituency himself (Forrester, 1976). He concluded that most studies indicated that the middle class was disproportionately represented amongst activists, but not necessarily amongst members. As to the decline of working-class activists over time he concluded that the evidence was inadequate to confirm or reject this argument.

However, there is indirect evidence which would support the Hindess thesis. There have been substantial changes in the occupational structure in Britain over the years leading to a decline in the numbers of manual workers. The survey of occupational mobility by Goldthorpe and his associates showed that some 43.8 per cent of the occupational structure was made up of manual workers in 1972 (Goldthorpe, 1980, p. 44). Respondents in their survey were asked about parents' occupation and their replies indicated that nearly 55 per cent of these parents were manual workers when the respondents were young. Thus vast changes in the occupational structure have been taking place over the years with many manual occupations disappearing altogether and being replaced by white collar service occupations. One might argue about how 'middle class' some of these service occupations are, but it is clear that they are not the traditional manual occupations and this is bound to have political as well as social repercussions. It would be surprising indeed if the social composition of Labour's local membership had not been affected by these changes in the social structure, making the membership more white collar, and hence to a point more middle class.

On this basis we shall argue that there has been a decline in working-class activism in the Labour Party and we shall also argue that this is one of the important reasons for the decline in party membership over time. The changing nature of the occupational structure may partly account for it, but there are also other reasons for this development.

One important reason for this decline can be observed in Table 3.2, and was discussed above in relation to the motives for joining. When these are instrumental and relate to the production of public goods they need nurturing or reinforcing by the successful implementation of those policies. Thus the individual who cited the fight against unemployment as the main reason for joining the party is much more vulnerable to defection than an individual who has diffused and generalized aims, at a time when the Labour government presided over increasing unemployment. Similarly, an individual concerned with improved social services is more likely to leave the party over cuts in these services, than someone with a general commitment to greater social justice. Thus in general individuals with instrumental motives are more likely to leave the party than individuals with expressive motives at a time of failing policy performance.

In recent years the Labour government presided over rising unemployment and inflation, cuts in welfare state, increased rather than decreased inequality (Bosanquet and Townsend, 1980), and as Stuart Holland has put it 'attempted to run the economy mainly by opposing its own supporters' (Holland, 1975, p. 144). Economic performance is a particularly salient issue for the voters as a whole, and it can be inferred that it is true for Labour Party members. Hence the instrumental members, who are disproportionately working class, are leaving the party as a result of these failures of policy performance.

This inference is supported by the classic study of affluent workers of Goldthorpe *et al.* (1969). The authors showed that affluent workers in the car industry in Luton retained their basic allegiance to the Labour Party, but they were much more instrumental than workers in traditional industries. They were more concerned with the performance of the party in power. Our delegates were much more likely to be skilled workers than they were to be unskilled, so the same reasoning could well apply to Labour activists. Roberts *et al.* (1977) reach a similar conclusion to Goldthorpe.

Hirschman's (1970) analysis of consumer responses to decline in firms, organizations and states is relevant in this context. There are three possible tactics when faced with declining performance: 'exit, voice or loyalty'. We might crudely summarize the situation in Labour's grassroots parties in response to the failures of Labour in office as follows: 'nearly everyone voices, but whilst the middle class remains loyal, the working class exits'. Clearly the Olson paradox tends to make instrumental members more likely to leave than expressive members, regardless of performance, simply because they are pursuing collective goals. But when this inherent vulnerability to defection is coupled with a wide-ranging failure of performance it becomes critical.

Other facts related to the class mix within local parties may also be influential in producing a working-class defection. Hindess (1971) showed that for middle-class activists the language of politics and the attitudes towards issues are very different from those of the working class. He argued that in the case of middle-class activists 'politics was seen basically as a matter of general principles, of broad policy outlines. Thereafter, it is a matter of administration, of getting suitably qualified personnel and of setting up the right sort of machinery to execute policy' (p. 136). On the other hand, for the working-class activists, politics is a question of 'unavoidable personal involvement, in consequence of political decision, to the experience of government . . . as an external or constraining and coercive organisation' (ibid.).

Thus middle-class activists tend to discuss politics in terms of general principles, whereas working-class activists see things in terms of specific events which affect the life of the individual.

These distinctions have been analysed more generally by Bernstein (1960) in his examination of the relationship between language and social class. Bernstein distinguishes between the 'elaborated' code of the middle class and the 'restricted' code of the working class. The archetypal elaborated code is characterized by complex sentence structure, a rich vocabulary, the use of abstractions, and it allows subtle distinctions of meaning and fine discrimination between concepts; on the other hand the restricted code is characterized by simple sentence structure, poor vocabulary, an emphasis on concrete descriptions rather than analytical reasoning and a limited range of expressions (see also Edwards, 1976).

It is fairly clear that the dominant language code in British politics is the middle-class code, and thus individuals proficient in this are likely to dominate local party meetings. This might well lead to a defection of working-class activists and members, who either find themselves excluded from proceedings, or forced to operate in what is very often to them an alien language code. Anyone who has observed the verbosity and circumlocution of a working-class trade unionist giving an interview to the media can appreciate the difficulties of a person socialized in one language code operating in another. Thus a small articulate group of middle-class activists might paradoxically drive out working-class activists. Similar processes may operate at the level of the electorate, where working-class voters see Labour politicians speaking in an ever-increasingly elaborate language code.

Thus both the language code of politics and the performance of Labour in office play a role in detaching working-class activists from the party. But what is the role of political ideology in this process? We examine this question next.

The decline of membership and ideology

We have seen that a significant relationship exists between instrumental motives for joining the Labour Party and social class. In Chapter 2 we observed a significant, though weak relationship between social class and political ideology; respondents in blue-collar occupations tended to be rather more left-wing than respondents in white-collar occupations. The obvious inference from this is that motives for joining the party and political ideology are related. We might postulate that 'instrumental' members tend to be more working class and this in turn tends to make them more left-wing. 'Expressive' individuals tend to be more middle class and this tends to make them more right-wing.

We test this hypothesis by examining the relationship between motives for joining the party and political ideology. This is done in Table 3.3, where the political ideology scale has again been recoded into four categories, and respondents not instrumental or expressive in their motives for joining are excluded. It is fairly clear in Table 3.3 that no statistically significant relationship exists between political ideology and motives for joining the party; instrumental respondents are no more likely to be left-wing than expressive respondents. The relationship between social class and ideology does not carry across to motives for joining the party. Therefore, if working-class activists are leaving the party it is not because they are disillusioned left-wingers. Given this, what role does political ideology play in attaching or detaching individuals from the party?

We can get a clue to the role of political ideology in maintaining attachment to the party from the earlier paper by Gordon and Whiteley (1979) which used the Labour councillors' data. This analysis showed that middle-class councillors were more ideologically homogeneous than working-class councillors, that is, their ideological structures were more coherent than those of the working class. This suggests a hypothesis linking attachment to the party, social class and political ideology. The hypothesis is that individuals with a high level of ideological structuring, whether they are left-wingers or right-wingers, are more likely to remain

Table 3.3 The relationship between ideology and political orientation for party conference delegates

Motives for joining the party	Political orientation					
	Left-wing	Centre-Left	Centre-Right	Right-wing		
Instrumental	22	22	30	18	92	(39.8)
Expressive	46	39	35	19	139	(60.2)
	68 (29.4)	61 (26.4)	65 (28.1)	37 (16.0)	231	

$\chi^2 = 4.23$, significant at the 0.25 level.

attached to the party than individuals with a low level of structuring. If the middle class has higher levels of structuring than the working class this should partly explain why it remains more loyal to the party than the latter. The reasoning behind this is rooted in the theory of cognitive dissonance developed by Festinger (1957). Cognitive dissonance refers to the inconsistency between an individual's attitudes and beliefs about the world, and the actual state of the world. A person will try to modify his attitudes or behaviour in order to reduce this dissonance. As Festinger argues: 'The presence of dissonance gives rise to pressure to reduce or eliminate the dissonance. The strength of the pressure to reduce the dissonance is a function of the magnitude of the dissonance' (1967, p. 350).

In our case the dissonance comes about as a result of the gap between the socialist ideals of party activists, and the actual performance of the Labour Party. In the extreme an individual can resolve this dissonance either by changing his ideals, or by leaving the party, or both. But it is clear that individuals with a highly structured set of beliefs will be more resistant to such a course of action than individuals with a low level of structuring. Festinger makes this point succinctly:

> To the extent that the element is consonant with a large number of other elements and to the extent that changing it would replace these consonances by dissonance, the elements will be resistant to change.   (1967, p. 355)

Consequently, if middle-class individuals have a high level of ideological structuring they should be less likely to abandon their beliefs or leave the party than individuals with a low level of structuring. This is because their attitudes are more closely integrated into a web of beliefs, each of which supports the others in the face of dissonant information. Similarly if working-class individuals have a low level of attitude structuring they should be more likely to abandon their beliefs in the face of dissonant information.

But do the working-class activists have a lower level of ideological structuring than the middle-class? We can test this by repeating the factor analysis of the attitude indicators for middle-class and working-class delegates separately. To do this we separated the unambiguously middle-class respondents (i.e. Registrar General's occupational status categories 1 and 2) from the working-class respondents (categories 3M, 4 and 5). The results of the factor analysis for these two groups of delegates appear in Tables 3.4 and 3.5. There is clear support for the hypothesis in these two tables. There are six significant factors in the case of middle-class delegates, and eight in the case of the working class. For middle-class delegates the first factor explains 52.9 per cent of the common variance (i.e. variance explained by all factors) and only 40.9 per cent of the

Table 3.4 Factor analysis of the attitudes of middle-class conference delegates
(*N* = 120)

Factor	Correlation between factors and variables	Percentage of variance explained by factor
1 *Political strategy and defence*		
Capture of middle ground	0.76	
Moderates against extremism	0.67	
Condemn political law breakers	0.65	
Support liberation groups	0.42	
Support Israel	0.66	
Withdraw from NATO	−0.59	
Retain nuclear weapons	0.67	
Reduce defence spending	−0.47	
Abolish the Monarchy	−0.56	33.5
2 *Class and public ownership*		
Central question of politics is class	0.61	
Nationalize for profit	0.65	
Implement Clause 4	0.62	
PLP accept conference decisions	0.56	
Return hived-off industry	0.72	
Take over the freeholds of land	0.56	
Nationalize Rolls-Royce	0.75	8.7
3 *Common Market*		
No interference in collective bargaining	0.63	
Withdraw from the EEC	0.77	
Boycott the European Parliament	0.81	
PLP accept conference decisions	0.58	6.2
4 *Health care and education*		
Take over the freeholds of land	0.40	
Support liberation groups	0.48	
Abolish private education	0.74	
Retain private health care	−0.69	5.4
5 *Trade union and incomes policy*		
Prices and incomes policy	0.58	
Trade unions have too much power	0.82	4.9
6 *Class and equality*		
Attack not ameliorate inequality	0.51	
Reduce defence spending	−0.49	
Not enough working-class MPs	0.65	4.6

Table 3.5 Factor analysis of the attitudes of working-class conference delegates (*N* = 57)

Factor	Correlation between factors and variables	Percentage of variance explained by factor
1 *Common Market and Defence*		
Withdraw from the Common Market	0.65	
Boycott the European Parliament	0.73	
PLP accept conference decisions	0.55	
Support Israel	−0.69	
Withdraw from NATO	0.67	30.2
2 *Political strategy and incomes policy*		
Labour capture the middle ground	0.72	
Moderates against extremism	0.57	
Condemn political law breakers	0.55	
Prices and incomes policy	0.66	
Retain nuclear weapons	0.47	
Not enough working-class MPs	−0.40	9.6
3 *Class and defence*		
Nationalize for profit	0.40	
Support liberation groups	0.87	
Withdraw from NATO	0.47	
Abolish the Monarchy	0.65	
Not enough working-class MPs	0.51	7.8
4 *Public ownership and class*		
Central question of politics in class	0.68	
Implement Clause 4	0.59	
Return hived-off industry	0.80	
Take over freeholds of land	0.75	6.2
5 *Public ownership and pay bargaining*		
Central question of politics in class	0.42	
Nationalize for profit	0.59	
No interference in bargaining	0.82	
Trade unions have too much power	−0.42	6.0
6 *Education and defence*		
Abolish private education	0.88	
Reduce defence spending	0.86	5.2
7 *Wealth and nuclear weapons*		
Retain nuclear weapons	0.62	
Retain private health care	0.82	
Nationalize Rolls-Royce	0.41	4.7
8 *Equality and trade unions*		
Attack not ameliorate inequality	0.89	
Trade unions have too much power	−0.64	4.3

common variance, in the case of working-class delegates. The political coherence of the factor structure is greater for the middle class in comparison with the working class. In the case of the former five of the public ownership indicators are clustered together on factor two whereas for the working class four of these are split between factors four and five, and the fifth is not highly related to any of the factors. Similarly, for the middle class, four of the defence indicators are clustered together on factor one, whereas these are split between three factors in the case of the working class. Finally, incomes policy and attitudes to trade union power are grouped together on one factor in the case of the middle class, but are different factors in the case of the working class. Clearly, there is a lower level of ideological structuring amongst working-class delegates in comparison with middle-class delegates. This makes them potentially more vulnerable to defection.

This analysis applies of course to the Labour elite, but we can also apply it to opinion leaders amongst the local party activists. We have seen in Chapter 2 that ordinary party members are not particularly ideological but if opinion leaders amongst the activists are more like the Labour elite in their ideological make-up, then ideology influences membership via elite activists. If these opinion leaders become disillusioned and defect this can drastically reduce the passive membership in a constituency party, because it is no longer properly serviced and maintained. The party then begins to decay and decline at the local level, which in turn can lead to a vicious circle of disillusionment and apathy for the remaining members.

We have seen that a number of separate forces act to increase the likelihood of working-class defection from the Labour Party in comparison with the middle class. We have attributed this phenomenon primarily to the poor performance of the Labour Party in power, in comparison with the aspirations of its activists. However, the argument up to now has remained largely theoretical. It remains to be shown that a relationship exists between policy performance and the decline of membership. We can examine this by developing a time series model of Labour membership.

Modelling the decline of membership

If the performance hypothesis is correct there should be a relationship between indicators of Labour's performance in office and the level of membership over time. In other words the level of individual membership should respond to the policy outputs of a Labour government, and a bad performance should produce an increased rate of defection. There is much poll evidence to suggest that the most salient issues from the point of view of the general public are economic issues (Butler and Stokes, 1974, pp. 369–404). In particular the rate of inflation and unemployment are always highly salient issues in surveys of public opinion. If we assume that these issues are also the most salient for Labour Party members, we can examine the relationship between economic performance and membership of the party over time as a test of the performance hypothesis. Of course this is only an approximate test, ideally we would require a panel sample of Labour members over time to fully examine this proposition. But it is a useful preliminary test in the absence of such individual level data.

If we refer again to Figure 3.1 in which the individual affiliated membership figures are plotted over time, we can see clear cycles in the series as well as a trend decline. There was a big increase in membership after the 1951 election defeat, but this peaked in 1953, and declined thereafter until 1955. After the General Election of 1955 membership picked up again, and peaked around 1957. It started to pick up in 1961, a period which coincided with the relative unpopularity of the Macmillan government, and peaked once again at the time of the 1964 General Election. From the time of this election victory until 1970 when Labour was defeated, the membership continued to decline. The party regained some members between 1970 and 1972, and once again at the time of the election of 1974; however, membership declined again after that.

One obvious problem of examining trends in Labour Party membership over time arises from the fact that we have to use the affiliated membership figures in the absence of an accurate longitudinal measure of true membership. Although the affiliated membership figures are a biased measure of the true membership figures they can still be used to identify trends, provided such biases are controlled as much as possible. This can be done by incorporating variables into a predictive model of trends in membership which are thought likely to influence it. To clarify the point it is useful to consider the relationship between the affiliated or published membership and the unknown true membership series. If the factors which cause the affiliated membership series to be a biased measure of the true membership series remain unchanged over time, then the existence of bias is irrelevant for estimating trends. This is because in that event the published and true figures will decline at the same time rate over time, making it possible to estimate that rate of decline from the published figures alone. (More technically, if we construct a regression model predicting membership from the number of years since 1950, then the slope coefficient of the regression using the published membership will equal the slope coefficient of the regression using the true membership, and only the intercept terms of the two models would differ.)

However, this is rather unlikely, and it is much more plausible that the published figures and the true figures will vary systematically in relation to each other over time. This is because there are a number of sources of variation in the true membership which might not be fully recorded in the published membership figures. For example, it is well known that the party in opposition tends on average to be more popular in the opinion polls than the party in power. The average lead of the opposition over the incumbent in the Gallup Polls from 1947 to 1975 was 3.6 per cent (Whiteley, 1979). On the assumption that trends in membership are influenced by trends in party popularity then incumbency should increase the rate of defection of members; but this might not be fully recorded in the affiliated membership figures. It is particularly likely not to be properly recorded after 1963 when the party introduced the minimum affiliation requirement for constituency parties of 1000 members. If a local party has to affiliate with 1000 members or not at all, it is likely to continue affiliation in the face of declining membership producing an ever-increasing bias in the figures over the years.

There are other factors which might possibly produce variations in the true membership figures over time which are not recorded. Faction fighting in public might lose members, and this might be partly responsible for the decline in membership during the period 1958 to 1961 when the party was riven by internal disputes over Clause 4 and nuclear disarmament. The parliamentary performance, and the effectiveness of the leadership, might influence the level of individual membership too. Clearly, there are many influences at work which affect the true level of membership.

With these points in mind we will investigate the relationship between aggregate economic indicators and the individual affiliated membership over the period 1950 to 1978 using a multiple regression model (see Appendix I). An attempt will be made to control the factors which might cause the published membership series to fluctuate relative to the true membership by incorporating three variables into the models. These variables act as controls, that is we can examine the influence of the economy on the membership whilst statistically holding constant these sources of variation. These controls are:

1 The average annual level of popularity of the Labour Party in the Gallup Polls. This should pick up a number of influences, including the performance of the party in Parliament, the influence of faction fighting and the success or otherwise of the Conservatives.
2 A dummy variable scoring zero up to 1962 and one thereafter to measure the bias in the series introduced by the minimum affiliation rule.
3 A dummy variable scoring one for years when Labour was in power and zero otherwise to pick up the influence of incumbency in government.

The influence of the economy on the level of membership was examined using two economic indicators. They were the rate of unemployment and the value of the index of retail prices as a measure of inflation. These variables are plotted against the membership data in Figures 3.2 and 3.3. In both cases there are curvilinear relationships (i.e. the relationship plotted on a graph is curved, as in Figures 3.2 and 3.3) between membership and the economic variables; above a value of approximately 700,000 members the relationship between membership, prices and unemployment is quite steeply negative, that is a high level of membership is associated with a low level of inflation or unemployment and vice versa; below this value the relationship is much less steep. We shall use a multiple regression model to examine the link between the economic variables and membership, controlling for the three variables mentioned above. The multiple regression model assumes linear relationships

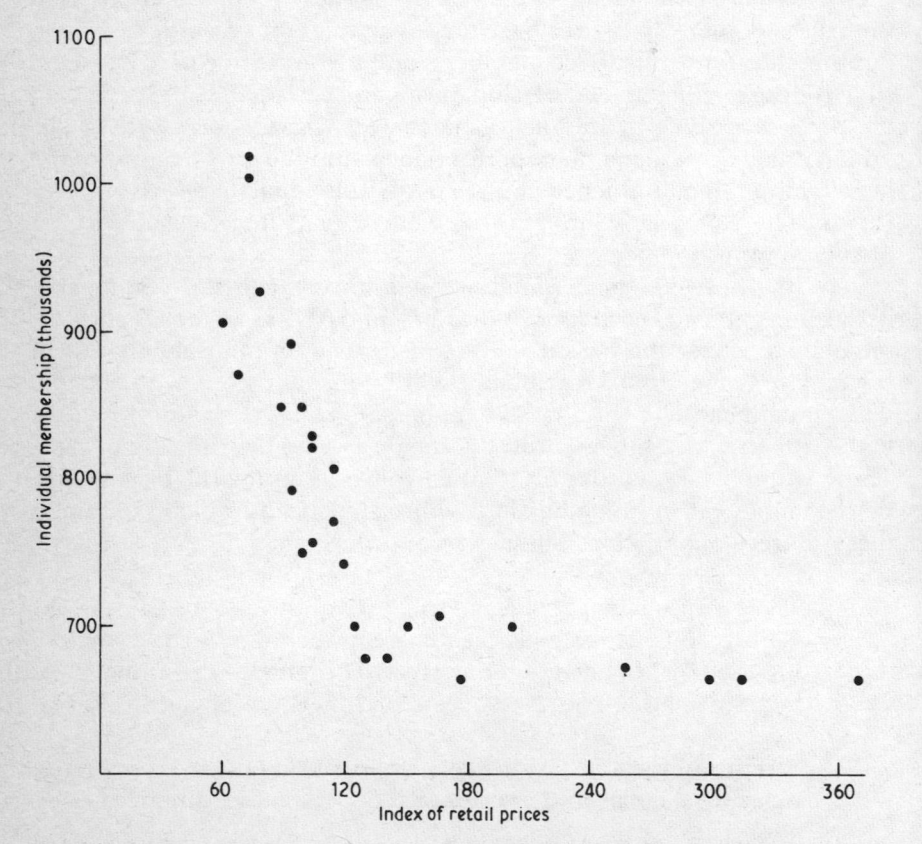

Figure 3.2   The relationship between individual party membership and inflation, 1950–78

Source: Labour Party headquarters.

(see Appendix I) between all the variables, and so it is necessary to transform the variables in Figures 3.2 and 3.3 in order to linearize them.

A variety of models and specifications were tested, and the results of
five different models appear in Table 3.6 and we shall discuss each of
these in turn. The first model in this table incorporates the three control
variables and the two economic variables without any modifications.
Each of the coefficients in the models measure the effect on membership
of a unit change in the predictor variable, so for example in model 1 an
increase in inflation of 1 per cent decreases membership by 0.65 thou-
sand, and Labour incumbency appears to increase membership rather
than decrease it by an average of 51,500. The R^2 or percentage variance
explained in the membership variable is quite high at 0.77 or 77 per cent.

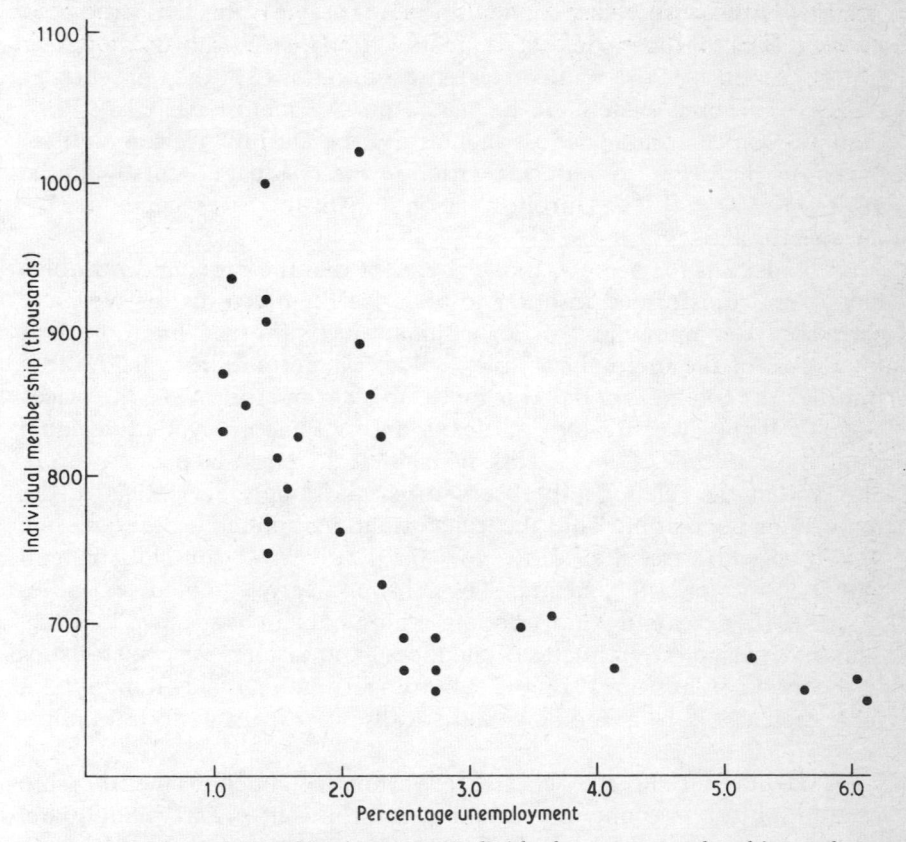

Figure 3.3 The relationship between individual party membership and unemployment, 1950–78

Source: Labour Party headquarters. Unemployment is calculated by
dividing the June unemployment figures by the total of the working
population, using various issues of the *Department of Employment
Gazette.*

However, in the first model neither unemployment nor inflation appear to be statistically significant, since the *t* statistics associated with those coefficients are not large enough.[2] This means that if we treat these data as a sample, then we cannot be sure that the state of the economy and membership are related in the underlying population from which this sample was taken. In other words the effects we observe in model 1 might be due just to chance. However, model 1 is inadequate for two reasons. Firstly, we know from Figures 3.2 and 3.3 that the economic variables should be transformed because they are curvilinear, but secondly the Durbin–Watson statistics tell us that the model is misspecified, i.e. important variables have been omitted.[3] The Durbin–Watson statistic measures relationships between successive residuals of the model (a residual is the observed membership minus the membership predicted by the model). If the model fits adequately then these residuals should be just a random series of uncorrelated observations. If they are not, it means that some systematic influence on the membership has been omitted from the model. More technically the Durbin–Watson statistic measures the degree of autocorrelation in the residuals (Koutsoyiannis, 1973, pp. 194–221). The Durbin–Watson statistic indicates that model 1 is misspecified.

Model 2 is the same as model 1 except that the economic variables have been transformed in order to linearize them. To do this we have expressed unemployment in logarithms, and expressed inflation as a reciprocal of the original variable. These transformations considerably improve the goodness of fit of the model to 0.84, and they make the prices variable highly statistically significant, and the unemployment variable significant at the 0.10 level. This means that there is a 90 per cent probability that the relationship observed in this sample also exists in the underlying population. Thus the transformations applied to the economic variables were essential. However, the Durbin–Watson statistic still shows positive autocorrelation; we have clearly omitted variables essential for explaining the variation in membership over time. This fact imparts error to the estimates of the model and distorts the test statistics of the model (Johnston, 1972, p. 249). Autocorrelation makes it likely that a coefficient will be accepted as statistically significant when in fact it is not.

We have attempted to control for various influences on membership in addition to the economic variables, but the controls are inadequate. There are a myriad of possible influences on membership and it is extremely difficult to measure and include everything which might be relevant. Fortunately, we do not need to estimate the precise relationship between the omitted variables and membership, we only need to control their influence so as to measure the relationship between economic conditions and membership efficiently. Consequently, we can use a 'proxy'

Table 3.6 Economic variables as predictors of Labour's individual membership, 1960–78, controlling for confounding influences – ordinary least squares estimates

Predictor	1	2	3	4	5
Labour incumbency dummy	51.56	13.34	30.44		
	(1.66)	(0.52)	(1.53)		
Labour popularity in the polls	10.69	7.65	7.38	5.38	5.38
	(3.24)	(2.66)	(3.61)	(2.67)	(3.45)
1963 dummy variable	−137.38	−48.94	−20.76		
	(4.62)	(1.38)	(0.82)		
Index of retail prices (1963 = 100)	−0.65				
	(1.42)				
Rate of unemployment	18.67				
	(0.78)				
Reciprocal of index of retail prices		25044.33	21925.28		21342.31
		(3.75)	(3.8)		(4.16)
Logarithm of unemployment		59.14	100.33		94.39
		(1.68)	(3.8)		(3.71)
Membership lagged one year			0.55	0.82	0.58
			(4.26)	(10.19)	(4.61)
Constant Term	413.27	197.13	−254.8	−104.24	−177.26
R^2	0.77	0.84	0.93	0.86	0.92
Durbin–Watson statistic	0.90	0.83	—	—	—
Durbin's h statistic	—	—	1.55	1.61	1.91
N	29	29	28	28	28

(t statistics in parenthesis, $t > \pm 1.96$ is significant at the 0.05 level)

Sources: Unemployment is calculated by dividing the June unemployment figures by the total of the working population, using various issues of the *Department of Employment Gazette*.

Prices are taken from Butler and Sloman (1980, p. 349, col. 5).

variable to represent all these omitted variables. The best proxy variable is membership lagged one period. Obviously all the omitted variables which are unmeasured in the model but which influence membership, will also influence membership lagged one period. The latter can therefore be used to control for these sources of variation in the dependent variable. Accordingly, we include membership lagged one period as a predictor in model 3.

If this is done the goodness of fit is improved still further to an excellent 0.93 per cent of the variance explained with the lagged dependent variable as a predictor the Durbin–Watson statistic is no longer an appropriate test for autocorrelation (Johnston, 1972, p. 309). Instead we use Durbin's h statistic, which was developed to deal specifically with models of this kind (Durbin, 1970). The h statistic is distributed as a standard normal distribution, so that values outside the range ±1.96 indicate the presence of autocorrelation. The h statistic associated with model 3 is well within the range enabling us to rule out autocorrelation. The use of the lagged dependent variable (i.e. all observations of the dependent variable up to and including the previous time period) has successfully controlled for other unmeasured influences on membership, and we can reliably interpret the coefficients of this model.

In the model the two economic variables are highly significant predictors of membership, as is membership lagged one period. However, including the latter has made the relationship between Labour incumbency, the 1963 dummy variable and membership non-significant. This is hardly surprising since by including lagged membership we are now in effect modelling the annual change in membership, something which can be clearly seen by moving the lagged membership variable to the left-hand side of the equation. Obviously current popularity in the opinion polls is likely to influence the change in membership, and this variable remains highly significant. But the incumbency and 1963 dummy variables measure rather long-term phenomena which are unlikely to influence the year to year changes in membership and for this reason become non-significant.

There are two other models in Table 3.6 which are included to facilitate the analysis. Model 4 includes the two control variables (popularity in the polls and lagged membership) which were statistically significant in model 3. These two variables alone explain 86 per cent of the variance in membership, but this is increased to 92 per cent by including the logarithm of unemployment and the reciprocal of prices as predictors as is done in model 5. Clearly, the economic variables make a significant contribution to improving the goodness of fit of the model overall. Moreover, the h statistic remains non-significant in both models.

In models 3 and 5 the t statistics indicate that the logarithm of unemployment and the reciprocal of prices inflation are highly significant predictors of membership, independent of the control variables. To consider price inflation first, the large value of the coefficient is caused by the reciprocal transformation, which also explains the positive sign; when prices rise, the reciprocal of prices falls and this produces a fall in membership so that the relationship between the reciprocal of prices and membership is positive. It is rather easier to interpret this coefficient in terms of the original prices variable rather than in terms of the reciprocal of prices; between 1963 and 1978 the index of retail prices increased from 100 to 365, according to the model this was associated with a fall in membership of approximately 159,000, a highly significant effect.

Unemployment and membership are positively related, so that as unemployment increases membership increases. The bivariate correlation between membership and the logarithm of unemployment is −0.69, which accords with the hypothesis that as unemployment rises membership falls, and at first sight the multivariate relationship appears paradoxical. But it is important to remember that the multivariate co-efficient measures the influence of unemployment on membership after Labour popularity, inflation and many other factors summarized by the lagged dependent variable have been controlled. A close examination of Figure 3.1 reveals a clear tendency for unemployment to increase under a Conservative government, compared with a Labour government, with the exception of the period after 1975 when the oil crisis had a deflation-ary effect on Western economies as a whole. Unemployment increased under a Conservative government as Labour membership increased on no less than four occasions prior to 1975; they were 1951–2, 1955–9, 1961–3 and 1970–2. Unemployment increased under Labour in the period 1966 to 1968 but the magnitude of the increase on this occasion was smaller than three out of the four cases of unemployment rising under the Conservatives. Thus the sign of the unemployment coefficient in the multivariate model is consistent with an anti-Conservative govern-ment surge in membership. Significantly, when unemployment rose during the Wilson government between 1966 and 1968 there was a sharp decline in Labour's membership. Unlike inflation which appears to have an adverse effect on membership whether or not Labour was incumbent, unemployment helps Labour to increase its membership in opposition but hurts it in government. The overall effect of these two tendencies is to produce a positive relationship between unemployment and member-ship.

The exception to this pattern occurred after 1975 when there was a rapid increase in unemployment between 1975 and 1978. Labour mem-bership was 675,000 in 1975 and 676,000 in 1978, therefore membership was hardly affected by this. There are two probable explanations for this. Firstly, the magnitude of the economic crisis after 1975 was much greater than any experienced since the war. The country entered a real recession for the first time since the 1930s. The sheer size of this change coupled with the fact that it was clearly associated with the OPEC oil price rises, changed the magnitude of the relationships between the state of the economy and membership. In a perverse way when unemployment is large enough members are increasingly likely to be aware that a Con-servative government represents a greater threat of further increases, than does the continuation of a Labour government. This makes them more loyal. Moreover, the reality of this expectation was borne out by events after the 1979 Conservative electoral victory. In other words when unemployment becomes a personal threat, rather than just a failure of ideological commitment, attitudes to the performance of Labour in com-parison with the Conservatives are likely to change.

A second point which influenced the membership figures in the late 1970s was the virtual disappearance of constituency parties who affiliated with more than the minimum membership. We saw earlier that only 14 per cent of constituencies affiliated with more than the minimum in 1978. It seems plausible that the published membership figures more accurately reflect the true membership for this group of constituencies, than for constituencies which affiliated with the minimum membership. Thus the bias in the published figures will become larger as the proportion of large constituency parties diminishes over time, as it did in the 1970s. This fact might well have masked a fall in the true membership figures between 1975 and 1978 which our control variables did not fully pick up. Therefore it is plausible that Labour's membership continued to be influenced by unemployment after 1975, but measurement error disguised this fact, because of the minimum affiliation rule.

In general these results show that economic policy outcomes have influenced the decline of Labour Party membership since the early 1950s, but unemployment and inflation have had different effects. In the case of inflation the performance of Labour in office is not distinguishable from the performance of the two-party system in general. Labour loses members because of inflation, whether it is in office or not. This may be partly due to the fact that electoral defeats for the party have traditionally led to extensive post-mortems, which in turn have produced faction fighting and internal wrangling. When the shortcomings of Labour in office are aired more in opposition than in power, this stimulates the decline in membership; such a process occurred in the years after the election defeat of 1970, and again in 1979. However, there may also be a factor of general disillusionment with politics as a whole when the record of both parties is one of persistent failure. This generalized cynicism would build up over many years and could affect the membership independently of Labour incumbency. However, this point can be overstated, since it is clear that unemployment influences membership differently depending on whether Labour is incumbent or in opposition. We know that Labour activists are much more concerned about unemployment than inflation; in the delegates' survey 39 per cent of respondents thought that unemployment was the most important issue facing the country, in comparison with 29 per cent who thought this was inflation (Whiteley, 1980). This greater saliency among activists makes it likely that they will be more sensitive to the issue and therefore more critical of the parties' performance in office than is true of inflation. Similarly, they are more ready to return to the fold when the Conservatives are incumbent, and are presiding over increased unemployment.

Aggregate analysis of this type has its limitations. Whilst we can observe the broad trends we cannot probe the detailed processes which operate to detach particular individuals from membership of the party. Ideally we require a panel sample of ex-Labour Party activists to investigate this fully. Psychological processes may be at work to detach members from the party, other than the performance of the party in power. Changes in society such as the decline of public meetings and the increasing dominance of the media in determining the nature and limits of political debates are also influential. The dominance of television as a means of providing political information at election times tends to reduce the importance of the activists. The rise of issue based pressure groups, particularly in the welfare field, might attract hitherto active Labour Party members who see more future in pursuing narrowly defined objectives than in the pursuit of broad strategies. The decline in the influence of the party conference during the Wilson years undoubtedly transmitted signals to the constituency parties about their relevance in the scheme of things, although this has changed in the late 1970s (Minkin, 1978). But having said all this it is clear that performance in office plays an important role in explaining the decline in membership.

Finally, it is clear that ideology plays a significant role in this. An individual with a strong, coherent ideological structure is much less likely to defect than an individual with a weak structure. This is not related to the degree of radicalism, but rather to the coherence of the ideological structure. For this reason the middle class with its expressive commitment to socialism tends to stay in the party, whereas the working class with its tendency towards instrumentalism tends to defect.

Conclusions

The decline in the individual membership of the Labour Party is explained in terms of the decline of working-class political activism at the grassroots level. There are a number of distinct factors which explain this decline, but perhaps the most important is the instrumental orientation towards politics of the working class. This contrasts with the affective orientation of the middle class. Individuals who join the party for instrumental reasons are inherently more likely to defect than those who join for affective reasons because of the 'free rider' problem. But this is made much worse by the persistent policy failures of the Labour Party in office. Over time, the policy failures, together with a number of other factors, have made the grassroots activists increasingly more middle class, more ideological in their approach to politics and less concerned with pragmatic instrumental questions. This has in turn contributed to the ideological dissensions in the party.

In this chapter we have discussed the crisis of Labour's declining membership, but there is a bigger, even more serious crisis which has emerged: the electoral crisis. We turn to this question next.

Notes

1 Clause 4 of the party constitution refers to the basic commitment to public ownership. The relevant section of this reads as follows: 'To secure for the

workers by hand or by brain the full fruits of their industry and the most equitable distribution thereof that may be possible upon the basis of the common ownership of the means of production, distribution and exchange, and the best obtainable system of popular administration and control of each industry or service.'

2 A *t* statistic is a measure of the statistical significance of a coefficient. A large *t* statistic means that its associated coefficient is most unlikely to have occurred due to chance in the sample being analysed. A small *t* statistic indicates that chance (i.e. the particular features of that sample) is the most likely explanation of the relationship. We refer to the *t* statistic because we wish to make statements about an underlying population from a random sample and the measure allows us to control for the unique characteristics of a sample when doing this.

3 Misspecification means that variables have been omitted from the model which should have been included, or that relationships are non-linear when they should be linear. Misspecification can produce biased estimates, so we cannot be sure that the coefficients in the model are accurate (Johnston, 1972, p. 168).

4

The electoral crisis

Perhaps the most serious of the crises facing the British Labour Party is the electoral crisis. The results of the 1983 General Election, together with the emergence of the SDP/Liberal Alliance, raise the spectre of permanent opposition. The weakness of Labour's electoral performance in 1979 has already been referred to in Chapter 1, but it can be further underlined by recalling that only 20.6 per cent of the total electorate voted Labour in 1983, the worst result since 1918.

   The aim of this chapter is to give an account of this electoral decline, which as we shall see is tied in with the performance of the party in power, and in the political system. Such an account can only be given within the context of a theory of electoral behaviour, since as we saw in Chapter 3, with any empirical model it is necessary to control for the behaviour of other relevant variables if we are to get an accurate picture. So we begin by reviewing the contemporary literature on electoral behaviour relevant to this issue, before specifying and testing a model of our own.

Explanation of voting behaviour

There are two broad traditions of research on voting behaviour which have come to dominate the literature in recent years. The first which might be characterized as the 'sociological' model of voting behaviour sees it as a product of social background and social–psychological factors in the electorate at the individual and group levels. The best known work on electoral behaviour in Britain by Butler and Stokes (1974) is squarely within this tradition, which has its origins in the work of Campbell and his associates at the University of Michigan (Campbell *et al.*, 1960).

   The second tradition of theoretical work on voting originated with Anthony Downs' seminal book *An Economic Theory of Democracy* (1957). This is the 'economic' or 'rational choice' model of electoral behaviour.

This tradition sees the voter as a rational utility-maximizing individual who votes for his most preferred party on the basis of past and future benefits received. This approach has given rise to rather more formal theoretical work than empirical work (Riker and Ordeshook, 1973) in comparison with the sociological model. But as we shall see it has strongly influenced the most recent research on voting behaviour in both Britain and the US. Our own model is essentially a synthesis of these two approaches, but before discussing that it is useful to review these traditions in more detail.

The sociological account of voting behaviour

Writing in 1967 Pulzer argued in a much quoted passage that 'class is the basis of British Party politics: all else is embellishment and detail' (p. 98). The relationship between social class and electoral behaviour is the central concern of the sociological model of voting in Britain. We can see this by examining the theoretical framework used by Butler and Stokes, which has been ably analysed by Crewe (1974).

The theoretical framework developed by Butler and Stokes centres on the concept of party identification. This refers to the long-term psychological attachment of the voter to one or other of the major political parties. This party identification is the most enduring feature of the voters' attitudes and political behaviour. It creates a process of selective perception in the mind of the voter which tends to filter out information at variance with this party identification, and accept information which reinforces it. It also tends to make voters develop attitudes towards issues which accord with the positions taken up by their parties. In this process the formative influences run from party identification to issue perceptions and not the other way round, for the great majority of voters.

For these reasons party identification tends to be self-reinforcing over time; so that an individual who supports a political party at a given election is more likely to do so at the next and subsequent elections. This means that younger voters who have not yet fully acquired their partisanship will more likely change their vote than older voters who have acquired a party identification. In the theory partisanship is a product of enduring social cleavages, principally social class. Thus the political and social environment in which the individual lives, and the experiences that he has, produce and reinforce partisanship along class lines.

Social class can be understood in subjective terms, that is in terms of how individual voters see it, or it can be understood in objective terms by some measure of the individual's position in the social structure. Butler and Stokes argued that the great majority of the electorate thought of themselves as members of a social class (1974, pp. 68–70), and most people measured class in terms of occupational status. Consequently, they used occupational status as the main indicator of social class. In their model social class and parental partisanship, which is itself a product of social class, are the main predictors of party identification and voting. So partisanship is strongly transmitted from one generation to another.

In the model political issues play a short-term role in influencing voting behaviour and really only then for individuals whose partisanship is weak. Such a weak partisanship is caused in two ways: firstly, if an individual's parents had mixed or weak partisanship then the process of intergenerational transmission would be inhibited; secondly, if individuals experience social mobility then they would move out of the social environment in which partisanship was created and sustained, thus weakening their identification. Butler and Stokes added a third rather *ad hoc* reason why partisanship might be weakened or disrupted. This was when a major economic or social upheaval occurred such as a major war or a severe depression. Such events might 're-educate' sufficient numbers of voters to cause a realignment of the party system. This third reason does not really follow from the earlier theoretical framework but was added on largely to explain the realignment of the party system after the First World War.

To summarize their model, social class largely explains party identification which in turn largely explains voting behaviour. To support this analysis they showed that in 1963 some 79 per cent of respondents in their survey with a middle-class self-image were Conservative identifiers, and 72 per cent with a working-class self-image were Labour identifiers (Butler and Stokes, 1974, p. 77). The relationship between social class and partisanship though not perfect appeared to be quite strong.

Crewe (1974) set out an extensive critique of this model. His central point in this critique was that Butler and Stokes had clearly failed to explain the secular decline in support for the two major parties since the 1950s. In an article with his co-researchers on the British election study (Crewe, Särlvik and Alt, 1977) he extended this critique pointing out that the Conservative and Labour parties had received the votes of 80.3 per cent of the total electorate in the 1951 election, and only 56.1 per cent in October 1974. There was nothing in Butler and Stokes' model which could explain this: between these elections there had been no major economic or social upheaval, some social mobility had taken place but it was 'glacially slow' (1974, p. 63) and there was no evidence of a breakdown in the intergenerational transmission of partisanship. Thus the model could not explain dealignment. If anything, with its emphasis on the self-reinforcing character of partisanship their model should predict a strengthening of partisanship rather than a decline.

Crewe does not provide a comprehensive explanation of the dealignment, but in his original article concentrated on calling into question the concept of party indentification. He criticizes the underlying model of the voter, who is seen rather as a passive automaton unable to make decisions and free choices and who adheres unquestioningly to one or other political party. In later work Crewe has stressed the importance of issues in electoral behaviour. In the article on partisan dealignment (Crewe, Särlvik and Alt, 1977) the authors argue that there was a growing rejection of the basic tenets of Labour Party policy by Labour voters. In particular Labour voters in 1974 were increasingly hostile towards the trade union movement, and by implication the links between the party and the trade unions. Similarly in an analysis of the issues in the 1979 election Crewe (1982) stresses the gap between the policy preferences of Labour identifiers and their perceptions of Labour's policy positions on a wide variety of issues. This type of analysis implies that dealignment at least in the case of the Labour Party is due to the gap between party policy and the issue preferences of the electorate. Harrop (1982) uses a similar argument.

Other writers have made criticisms of the original Butler and Stokes model. Rose (1974) argues that social class is more complex than Butler and Stokes would suggest with their emphasis on occupational status. In his view the critical determinant of voting behaviour in a constituency is the local concentration of core classes in that constituency. Core classes are multidimensional, so that for example an ideal type member of the core working class has five different characteristics: minimum education, trade union family, council house tenancy, manual occupation and working-class identification. Individuals with these characteristics are the core members of the 'anti-controllers' class as distinct from the 'controllers' class who have the polar opposite social characteristics. Miller (1977, p. 148) has shown that the percentage of employers and managers in a constituency is a very strong predictor of the Conservative two-party vote in post-war elections. This group represent the controllers class, and so Miller's evidence strongly supports this interpretation. Gordon and Whiteley (1981) found similar evidence to support this in an analysis of the European and General Elections in Britain of 1979. The 'controllers' and 'anti-controllers' classes are relatively small minorities in the electorate, and it could be argued that since large changes have taken place over time in some of the variables defining core class membership, this could partly explain dealignment. For example the increase in owner occupation over time obviously influences one important variable which defines core class membership.

Dunleavy (1979, 1980a, 1980b) makes a similar criticism that Butler and Stokes rely on a simplistic notion of class. He introduces the notion of production and consumption sectors as having an influence on voting behaviour independent of social class. The notion of a sector was developed by O'Connor (1973) and Habermas (1976) to describe vertical divisions in society which represent cleavages that cross-cut social class. In production, these sectors represent different ways in which capital is organized which in turn influence the labour market and the degree of working-class organization. Dunleavy (1980a, pp. 380–2) discusses three production sectors. The corporate sector is characterized by large scale capital, high levels of investment, large firms, administered prices and a high level of unionization in the work force. The market sector is characterized by small firms, involving small scale capital, market determined prices, low investment and weak unionization. Finally, the public sector is labour rather than capital intensive, with politically determined prices, a rapid growth in size in recent years, and is highly unionized with a highly politicized wage-bargaining system. His discussion of consumption sectors (1979) concentrates on the distinction between owner occupiers and tenants in the housing arena, and car owners and public transport users in the transport area.

Dunleavy does not directly apply his model to the question of partisan dealignment but speculates that vast changes in production and consumption sectors in the postwar period could have had major electoral effects. In the production sector the major development has been the rise of public sector employment. He points out that 31 per cent of the work force were in the public services or public corporations in 1976, compared with 24 per cent in 1961, a rise of nearly two-thirds (1980a, p. 366). In the consumption sector about 30 per cent of households were owner occupiers in 1950, rising to 53 per cent in 1976 (1979, p. 411). These changes are significant by any standards and clearly provide a possible explanation for dealignment.

The empirical evidence for the sectoral analysis provides stronger support for the theory in the case of consumption sectors rather than production sectors. Dunleavy argues that the consumption sector effects of housing and car ownership are comparable to occupational status in their influence on voting behaviour. His results have been heavily criticized (Harrop, 1980) for failing to control for confounding influences such as age and income, and also for failing to examine any attitudinal differences between individuals in different sectors which could support the hypothesized political differences. The evidence relating to production sectors showed no direct link between sector and voting behaviour, but demonstrated an indirect link operating via social class and unionization (Dunleavy, 1980b, pp. 544–7). Further research has however demonstrated a link between membership of the public sector and voting behaviour (Alt and Turner, 1982). It appears that the rise in the Labour middle-class vote has a lot to do with the rise in public sector professional employment. The rise in the Labour middle-class vote (Crewe, Särlvik and Alt, 1977; Rallings, 1975) is an important aspect of dealignment, but if the sectoral model can partly account for this it cannot account for the fall in the working-class Labour vote. In the 1979 General Election the Conservatives obtained 44 per cent of the skilled manual workers, compared with Labour's 45 per cent (Crewe, 1981, p. 280). It might be argued that the consumption sector theory can explain this. But apart from Harrop's criticisms of this theory referred to earlier, such an interpretation does not accord with the findings of Goldthorpe and his associates (Goldthorpe *et al.*, 1969). Their classic study of affluent workers showed that increased affluence, and the acquisition of consumer goods along with it, did not bring a change of political allegiance in the affluent working class. It seems clear that the sectoral analysis though interesting does not give a full account of the process of dealignment.

One final problem facing the Butler–Stokes model is a methodological issue. It does not appear possible to measure party identification independently of voting behaviour. There are standard survey questions designed to measure party identification and voting intentions, and voters appear to respond in a similar way to both (Mughan, 1981). This is not true in the United States where voting intentions and party identification are empirically independent of each other (Nie *et al.*, 1976). Since the concept of party identification is so central to the theory, then the inability to measure it accurately makes the theory untestable; we do not know if party identification is or is not a key factor in explaining voting behaviour. Some writers have suggested that social background variables can be used to measure the long term predispositions of voters, as a kind of proxy measure of party identification (Budge and Farlie, 1977) but this involves a major departure from Butler and Stokes' theoretical analysis.

In conclusion Butler and Stokes' theoretical model is fundamentally inadequate in explaining political change in Britain. Various criticisms of it have been made and amendments suggested within the basic sociological paradigm. Some of these, particularly the sectoral theory, throw useful light on aspects of partisan dealignment, but none give a wholly satisfactory account. The basic problem with the sociological paradigm is that its fundamental conception of human behaviour is flawed. It disregards to a great extent the ability of individuals to make autonomous choices in the light of their own preferences and experiences. It tends to see voters as automata, driven by outside social forces without any willingness or ability to make their own decisions. This is why purely sociological accounts of electoral behaviour will never be wholly satisfactory.

The economic theory of voting behaviour

The economic or rational choice theory of voting really made its first impact in political science with the publication of Downs' book, although similar work had been done earlier in the field of formal political theory

(Black, 1958). In the economic model voters are rational utility maximizers who vote in order to promote their most preferred policies. In order to do this they vote for the political party which is closest to their own most preferred policy position. They are pure issue voters who will rapidly switch support between parties if a new party emerges or an old party changes its policies to a position closer to their preferences. Thus there is no party identification in the Downsian model.

In the original analysis (Downs, 1957, pp. 114–41) it was assumed that the electorate were distributed along a single left–right dimension, and the political parties manoeuvred along this dimension in order to maximize votes. The left–right dimension represents all the issues which figure in electoral politics, and thus an implicit assumption of the theory is that the attitudes of voters are highly constrained, since every issue is related to every other issue. If the electoral space was multidimensional, with separate dimensions for economic policy, social policy, foreign policy and so on, the theory breaks down. This is because a multidimensional policy space is pervaded by policy cycles (Schofield, 1978a; Riker, 1980). This means that whenever a party adopts a set of policies which are supported by a majority of the electorate, a second party can always attract a majority also with a different set of policies. The first party can then attract a majority back by another set of policies and so on, so that no stable majority can be maintained by any party. This problem feeds back into the electorate since voters cannot reliably support a party which comes closest to their preferences when parties are constantly shifting ground in order to outflank their rivals. In this situation the entire model breaks down. These results are purely theoretical but are of great interest because they demonstrate that if voters actually behaved according to the tenets of classical democratic theory and voted purely on policies then, unless they were all ideologues, democratic politics would be impossible. Therefore, the underlying social cleavages such as social class which give rise to political cleavages not based purely on policy help to keep the system stable.

Much of the original work derived from Downs was purely formal with little or no empirical content (Riker and Ordeshook, 1973; Mueller, 1979). Such work is useful for analysing the basic logic of collective action, but it cannot provide an adequate account of electoral behaviour (Budge and Farlie, 1977, pp. 156–84). Thus the most fruitful work arising from the rational choice tradition has sought to modify and adapt the theory to make it accord more realistically with the actual world of electoral politics.

One example of this is Robertson's theory of party competition (1976) which attempts to synthesize the rational choice and sociological approaches to voting behaviour. His model contains two attitude spaces, analogous to Downs' left–right dimension. The first is a policy aims space which measures the voters' concerns with policy outcomes, e.g. greater social equality in society. The second is a policy methods space which measures the concern of politicians which bring about the policy aims, e.g. by introducing a wealth tax. In this model voters are concerned only with policy aims, and not with policy methods which are the concern of the elite decision makers. Information about politics is seen as costly to acquire, and the electorate are willing to delegate the details of policy making to the leadership of their party for this reason. They only begin to take an interest in aims and methods if significant changes occur in their own preferred parties' policies. Parties manoeuvre for support in the policy aims space but the costs of information coupled with the fact that parties cannot move anywhere in the space, allows them to maintain reasonably stable coalitions of voters. Restrictions of party movements are assumed because it is most unlikely in practice for a political party to adopt any policy which might win votes. For example, the Conservative Party could not credibly adopt nationalization as a policy, even if this might increase its vote. Robertson argues from an empirical analysis of party manifestos over many years that the policy aims space is two dimensional, and this, coupled with the other restrictions we have mentioned on party movements, makes electoral politics in Britain reasonably stable.

Budge and Farlie (1977) have further developed this spatial model of electoral behaviour. Their model contains no less than eleven distinct spaces relevant to the analysis of electoral choice (p. 221). However, for questions purely of voting behaviour only two of these are really important, the policy formation space and the background characteristics space. The former reflects short-term electoral issues, and the latter long-term predispositions for supporting one party rather than another. They use a multivariate technique to investigate the relative importance of social background characteristics and the attitudes of voters towards issues in influencing voting behaviour in Britain (Budge *et al.*, 1976, pp. 103–26). They conclude that background characteristics such as social class, education and so on had slightly more predictive power than issues in determining voting behaviour in 1963 (p. 119).

A third model which is rooted in social psychology but which draws on the rational choice literature is by Himmelweit and her associates (1981). The theory has its origins in the work of Fishbein on predicting behaviour from attitudes (Fishbein, Thomas and Jaccard, 1976; Ajzen and Fishbein, 1980). The model combines the expected utility calculations of the rational choice theorists with the social background variables of the sociological theorists (Himmelweit *et al.*, 1981, pp. 112–29). The decision to vote is treated as being analogous to any problem of consumer choice in which the voter has to choose a party from an array of competing parties, much as the consumer has to choose soapflakes from an array of competing brands. The overall 'worth' of attractiveness of the party depends on the desirability of its policies and the likelihood that it will implement those policies in office. The more a voter cares about an issue, and the stronger his belief that one party will implement it rather than another, the more likely he is to vote for it. The model is used to predict the vote from various issue indicators and the voter's previous voting history using a panel sample of males, and it gives an 80 per cent correct prediction of the voting behaviour of their sample in 1974 (p. 127). The model is quite interesting but the empirical analysis is unreliable in view of the unrepresentative nature of the sample, which by 1974 consisted of a small sample of middle-class males.

These are examples of rational choice type models applied to Britain. They are distinguished from the sociological theories discussed earlier in allowing the voter an autonomous ability to choose in the light of his or her experiences and aspirations. In the light of this literature we shall now develop our own model of electoral behaviour in Britain with the aim of trying to explain partisan dealignment.

A theory of electoral behaviour in Britain

Any theoretical synthesis of the work on electoral behaviour needs to take into account the long-term predisposition of voters in supporting a given party, as well as the short-term issues which influence voting behaviour. In doing this we shall abandon the concept of party identification in the sense in which it has been traditionally used because of the conceptual and methodological problems it faces. As we have seen it is both theoretically unclear (Crewe, 1974) and empirically inseparable (Mughan, 1981) from voting intentions.

The theoretical model of voting behaviour we shall use is summarized diagrammatically in Figure 4.1, and we shall discuss it conceptually before examining empirical evidence. The straight line arrows in Figure 4.1 denote a causal relationship between variables, and a curved double headed arrow denotes a statistical association with no specified causal path. In the model the dependent variable is the probability of an individual voting Labour which, like all probabilities varies from 1 (certainty) to 0 (impossibility). There are two broad classes of factors which are used to explain the probability of voting Labour. Firstly, there are the individual's social attributes, which in the model measure the individual's relationship to the means of production and consumption. Secondly, there are subjective evaluations which measure the individual's attitudes to the Labour Party, its policies and performance.

The model should be considered as merely part of a wider and more general model of the political system. System models of politics have been extensively developed at the theoretical level (Easton, 1965;

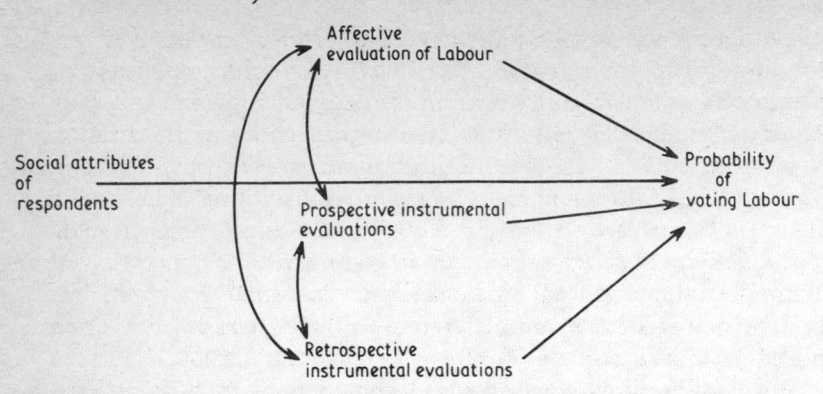

Figure 4.1 A theoretical model of voting in Britain

Deutsch, 1963) but have been applied largely in the literature on policy analysis (Lindblom, 1968) and political development (Almond and Powell, 1966). In the present case electoral behaviour is seen as an input into the political system which provides support and legitimacy to democratic politics, but is strongly influenced by policy outcomes. There is a growing literature which examines the link between policy outputs, political support and electoral behaviour (Whiteley, 1980; Hibbs and Fassbender, 1981) and we shall make this link a key factor in the theory.

The central assumption of the model is that voters support a political party because it brings them objective and subjective benefits at the individual and collective levels. The electorate can be subdivided into various groups or collectives along certain well-defined social cleavages such as social class, sector of production, region of the country and so on. Individuals within these collective groups have interests which are a product of this collective membership. For example members of a trade union have an interest in protecting their right to organize under the law, owner occupiers have an interest in state subsidies for mortgage payments and so on. Any one individual will be a member of several collectives whose interests may be mutually antagonistic. Thus car owners have an interest that state subsidies should go to roads rather than to public transport, but those car owners who are commuters have an interest in subsidies for the railways. These interests are a product of the individuals' membership of the collective and are organized into demands made upon the political system with varying degrees of efficiency by the collective action of pressure groups and the political parties. In addition political parties have the role of mobilizing bias in favour of certain collectives at the expense of others when they are in office. Thus as well as making demands, political parties are in a position to influence the supply of policy outputs in favour of some collectives rather than others. They achieve a bias in 'who gets what, when and how' (Lasswell, 1936) in favour of particular collective groups in exchange for electoral and other types of support from those groups. A political party which is interested in power faces the problem of balancing the often antagonistic needs of various collectives in order to construct a winning coalition of support in electoral terms. In this analysis so long as Labour represents the objective needs of, say, unskilled manual workers in the political system, by achieving a bias in their favour, it will retain their support. If it fails to do this it will in the long run lose their support to other parties.

The main source of differences in collective interests in our society originate from the individual's relationship to the means of production and consumption. Different production and consumption locations give rise to different objective needs and interests which in turn become translated into policies and policy outcomes via the political system. Therefore the link between production and consumption locations and electoral behaviour operates via the political system and the success or otherwise of political parties in meeting those interests. Individuals within these collectives learn, often over many years, how their relationship to the means of production and consumption are influenced by the party system. This learning process takes place partly within the collective by group socialization and partly outside via the media. The link between the party system and collective interests is slow to construct and slow to dismantle, but it needs to be sustained by a two-way interaction of supports and policy outcomes in the long run.

Subjective interests and needs are those which individuals articulate at any one point of time and they are not necessarily the same thing as objective needs. This is true for a number of reasons. Individuals may not know that they benefit from a given set of policies rather than another, and in a complex political system this can often be difficult to determine, even by experts. Secondly, there may be no real choice between the parties in terms of supporting particular collective interests and so people can become confused about whether their interests can be supported by a particular party. Thirdly, the political system frequently has to deal with paradoxes of collective action (Olson, 1965) which make the interests of particular individuals in a collective ambiguous. For example, it is in the interests of workers as a whole to link the growth in incomes to the growth in productivity in order to avoid inflation, but it is in the interests of particular workers to achieve pay rises well above inflation. At the same time if everyone achieves big increases this will accelerate inflation. In this situation the interests of workers are ambiguous or fragmented depending on their bargaining power, and for this reason subjective and objective interests might diverge. Fourthly, some individuals might support policies which they recognize as being in the collective interest but not in their own personal interests; this has been described as sociotropic voting (Kinder and Kiewet, 1981). Finally, individuals can have false consciousness and support policies which are not in their own objective interests, but which reflect the dominant ideology in society (Parkin, 1971). In general the transmission of objective needs and interests into party support and thence into policy outcomes will be mediated by a complex set of subjective factors not necessarily directly related to the individual's objective situation in the social structure. We might hypothesize that in the long run, subjective and objective needs will coincide, but politics and policy are characterized by a series of short runs in which such interests do not necessarily coincide. However, for society as a whole, as distinct from particular individuals, objective and subjective interests will be significantly if imperfectly linked in the political system.

The subjective interests which mediate between objective needs and voting behaviour in our model are of two types. Firstly, there are affective evaluations which measure how individuals feel about a political party, whether they like or dislike the image of that party. Secondly, there are instrumental evaluations which are concerned with the voters' assessments of the performance of that party. Following Fiorina (1977, 1981) we distinguish between prospective and retrospective evaluations. Prospective evaluations refer to the voters' assessment of the future policies adopted by a party, and the relationship between these and their own policy preferences. Retrospective evaluations refer to the voters' assessment of the past performance of the party in implementing those policies once it is in power; it can also refer to the voters' hypothetical judgement of how a party would have performed had it been in power.

The notion of affective evaluations is much more general than the notion of party identification. It is not just concerned with the individuals' partisanship but how they feel in general about one party compared with another. Thus two respondents could identify with the Labour Party, one of them strongly disliking the Conservatives, and the other regarding them in neutral terms. Similarly, an individual might not identify with any party but dislike Labour more than the Conservatives. Clearly affective evaluations are related to instrumental evaluations, which is why we do not assign a causal sequence to these variables in the model but just regard them as interacting. Affective evaluations are influenced by the performance and personality of the party leadership, its historical associations and the kind of people voters feel support that party. Ultimately affective evaluations will be influenced strongly by objective interests. But at any one point of time the relationship between these two is likely to be cross-cut by a complex set of factors, some of which were discussed earlier. Nevertheless, we should expect to see a link between social attributes and affective evaluations.

Retrospective and prospective evaluations are analytically and empirically related but conceptually distinct. In a purely rational choice model individuals are more likely to use retrospective evaluations than prospective evaluations in assessing the political parties. Downs explains why when he discusses the voter's choice in a two-party system:

> (The voter) must either compare (1) two hypothetical future utility incomes or (2) one actual present utility income and one hypothetical present one. Without question, the latter comparison allows him to make more direct use of concrete facts than the former. Not only is one of its terms a real entity, but the other can be calculated in full view of the situation from which it springs. If he compares future utility incomes, he enjoys neither of these advantages. Therefore we believe it is more rational for him to ground his voting decision on current events than purely on future ones.   (1957, p. 40)

Thus rational voters are more likely to be guided by retrospective rather than prospective evaluations, since the former are more tangible and certain than the latter. Once again retrospective and prospective evaluations will be influenced by social attributes. The link between policy outcomes and instrumental evaluations is outside the scope of this particular model, but we shall take up this issue again in a later chapter.

In the light of this model our theoretical explanation of long term partisan dealignment is clear. The party system increasingly fails to represent the objective and subjective interests of the electorate. This is partly due to changes in those objective needs which in the case of Labour creates serious problems for the party in terms of its policy outputs. To give a simple example, a policy bias which favours Council tenants at the expense of owner occupiers is likely to become an increasing electoral liability as the owner-occupier sector grows over time. But also the dealignment is due to the failure of the party to achieve policy outcomes which do promote the interests of its support groups, such as full employment, regardless of any changes in the make up of these support groups. A third point is that the paradoxes of collective action referred to earlier, particularly in relation to incomes, are getting greater over time. As the public and corporate section grow at the expense of the market sector then wage bargaining and the allocation of incomes becomes more politically determined rather than market determined. Many years ago governments were not held responsible for the allocation of incomes in society because to a very large extent these were determined by the market. This is no longer the case, and now government is held responsible for this even though it may have great difficulty in controlling such allocations. As we said earlier objective interests are ambiguous or fragmented in this case, which produces a situation where the government loses politically whatever it does.

Subjective interests tend to follow objective interests, but they can also operate independently. If the link between objective interests and voting behaviour is weakened then subjective interests can be manipulated more easily by the media and Labour's political opponents. The bias in the media against trade unions and the Labour movement is now well documented (Glasgow Media Group, 1976), and this becomes more important in undermining Labour support when the objective basis of this support is weaker. Moreover, the weakening of support tends to make Labour in office more timid and less willing to pursue policies such as a wealth tax which are in the objective interests of its support groups. This further weakens support, creating a vicious circle of cause and effect.

The evidence for the proposition that the Labour Party increasingly does not represent the objective interests of its support groups will be discussed more fully in a later chapter, but for now we can examine the implications of the argument. We should expect to see a weakening of the links between social attributes and party support in the electorate as a whole. We should also expect to see an increase in retrospective dissatisfaction with the performance of the party in office. There may be evidence of increasing dissatisfaction with the party's prospective policy position also but the link between this and declining support is likely to be rather weak, playing only a minor role. This is true for two broad reasons. Firstly, there has been a gap between the policy preferences of Labour voters, and the position taken by the party on many issues over a long period, well before dealignment took place (Milne and Mackenzie, 1954; Abrams *et al.*, 1960). Consequently it is difficult to attribute dealignment to it. Secondly, because prospective issues can often be remote from the personal experiences of voters, responses to survey questions about such issues are much more likely to reflect the dominant ideology than are issues closer to the everyday experience of voters. Dunleavy (1980b, p. 533) cites some evidence which supports this interpretation. In a survey carried out in 1975 some 66 per cent of trade unionists agreed that 'trade unions have too much power'. At the same time 80 per cent of respondents in all occupational groups denied that their own union had too much power. Thus the response to the generalized question was much more likely to reflect the dominant ideology that trade unions are too powerful and are economically disruptive, than the response to the specific question which was placed within the individual's direct experience, and frame of reference. For these reasons we should expect retrospective evaluations to be more significant than prospective evaluations as explanations of dealignment. In the light of this analysis we can examine the empirical evidence in support of the model.

Testing the theory of voting

The model will be tested using the data from the 1979 British Election Study cross section sample. Ideally it should be tested with time series panel data, but the variables in the panel sample of the British Election Study 1974–9 are not adequate for our purposes. The 1979 cross section sample contained retrospective issue indicators not previously available. Similarly, indicators of production sector membership were not available before this year. Finally, the prospective indicators used in the present analysis were in most cases introduced for the first time in 1979. For these reasons we shall use cross sectional data.

The dependent variable in the model is the probability of an individual voting Labour. In the model this is a dummy variable scoring one for Labour voters and zero for all others which includes Conservatives, Liberals, minor party voters and non-voters. The social attributes consist of six variables which measure the relationship of the individual to the means of production and consumption. Six of these variables are production sector variables; these are the respondent's occupational status measured using the same six point scale as Butler and Stokes (1974, pp. 68–73), a dummy variable (coded 1 and 0)[1] measuring whether or not the respondent was a trade union member, and four dummy variables measuring the respondent's employment sector: market, corporate, public services and public corporations. Membership of the market sector meant that the respondent worked in a private firm with fewer than 25 employees; membership of the corporate sector meant employment in a private firm with more than 100 employees; membership of the public service sector meant employment in national or local government; and membership of the public corporation sector meant employment in the nationalized industries. There were two indicators of consumption sector status; whether or not the respondent was an owner occupier, and whether or not he or she owned a car. Altogether then we used eight separate variables to measure the respondent's relationship to the means of production and consumption.

The affective evaluation indicator was provided by a question which asked the respondents: 'Let us say that you gave each of the parties a mark out of ten points – a mark according to how much or how little you like it. You can give each party any mark from 0 out of 10 to 10 out of 10.' Each respondent's score out of ten for the Labour Party was used to measure his affective evaluation. The retrospective evaluations were measured with four variables relating to inflation, unemployment, strikes and law and order. In the case of unemployment for example, respondents were asked: 'How well do you think the recent Labour government handled the problem of unemployment – very well, fairly well, not very well, or not at all well?' The prospective evaluations had to be selected from a large number, since as we saw in Chapter 2 there were no less than 41 possible measures. However, a sample of these measures were accompanied by a question asking voters to indicate the importance of that issue in their decision to vote. In the case of five of these prospective issues at least 50 per cent of the sample said that the issue was extremely important or fairly important in influencing their vote. These issues were cuts in social services, taxation versus government spending, legal curbs on trade unions, the economic policy of the common market, and free collective bargaining or government intervention in wage determination. Consequently we used these five variables as indicators of prospective evaluations.

It is interesting to look at the pattern of responses for these eighteen variables cross-tabulated by the dependent variable. This is done in Table 4.1. The percentages in Table 4.1 refer to the percentage of respondents with that particular attribute in 1979 who either did or did not vote Labour. For example 48.8 per cent of union members voted Labour, and 51.2 per cent did not, quite a surprising figure. Similarly 31 per cent of non-union members voted Labour and 69 per cent did not. This table includes the correlation between the dependent variable and each of the eighteen variables in parenthesis beneath each sub-table. This correlation assumes that all variables are quantitative, which is quite a legitimate assumption in the case of the dummy variables and is fairly orthodox in the cases of the ordinal attitude variables. An ordinal variable is one in which the scores represent rankings from a 'high' to 'low' scale rather than numerical values. For example in variable 14, respondents who argue that benefits should be cut back a lot rank higher than those who think they should remain the same, but we cannot say anything about the numerical distance between these rankings.

To consider social attributes first, the strongest relationships in Table 4.1 are between the consumption indicators and voting behaviour. Only 30.3 per cent of the car owners were Labour compared with 48.7 per cent of non-owners. Similarly, 26 per cent of home owners were Labour compared with 51.3 per cent of non-owners or council and private tenants. Compared with this, the production sector variables are not significantly related to voting. This confirms Dunleavy's findings (1980b) that no direct relationship existed between sector and voting, although indirect links did exist via other variables. The relationship between occupational status and voting is significant but not very strong, with a correlation of only 0.23. Finally, there is a clear relationship between union membership and Labour voting, which is about the same strength as the link between voting and car ownership.

The retrospective voting indicators are quite strongly related to voting. It is no surprise that Labour voters are much more likely to think that the party handled the economy better than the others. The price inflation, unemployment and strikes variables are approximately equally related to Labour voting, and law and order is slightly less so, but nevertheless it is more significant than social attributes. The affective evaluation scale is more strongly related to voting than any other variable; its

Table 4.1 The relationship between social attributes, affective, prospective and retrospective evaluations and Labour voting, 1979 (N = 1893). The percentage of respondents with attribute who are Labour, or not Labour (correlations of variable and Labour vote in parenthesis)

Variable	Coding	Labour	Not Labour
1 Unionization	Union member	48.8	51.2
	Not union member	31.0	69.0
		(0.17)	
2 Home ownership	Home owner	26.0	74.0
	Not home owner	51.3	48.7
		(−0.26)	
3 Car ownership	Car owner	30.3	73.2
	Not car owner	48.7	51.3
		(0.18)	
4 Occupational status	Higher managerial (A)	17.1	82.9
	Middle managerial (B)	25.5	74.5
	Skilled non-manual (CIA)	18.7	81.3
	Lower non-manual (CIB)	33.0	67.0
	Skilled manual (C2)	46.6	53.4
	Un- or semiskilled (D)	49.4	50.6
	Manual	(0.23)	
5 Membership of market sector	Member	34.1	65.9
	Not member	36.7	63.3
		(−0.02)	
6 Membership of corporate sector	Member	39.5	60.5
	Not member	35.3	64.7
		(0.04)	
7 Membership of public service sector	Member	36.8	63.2
	Not member	36.4	63.6
		(0.00)	
8 Membership of public corporation sector	Member	48.4	51.6
	Not member	35.2	64.8
		(0.08)	
9 Labour's handling of prices	Very well	67.3	32.7
	Fairly well	44.1	55.9
	Not very well	16.7	83.3
	Not at all well	10.6	89.4
		(−0.37)	
10 Labour's handling of unemployment	Very well	78.5	21.5
	Fairly well	50.2	49.8
	Not very well	21.6	78.4
	Not at all well	7.4	92.6
		(−0.41)	

Table 4.1—(cont.)

Variable	Coding	Labour	Not Labour
11 Labour's handling of strikes	Very well	73.9	26.1
	Fairly well	58.2	41.8
	Not very well	26.1	73.9
	Not at all well	11.7	88.3
		(−0.42)	
12 Labour's handling of law and order	Very well	60.0	40.0
	Fairly well	48.0	52.0
	Not very well	24.4	75.6
	Not at all well	13.9	86.1
		(−0.31)	
13 Mark out of ten for Labour	0	1.5	98.5
	1	3.7	96.3
	2	0.0	100.0
	3	2.5	97.5
	4	1.6	98.4
	5	5.9	94.1
	6	14.5	85.5
	7	48.9	51.1
	8	75.3	24.7
	9	81.0	19.0
	10	92.7	7.3
		(0.63)	
14 Respondent's view of social services and benefits			
Benefits:	Cut back a lot	18.7	81.3
	Cut back a bit	25.6	74.4
	Stay as they are	49.9	50.1
	More are needed	54.8	45.2
		(0.29)	
15 Respondent's view of taxes and government services			
Taxes and services should be cut:	Very strongly favour	20.5	79.5
	Fairly strongly favour	18.8	81.2
	Mildly favour	14.8	85.2
	Doesn't matter	36.0	64.0
Taxes and services should be maintained:	Mildly favour	32.0	68.0
	Fairly strongly favour	42.1	57.9
	Very strongly favour	53.7	46.3
		(0.25)	
16 Respondent's view of how wages and salaries should be settled			
The government should set guidelines:	Very strongly favour	44.1	55.9
	Fairly strongly favour	31.5	68.5
	Mildly favour	30.3	69.7
	Things left as they are	46.0	54.0

Table 4.1—cont.

Variable	Coding	Labour	Not Labour
Employers and trade unions should settle wages alone:	Mildly favour	25.5	74.5
	Fairly strongly favour	36.4	63.6
	Very strongly favour	44.8	55.2
	(0.33)		
17 Respondent's view on the economic policy of the Common Market			
Britain should be more willing to go along with the EEC:	Very strongly favour	31.2	68.7
	Fairly strongly favour	25.3	74.7
	Mildly favour	26.8	73.2
	No need for change	45.0	55.0
Britain should oppose EEC economic policies:	Mildly favour	26.8	73.2
	Fairly strongly favour	39.2	60.8
	Very strongly favour	44.1	55.9
	(0.11)		
18 Respondent's view of stricter laws to regulate trade unions			
There should be stricter laws:	Very strongly favour	17.9	82.1
	Fairly strongly favour	29.6	70.4
	Mildly favour	40.0	60.0
	Doesn't matter	67.9	32.1
No need for stricter laws:	Mildly favour	54.3	45.7
	Fairly strongly favour	71.8	28.2
	Very strongly favour	82.7	17.3
	(0.43)		

correlation with voting is 0.63, which is highly significant. Finally, the prospective evaluation indicators are more weakly related to voting than the retrospective evaluation indicators, but with the exception of the Common Market issue they are more strongly related to voting than the social attributes. Attitudes to trade union laws stand out among the prospective indicators as being particularly significant. No doubt this is partly due to the context of the 1979 election following as it did the period of industrial conflict which became known as the 'winter of discontent'.

The results in Table 4.1 are very interesting but they cannot be used to make reliable inferences about the comparative importance of evaluations and social attributes in predicting the vote. We need to examine the influence of each variable on the probability of voting Labour, controlling for the influence of the other variables. In this way we can identify the unique contribution of each variable in explaining the Labour vote. As in previous chapters we can do this using a multiple regression analysis.

The multivariate analysis of the vote model

To reiterate, the dependent variable in the multiple regression analysis is the probability of voting Labour. This probability can be measured using elaborate probability functions such as a probit or logit function (Pindyck and Rubinfeld, 1976, pp. 237–64). This however makes the interpretation of the results difficult. Accordingly, we use a linear probability model in which Labour voters score one, and non-Labour voters zero. The eighteen independent variables can then be used to predict the probability of voting Labour which produces a probability figure for each voter, varying between one and zero. There can be statistical problems with such a model (Fiorina, 1981, pp. 213–15), but a reanalysis of the results with the more powerful probit model revealed no significant differences.[2] We can therefore interpret the results with reasonable confidence.

In Table 4.2 we examine the predictive power and statistical significance of social attributes and evaluations as separate predictors of the probability of voting Labour. In the case of social attributes they explained only 14 per cent of the variation in the probability of voting Labour. There are four separate models using the social attributes with one production sector indicator omitted from the model in turn. This is done to avoid statistical problems arising from multi-collinearity, which occurs when variables are highly interrelated with each other.[3] The *t* statistics in parenthesis measure the statistical significance of each of the coefficients. A *t* statistic less than 1.65 indicates that a coefficient of that magnitude has more than a one in ten probability of occurring due to chance, and so we cannot assume it measures a reliable effect. As before this provides a criterion for judging the effects of each variable. Each coefficient should be interpreted in the same way as a correlation, except that it measures the independent effect of that variable on the Labour vote, controlling for the other variables in the model.

The strongest effect in the social attribute models in Table 4.2 is unionization, closely followed by the consumption sector variables, home and car ownership; occupational status has about the same effect as car ownership and is rather weaker than home ownership. Only one of the production sector variables is statistically significant, corporate sector membership; thus there is a slight tendency for corporate sector workers to vote Labour because of their employment sector. Interestingly enough the significant division is not between the public and private sectors but between large scale private capital and the rest.

The evaluation variables are much better predictors of the probability of voting Labour than social attributes. The most significant predictor is the affective evaluation scale, followed by the retrospective and prospective evaluation indicators in that order. All the retrospective evaluation indicators are highly statistically significant, as are the prospective

Table 4.2 Social attributes, affective, prospective and retrospective evaluations as predictors of the probability of voting Labour

Predictors	Standardized coefficients			
1 Social, attributes				
Unionization	0.20	0.19	0.20	0.18
	(7.05)	(6.83)	(6.89)	(6.24)
Home ownership	−0.16	−0.16	−0.16	−0.16
	(5.43)	(5.44)	(5.38)	(5.47)
Car ownership	−0.12	−0.12	−0.12	−0.12
	(4.24)	(4.20)	(4.16)	(4.10)
Occupational status	0.11	0.11	0.12	0.11
	(3.84)	(3.62)	(3.87)	(3.86)
Market sector	0.03	0.03	0.01	—
	(0.86)	(1.00)	(0.43)	
Corporate sector	0.06	0.06	—	0.06
	(1.88)	(2.13)		(2.03)
Public service sector	0.01	—	0.00	0.02
	(0.46)		(0.00)	(0.65)
Public corporation sector	—	0.04	0.02	0.04
		(1.27)	(0.66)	(1.25)
R^2	0.14	0.14	0.13	0.14
2 Retrospective, prospective and affective evaluations				
Labour's handling of prices	−0.14			
	(5.24)			
Labour's handling of unemployment	−0.22			
	(8.23)			
Labour's handling of strikes	−0.21			
	(7.96)			
Labour's handling of law and order	−0.11			
	(4.53)			
Social services and benefits		0.17		
		(6.53)		
Taxes and government services		0.15		
		(5.87)		
Wages and salaries		−0.02		
		(0.79)		
Common Market economic policy		0.05		
		(1.86)		
Laws to regulate unions		0.34		
		(13.07)		
Affective evaluation of Labour			0.63	
			(32.34)	
R^2	0.27	0.24	0.40	

t statistics in parenthesis, $t \geq 1.96$, $t \geq 1.65$ significant at 0.05 and 0.10 levels respectively.

evaluation measures apart from the wages and salaries indicator. Once again attitudes to trade union laws are very highly significant.

The models in Table 4.2 indicate how attitudinal indicators are much more significant than social attributes in predicting the Labour vote. But to assess the relative importance of particular variables we have to include all predictors in the model simultaneously, this is done in Table 4.3. The first model in this table includes all the variables which appeared in the earlier tables with the exception of one non-significant production sector variable. Again this is excluded to avoid statistical degeneracy. Overall the seventeen variables explain 47 per cent of the variation in the probability of voting Labour, which is quite a good fit for individual level survey data.

In Table 4.3 the affective evaluation scale is the strongest predictor of the Labour vote. All the retrospective evaluation measures are statistically significant, apart from the law and order indicator. Apart from the trade union indicator none of the prospective evaluation indicators are statistically significant. This implies that the retrospective evaluation indicators dominate the prospective evaluation indicators when it comes to predicting voting behaviour. Voters judge Labour on its record not on its future policies, apart that is from the trade union issue.

Only three of the social attribute indicators remain statistically significant in the full model; they are unionization and home and car ownership. Union membership significantly increases the probability of an individual voting Labour, and home and car ownership significantly decrease it. Occupational status is not statistically significant in this model, so we cannot be sure that it has an independent effect on the vote apart from the other variables.

To test the robustness of these findings we re-estimated the model after transforming the retrospective and prospective evaluation indicators. In the case of the retrospective indicators we measured the difference between the respondent's evaluation of Labour and his or her evaluation of the Conservatives' hypothetical record on that issue. This difference was then weighted by the importance of that issue in influencing the respondent's vote.[4] Thus the transformed variable measures the difference between the respondent's evaluations of the major parties, weighted by the importance of that issue to the respondent. In the case of the prospective evaluations we measured the difference between the respondent's preferences on that issue, and their perceptions of Labour's position on the issue, once again weighted by the importance of that issue in influencing the vote. The results appear in Table 4.3.

If we repeat the multiple regression analysis with the transformed model the results do not change our earlier conclusions. The affective evaluation scale remains most important, followed by the retrospective evaluations, which are in turn followed by the social attributes. Apart

Table 4.3 Social attributes, affective, prospective and retrospective evaluations altogether as predictors of the probability of voting Labour

Predictors	Standardized coefficients	
	Original model	Transformed model[a]
Unionization	0.08	0.09
	(3.13)	(3.37)
Home ownership	−0.06	−0.04
	(2.34)	(1.51)
Car ownership	−0.09	−0.10
	(3.27)	(3.81)
Occupational status	0.02	0.02
	(0.56)	(0.82)
Market sector	0.00	0.01
	(0.00)	(0.46)
Corporate sector	0.02	0.04
	(0.84)	(1.31)
Public service sector	−0.02	−0.02
	(0.65)	(0.55)
Labour's handling of prices	−0.06	−0.08
	(1.91)	(2.46)
Labour's handling of unemployment	−0.08	−0.11
	(2.87)	(3.75)
Labour's handling of strikes	−0.07	−0.07
	(2.16)	(2.10)
Labour's handling of law and order	−0.03	−0.01
	(1.11)	(0.37)
Social services and benefits	0.03	−0.01
	(1.15)	(0.44)
Taxes and government services	0.03	−0.04
	(1.06)	(1.28)
Wages and salaries	0.01	−0.02
	(0.60)	(0.59)
Common Market economic policy	0.03	−0.03
	(1.35)	(1.04)
Laws to regulate unions	0.17	−0.11
	(6.13)	(3.45)
Affective evaluation scale	0.36	0.38
	(9.93)	(10.96)
R^2	0.47	0.46

t statistics: $t \geq 1.96$, $t \geq 1.65$ significant at the 0.05 and 0.01 levels.
[a] See text for explanation of transformations.

from the trade union issue none of the prospective evaluations are significant. In general, consumption sector and trade union membership, retrospective and affective evaluations explain Labour voting. There is some evidence of an indirect link between production sector and voting, operating via trade union membership. The correlation between market sector membership and trade union membership was −0.19 which suggests that workers in the market sector are less likely to be unionized than other workers, and therefore less likely to vote Labour. In the case of the public service and public corporation sectors, the correlations with unionization were 0.16 and 0.22 respectively, and so the effect operates in the opposite direction in these sectors. There are also indirect links between occupational status and voting behaviour which operate via home and car ownership.

If we compare the objective and subjective indicators in these models clearly the latter dominate the former. In the models we see an instrumental electorate motivated by performance rather than promises, which is much less influenced by sociological characteristics in determining its voting behaviour than the traditional theory would suggest. We have seen earlier that the two significant consumption sector indicators, home and car ownership, have undergone enormous changes in the post-war years. If these were significant predictors of Labour voting in the 1950s, which seems very likely, then the rise in home and car ownership since then could partly explain dealignment. However, consumption sector variables are also bound up with retrospective evaluations when it comes to voting behaviour. The performance of the party in office in managing the economy influences both retrospective evaluations and consumption sector status, which could make the latter more salient in influencing electoral behaviour.

The only favourable trend for Labour in the social background variables is the growth in trade union membership (Caves and Krause, 1980, pp. 81–106). Since this positively affects the Labour vote, the trend ought to offset to some extent the adverse effects of increased owner occupation and car ownership. However, as we saw in Table 4.1 only 48.8 per cent of union members were Labour voters, so the party has a long way to go before it can automatically assume the support of trade unionists.

Affective and retrospective evaluations are also likely to be significantly related. The correlations between the various evaluation indicators, which appear in Table 4.4, confirm this. The correlations between affective and retrospective evaluations are consistently higher than the correlations between the former and prospective evaluations. It seems plausible that the magnitude of the relationship between voting and affective evaluations is partly due to the influence of retrospective evaluations. For this reason and because of the results in Table 4.4, it seems

Table 4.4 Correlations between affective, retrospective and prospective evaluations of issues

	1	2	3	4	5	6	7	8	9	10
1 Labour's handling of prices	1.0									
2 Labour's handling of unemployment	0.43	1.0								
3 Labour's handling of strikes	0.45	0.44	1.0							
4 Labour's handling of law and order	0.33	0.33	0.38	1.0						
5 Social services and benefits	−0.15	−0.22	−0.25	−0.24	1.0					
6 Taxes and government services	−0.18	−0.22	−0.20	−0.22	0.20	1.0				
7 Wages and salaries	0.07	0.11	0.06	−0.00	0.00	−0.06	1.0			
8 German market economy	−0.10	−0.04	−0.10	−0.09	0.10	0.19	0.04	1.0		
9 Laws to regulate unions	−0.21	−0.26	−0.33	−0.27	0.30	0.22	0.05	0.12	1.0	
10 Affective evaluations scale	−0.50	−0.51	−0.52	−0.46	0.37	0.34	−0.10	0.16	0.43	1.0
	retrospective evaluations				prospective evaluations					

clear that dealignment is largely explained by the retrospective evaluations of voters, although changes in social attributes also are a factor. There is increasing aggregate time series evidence that voting behaviour and electoral popularity are significantly influenced by the state of the economy (Alt, 1979; Whiteley, 1980; Pissarides, 1980; Frey and Schneider, 1978). Such evidence is compatible with a secular decline in party support which arises from the parties' inabilities to satisfy the economic expectations of the electorate.

To summarize, partisan dealignment affects the Labour Party in three different ways. Firstly, changes in the social structure such as the rise of consumption sector private ownership cross-cut and weaken the link between party and class, which make retrospective evaluations more salient over time. Secondly, the secular decline in Britain's economic performance with rising unemployment and inflation and lower growth also make retrospective evaluations more salient and more adverse for Labour both when it is incumbent and in opposition. Thirdly, retrospective evaluations and the associated affective evaluations may serve to weaken the class–party tie independently of autonomous changes in the social structure. Thus affluent workers, despite Goldthorpe *et al.*'s findings (1969), will increasingly desert the party if they do not believe it can meet their economic aspirations. The importance of consumption sector variables as well as retrospective evaluations all point to an increasingly instrumental electorate whose partisanship cannot be taken for granted by any party.

Conclusions

We have reviewed all the major literature on electoral behaviour in Britain, and concluded that none of this literature provides an adequate explanation of electoral dealignment. Our own model explains electoral support as a product of objective social circumstances and subjective judgements on the part of the individual. It is clear from the evidence that subjective judgements are better predictors of voting behaviour than objective factors, and within the former category affective evaluations are the most important influences. Subjective instrumental evaluations are divided into two categories: retrospective and prospective evaluations. The evidence shows that the former are much more significant than the latter in explaining support for the Labour Party. This is consistent with the performance hypothesis in which voters are passing judgement on Labour's record in office, rather than on its future policy proposals. Thus dealignment is explained by the failure of the party to represent adequately the objective and subjective interests of its supporters.

This chapter completes our examination of the three crises facing the Labour Party which we set out in Chapter 1. These crises are all linked directly or indirectly to the performance hypothesis. Why has Labour in office failed to manage the economy successfully, so as to produce these electoral and ideological crises? Could any set of policies deal with the intractable problems of the British economy? We turn our attention to those questions in the next three chapters.

Notes

1 A dummy variable allows us to treat a category variable as though it were a quantitative variable. In effect it transforms a category variable into a probability scale. For example:

   1 trade union member
   0 not trade union member

In this variable the probability that a respondent is a trade union member is 1 (i.e. certain) or 0 (i.e. impossible). We are able to calculate the probability that a respondent selected from the sample at random is a trade unionist from the expression:

No. of trade unionists

———————————————

No. of respondents

and in other ways treat the variable as though it were numerical rather than categorical.

2 Probit analysis assumes that the dichotomous dependent variable is an imperfect measure of an underlying quantitative probability distribution, and so the dependent variable is transformed into a non-linear probit function of the independent variables. This corrects the problem of heteroscedasticity which is associated with the linear probability model, but it makes the coefficients of the model difficult to interpret. See Finney (1964) for a full explanation of the probit model.

3 The four dummy variables divide the sample into discrete subsets. Any one dummy is therefore a linear function of the others, which results in multicollinearity. This means that it is impossible to separate the different effects of each dummy variable if they are included in the model altogether. See Johnston (1972, pp. 159–68).

4 For example the transformed prices variable was calculated as follows:

(Labour's record on prices – Conservative's hypothetical record) × importance of prices in vote.

The Conservative hypothetical record was coded the same as Labour's record in Table 4.3, and the importance of prices in the vote was coded: extremely important = 3, fairly important = 2, not very important = 1.

II
The political economy
of the crisis

5

Labour's policy goals

In this and subsequent chapters we change the focus of the analysis from the political sociology to the political economy of the Labour Party. Instead of examining the party's internal conflicts, changes in its membership and electoral support, we begin to look at the performance in achieving its short- and long-term goals or policy outputs. Traditional political sociology has neglected the analysis of policy making and policy outputs, concentrating on inputs into the political system such as electoral support, and political socialization and recruitment. To understand Labour's current problems we need to examine both inputs and outputs to the political system.

What then are the goals of the Labour Party? Historically what has it tried to achieve in the British political system? Such questions are an essential prerequisite for understanding the party's policy performance; to assess what the party has achieved we need to know what it has tried to achieve.

There are several difficulties in trying to define the goals of a political party. A party is not a homogeneous entity and different factions have different aims. Party programmes contain mixtures of general philosophical statements, attacks on opponents, slogans included for the benefit of the faithful as well as concrete policy proposals. All of these can impinge on party policy as it is formulated over time. It is also true that the goals of a political party can be articulated at different levels. At one level broad examinations of the nature of socialism by writers like Tawney (1931, 1933), Strachey (1936) and Crosland (1956) have been very influential in setting the policy agenda of the party. At another level the writings of politicians concerned with more practical questions of day to day politics such as Attlee (1937), Bevan (1961) and Crossman (1964) have also been influential. There is also of course a huge mass of literature on particular aspects of policy emanating from the Fabian Society, the independent Labour Research Department and the Labour Party itself. Similarly the experience of Labour policy makers in office has often drastically altered their goals and so from one point of view the goals of the party are inextricably linked to its political experiences over the years.

One of the main difficulties in defining Labour's goals is that they spring from a doctrine, democratic socialism, which is far from being coherent and well defined. Democratic socialism is an amalgam of different·strands of thought, and as such has been defined in different ways by different writers. At its most general socialism is a critique of the values and practical effects of industrial capitalism, together with an alternative perspective on how society could operate to promote the common welfare. According to Berki (1975) this critique contains four distinct elements. Firstly, there is the notion of equality and the ideal of co-operation between equals for the common good. Secondly, there is the moralistic attack on capitalism which criticizes the basic selfishness of the notion of individual self-interest, as well as the inhuman conditions which it produced in the factory system. Thirdly, there is rationalism, or the idea that a planned approach to production will eliminate the waste and chaos of the market system. Finally, there is libertarianism which emphasizes individual liberation from the oppressive nature of capitalist society.

All these elements can be discerned in the writings of Labour leaders and intellectuals over the years (Bealey, 1970). Of course different people emphasize different things. For example Attlee (1937) lists a number of socialist objectives such as freedom, security, equality, democracy and common ownership. But he tends to emphasize the importance of freedom above the others, particularly freedom from unemployment and poverty. Strachey (1936) on the other hand emphasizes the desirability of rational planning, and the large increases in production which he feels could be achieved by a comprehensive national plan. Bevan (1961) tends to emphasize the immorality of industrial capitalism, particularly the application of the market philosophy to health care. Finally, Crosland (1956) argues that equality is the main aim of socialism.

In the light of these problems in defining Labour's goals, we will focus particularly on key party documents and election manifestos, while recognizing that these do not give a complete statement of party objectives in practice. To put contemporary debates in perspective we need to go back to the origins, to the first comprehensive statement of the party's socialist goals in 1918. There is a good deal of continuity in Labour's policy goals from that time up to the 1945 Labour government and so we will examine the entire interwar period together. Developments after 1945 will be examined separately.

From the origins up to 1945

Before the First World War Labour was not officially a socialist party. As Cole points out (1948) this was largely because many of the leading trade unionists in the party were not socialists, and it was only the advent of the new unionism, and the replacement of the old craft union leadership by a more radical leadership, which opened the way to a formal commitment to socialism.

The first comprehensive statement of Labour's socialist objectives appeared in *Labour and the New Social Order* written in 1918 by Sidney Webb (Labour Party, 1918). This document was very influential, and the substance of it was incorporated into a series of resolutions accepted by the party conference in June 1918. These resolutions set the agenda of Labour's policy goals up to the time of the 1945 government. Cole writes:

> Labour and the new Social order, looked at in retrospect nearly thirty years later, is seen to contain in substance by far the greater part of what has been put forward in respect of home policy in subsequent Labour programmes, and of the actual policy which the Labour Government of 1945 began vigorously to carry into effect.
>
> (1948, p. 56)

The document reviewed the entire field of policy from the domestic economy and employment, to education, social welfare and foreign policy. It made a number of detailed policy proposals many of which were later implemented, though some have still not been implemented today.

The first striking characteristic of *Labour and the New Social Order* in comparison with contemporary party documents is its powerful and unrelenting attack on capitalism. For example it stated:

> The individualistic system of capitalist production, based on the private ownership and competitive administration of land and capital, with its reckless 'profiteering' and wage slavery; with its glorification of the unhampered struggle for the means of life and its hypocritical pretence of the 'survival of the fittest'; with the monstrous inequality of circumstances which it produces and the degradation and brutalisation both moral and spiritual, resulting therefrom, may we hope, indeed have received a death blow.
>
> (pp. 4–5)

This was of course written before the Bolshevik revolution and before the breach with the Communist Party, but with this kind of language it is easy to see that Labour was at that time an anti-system party. In terms of Labour's long-term goals Webb sets out four broad objectives or, as he puts it, 'the Four Pillars of the House of Tomorrow'. In his words these were:

(a) The Universal Enforcement of the National Minimum
(b) Democratic Control of Industry

(c) The Revolution in National Finance; and

(d) The Surplus Wealth for the Common Good.   (p. 4)

To consider these points in turn, the national minimum meant a policy to ensure a minimum standard of living for all workers obtained by full employment and the enforcement of a living wage. The document called on the government to undertake public works so as to maintain investment and employment, and to eliminate fluctuations in economic activity associated with the trade cycle.

The democratic control of industry meant primarily the safeguarding of trade union rights, and the development of planning in industry via public ownership. There was a demand for the immediate nationalization of the railways, mines and the electrical power industry together with an open-ended though unspecific demand for extensive planning in industry. It stated: 'Chaos and disorganisation must be replaced by ordered planning. The only basis on which ordered planning of industry and trade can be carried out is that of public ownership and control' (p. 10).

The revolution in national finance referred to a radical reform of the tax system to ensure the progressive taxation of incomes, and redistribution from the proceeds. There were specific proposals for a levy on capital in order to pay off the war debt, and an inheritance and wealth tax together with a profits tax in industry.

The surplus for the common good meant the promotion of greater equality by a system of social security, and greater access to education at all levels from nursery education to higher education. The document also speaks of the development of civilization and culture based on the idea of co-operation for the common good.

The basic arguments of *Labour and the New Social Order* were translated into some twenty-six resolutions at the 1918 party conference, with remarkably little dissent. The resolutions fall into five main groups, with a sixth group of miscellaneous resolutions. The first group was concerned with social welfare and contained resolutions calling for minimum wages, full employment, unemployment insurance, comprehensive education, municipal house building, a municipal health service and the abolition of the Poor Law. The second group concerned with public ownership varied from resolutions specifically proposing the nationalization of railways and canals, the mines and electricity supply to those expressed in more general terms calling for nationalization as a means of avoiding inefficiency and waste. There was also a resolution calling for the nationalization of life assurance.

A third group of resolutions dealt with constitutional reform including the introduction of universal adult suffrage, the emancipation of women and equal pay, home rule for Ireland, devolution with separate

legislative assemblies for Scotland, Wales and England, and a reorganization of local government giving local authorities greater powers to
extend municipal services and planning. A fourth group dealt specifically
with the problems arising from the war in connection with the demobiliz-
ation of troops, the discharge of civilian war workers and the restoration
of traditional trade union bargaining rights. Finally, there was a resolution calling for the introduction of income, wealth, property and profits
taxation. In particular the wealth tax proposal was fairly radical, proposing an exemption level below £1000 in wealth, and a graduated scale for
larger totals.

The 1918 Labour election manifesto was in common with all party
manifestos at that time, rather brief, but it did reflect quite accurately the
proposals from Labour and the new social order. It called for indepen-
dence for Ireland, a levy on capital, land nationalization and: 'the
immediate nationalization and democratic control of vital public services,
such as mines, railways, shipping, armaments, and electrical power'
(Craig, 1975, p. 32). Thus the proposals for nationalization in the manifesto went further in some respects than the proposals in Sidney Webb's
document. It called for a 'comprehensive Public Health Act' and for the
building of a million new homes at the state's expense. It also made a
specific appeal to women, most of whom received the vote for the first
time in 1918.

During the interwar years Labour produced broad statements of its
policy goals on two occasions, both after experiencing political defeat.
The first was in 1928 when *Labour and the Nation* was published following
the brief experience of the first Labour government of 1924, and the
debacle of the General Strike in 1926. The second occasion was in 1933
after the demoralizing experience of the second Labour government and
the MacDonald betrayal, when the party published *Socialism and the
Condition of the People*. Both documents represented a toning down of the
attack on capitalism which appeared in *Labour and the New Social Order*,
as well as an elaboration and modification of the basic policy proposals
made in that document.

The experience of government and the trauma of the General Strike
had influenced Labour's leadership in their approach to socialism. The
first Labour government was a minority government subject to the
control of the Asquith liberals. It lasted nine months and made some
modest reforms, although none of these were particularly socialist in
character. Cole sums it up as follows:

> It attempted no single measure of socialisation, or, with the excep-
> tion of building materials, of state control over industry . . . what it
> could and did achieve was to undo many of the administrative
> effects of the 'Geddes Axe', to pass several valuable measures of

social reform, and to make a somewhat faint-hearted attempt at coping with the unemployment problems by the institution of public works.   (Cole, 1948, p. 163)

The Labour Party stood on the sidelines during the General Strike, the leadership playing no significant role in events. However, it was significantly affected by the employer's backlash, in particular the Trades Disputes Act of 1927 which was designed to curb the right to strike, and to cut off funds to the Labour Party by changing the system of contracting out of the political levy to one of contracting in. This reduced the trade union membership of the party by 1.2 million in a single year. After the first Labour government much of the running on policy was made by the Independent Labour Party which developed a series of policy statements at its own annual conference, and then subsequently tried to influence the policy of the Labour Party. The proposals concerned finance, agriculture, parliamentary reform, unemployment and the minimum wage. The ILP proposals were for the most part unacceptable to MacDonald, Snowden and the other Labour leaders, and MacDonald made a scathing attack on them at the 1927 annual conference. He used an argument that was to become a familiar one in later years, namely that the proposals would frighten the electorate and ensure the party's defeat. The ILP proposals were for the most part defeated receiving a particularly severe setback in 1928 when the annual conference threw out their resolution on the living wage.

Labour and the Nation (Labour Party, 1928) was designed to be a restatement of the goals set out in 1918 rather than an immediate programme for the party. But it introduced for the first time a note of vagueness and ambiguity in the party programme, in sharp contrast with the ILP proposals. This reflected the fact that MacDonald was becoming more and more devoted to rhetoric about socialism, and less and less interested in specific proposals to bring it about. The document set out five principles aimed at guiding the party in power. These principles were concerned with the living wage, social security, co-operation in industry, taxation and peace and freedom. Their general character can be judged from the first which was: 'to secure to every member of the community the standards of life and employment which are necessary to a healthy, independent and self respecting existence' (p. 16). In other words they were worthy, but vague.

Labour and the Nation carried over many of the proposals made in *Labour and the New Social Order*, but they were couched with reservations and were distinctly unclear about the details of their implementation. For example after reaffirming the intention to nationalize land, coal, power, transport and credit it went on to say that the proposals would be implemented: 'without haste, but without rest, with careful preparation, with the use of the best technical knowledge and management skill and with due compensation for the persons affected' (p. 26).

Thus the commitment was there, but so were the escape clauses for doing nothing. A more telling illustration of this concerned the strategy for dealing with the severe economic crisis. The document proposed the setting up of a 'National Economic Committee, acting under the direction of the Prime Minister, which will be his eyes and ears on economic questions. . . . It would thus ensure that economic policy was accurately adjusted to the needs of the moment' (p. 23). The only concrete suggestions for dealing with the depression apart from relying on this Committee of experts was a proposal to set up an 'Employment and Development Board' to undertake land drainage and afforestation schemes, with a vague suggestion that it might get involved in slum clearance and road building. It looked very much like the limited and not very successful programme of public works undertaken by the first Labour government all over again. The rigid financial orthodoxy of the second Labour government is not too difficult to understand given this very limited set of proposals for dealing with a rapidly worsening economic crisis.

After the General Election of 1929 Labour was for the first time the largest party in the House of Commons. The toning down of socialist goals compared with 1918 can be seen by examining the 1929 manifesto. The proposals to nationalize railways, shipping, armaments and power were dropped and only the commitment to the public ownership of mines was unequivocally retained. There was no mention of a public health act or of the building of a million new homes. The proposal which appeared in 1918 for the 'Conscription of Wealth' was replaced by a proposal for income and surtax, and wealth taxation was not mentioned. The major innovation in 1929 which arguably had an important influence on the party's electoral performance was a section on the problem of unemployment. It stated: 'The Labour Party gives an unqualified pledge to deal immediately and practically with this question. Its record on unemployment is a guarantee that this pledge will be kept' (Craig, 1975, p. 82).

In fact the second Labour government was a government of almost unremitting failure, particularly with regard to unemployment. Unemployment went from 1.2 million in June 1929 to 2.9 million in September 1931 (Butler and Sloman, 1980, pp. 340–1), thus it more than doubled during Labour's period in office. This was a product of the Chancellor Snowden's orthodox policy of defending the Gold Standard and balancing the budget, at a time when the need was for deficit spending in order to reflate the economy. The initial proposals on other aspects of domestic policy were very modest even by the standards of the 1929 manifesto. The party proposed to amend the Trades Disputes Act of 1927 and to make provision for modest public works including house building and slum clearance.

The mounting unemployment produced a revolt in the party led by Mosley who put forward a memorandum in 1930 setting out an alternative economic strategy to that of Snowden. His plan called for the stimulation of demand by extensive public works, an expansion of social services and pensions, nationalization and import restrictions. It has often been described as a Keynesian policy, and it did have some of the features of what later became known as Keynesianism. However, unlike Keynes the proposals emphasized economic nationalism both with respect to public ownership and import controls. Such was the disquiet in the party by 1930 at the government's economic performance that it was only narrowly defeated at the 1930 conference by 1,251,000 votes to 1,046,000 (Cole, 1948, p. 241).

In the four short years after 1930 until *Socialism and the Condition of the People* was adopted by the party conference of 1934, a great deal happened to the party. It experienced the traumatic betrayal of Mac-Donald, Snowden and others who left the party to form the National government after failing to get their Cabinet colleagues to accept drastic cuts in the social services. It experienced an unprecedented election defeat reducing the parliamentary party from 288 MPs in 1929 to 52 in 1931 (Butler and Sloman, 1980, p. 207). The Independent Labour Party disaffiliated in 1932 ostensibly over the issue of the rights of MPs, but fundamentally over its failure to influence Labour policies in a more socialist direction. It is interesting to see the impact of these series of convulsions on the party's policy goals as set out in *Socialism and the Condition of the People* (1933).

Once again *Socialism and the Condition of the People* carried forward a number of the proposals initiated in 1918. However, it was very innovative in one major respect. For the first time it introduced a theoretical analysis of the causes of the great depression, and concrete policy proposals for dealing with it which went beyond the earlier rhetoric about planning. The analysis and strategy was Keynesian in a way in which the earlier talk about public works and municipal enterprise was not. This was because it had a clear conception of the macroeconomic behaviour of the economy and the need to consider aggregate consumption, investment and savings. Some of the passages in the document could almost be taken directly from Keynes' *General Theory of Employment, Interest and Money* (1936) even though this was not published for another two years. In particular it had a clear under-consumptionist theory of the depression, as did Keynes. That is, it attributed the declining production and increasing unemployment to a lack of what later would be called effective demand. It stated:

> Money forthcoming for the purchase of goods falls short of the money spent on their production, and there is a fall in prices and a

decline in employment. . . . If money is spent on capital goods faster than actual savings are accruing for investment, there comes the opposite result: demand for goods for immediate consumption is greater than immediate supply; there is a rise in prices, profits and employment. (Labour Party, 1933, p. 9)

In Keynes' general theory the equality of aggregate income or production and aggregate expenditure at full employment implied an equality of savings and investment. If individuals planned to save more than businessmen planned to invest, the reduction in expenditure which this implied would lead to falling production and employment. Savers and investors were not properly co-ordinated and Keynes argued that this could produce a stable level of production well below full employment leading to a permanent pool of unemployment (Keynes, 1936; Ball, 1982). The economy would remain stuck permanently at this level because of the lack of effective demand. The authors of *Socialism and the Condition of the People* showed a real awareness of this lack of co-ordination between savers and investors when they stated, 'The object of the National Control of investment is to make investment equal to savings' (p. 10).

In a section headed 'Planned Development of National Resources' the document set out a number of proposals for remedying the lack of effective demand including investment in industry, electrification of the railways, oil extraction from coal, road, house, school and hospital building which altogether amounted to a massive programme of public works. The proposals were much more comprehensive and more concrete than had appeared in *Labour and the Nation*. They were also more confidently stated because unlike the earlier document they contained a relatively coherent theory of why the depression had occurred. It was obvious that the Mosley memorandum together with Snowden's failure had fundamentally changed Labour's perspective. The document did not however accept Mosley's proposals without amendment. In particular it criticized the development of economic nationalism in the form of tariff barriers and import controls, and argued that these were partly responsible for the world recession.

In retrospect the major importance of *Socialism and the Condition of the People* is that it represented Labour's acceptance of essentially liberal economic theory. The Keynesian analysis is not merely rooted in the classical liberal economic theory of Adam Smith and Alfred Marshall, but it does not represent a significant departure from the classical model. Recent theoretical work has shown that the Keynesian model is essentially the classical model modified slightly by imposing certain restrictive assumptions, notably the downward rigidity of wages. Leijonhufvud, in a brilliant analysis of Keynes' theories and the ideas of the Keynesians, concluded that:

> Keynes' theory is quite distinct from the Keynesian income expenditure theory. . . . It is possible to describe, at least in rough outline, a model (or class of models) with substantially different structure from that of the income expenditure model, that is more consistent with the textual evidence of Keynes' two major works – and with pre-Keynesian 'classical' theories.   (1968, p. 8)

Thus when Labour embraced Keynes' theories it accepted classical liberal economic theory in a slightly new form. After 1934 Labour had no distinctive macroeconomic policy of a socialist character. It still spoke of the need for planning and public ownership, but much of this was basically rhetoric when it came to the question of planning the entire economy.

To be fair to the party leadership, then as now, there is no politically acceptable democratic socialist approach to the macroeconomic management of the economy, anything like comparable to Keynes' general theory. Economic analysis outside the mainstream has provided little or no guidance to policy makers grappling with the problems of macroeconomic management. Marxist or radical economics has experienced a recent revival (Howard and King, 1975; Desai, 1974) but this is fundamentally flawed in practical applications because it adheres to an obsolete labour theory of value. The essential problem with the labour theory of value is that it ignores the role of consumer demand in influencing prices and thus the value of goods and services. A large amount of labour power might be expended on a product, but if there is no demand for this product it has no value. Much effort has been fruitlessly expended by Marxist writers and others to circumvent this simple but fundamental truth. Once the labour theory of value is undermined, so is the theory of exploitation and other important features of the Marxist paradigm. Undoubtedly exploitation exists, but it cannot be inferred using the labour theory of value. The alternative of a centrally planned economy along Eastern European lines was advocated by a few Labour writers in the 1930s, notably Strachey (1936). But the postwar performance of these economies, let alone the political and economic changes required to introduce that type of planning, make it politically unfeasible in Britain.

The Labour Party came to power in 1945 with a programme based on three broad components. Firstly, there was the Keynesian strategy of macroeconomic management which among other reasons thanks to Keynes' own persuasive talents (Harrod, 1972) had by 1945 overturned the Treasury orthodoxy. Secondly, there was the radical liberal strategy for the reform of social insurance set out in the Beveridge report, *Social Insurance and Allied Services* (HMSO, 1942). These two were related as Beveridge himself acknowledged in his report on employment policy

(HMSO, 1944a). The social insurance provisions would not work without full employment because they could not be financed. Thus an essential precondition for the successful implementation of Beveridge was a fully employed growing economy to be maintained by Keynesian methods. Finally, there were the distinctive socialist policies of public ownership applying to fuel and power, the railways and steel, and the establishment of the National Health Service.

All of these elements had appeared at different stages in prewar policy documents, although the details of their implementation had obviously not been fully worked out then. Taken together these policy aims represented a distinctive social democratic, and to a limited extent, socialist alternative to the paucity of Conservative policy goals in 1945. By 1948 Keynesian methods had become the new orthodoxy, and most though not all of the Beveridge proposals had been implemented; the limited socialist programme had also by then been established. After 1948 the basic programme which had been developed in the interwar period was exhausted, and the Labour government ran out of steam.

To summarize, the Labour Party had set out a broad programme in 1918 which was modified and developed in the interwar years and for the most part implemented in 1945–8. The major omission of this programme had been any coherent strategy for the macroeconomic management of the economy, which went beyond mere rhetoric about planning. This had led both the Labour governments of the interwar years to pursue rigid orthodox financial policies, tempered by half-hearted attempts at public works. In the case of the 1929–31 government this had completely wrecked any radical initiatives which it might have made, and ultimately led to its own downfall. By 1934 however the party had accepted Keynesianism, and this together with the Beveridge proposals and a limited socialist programme laid the basis for the success of the 1945 Labour government. The 1945 to 1951 Labour government made only limited advances in the direction of distinctively socialist policies but in the realm of social welfare which had been the most important issue in the 1918 programme its achievements were not far short of the original policy aims. The party found itself in opposition in 1951 with no very clear idea of what it wanted to do next, other than more of the same, and this paved the way for the revisionist alternative.

The revisionist era, 1951–70

In 1951 just before the General Election which put Labour in opposition Aneurin Bevan resigned from the government along with Harold Wilson, the President of the Board of Trade, and John Freeman, a junior minister. The resignation marked the start of the Bevanite revolt, and was a result of the Labour government's huge arms spending programme. The Bevanite revolt had its origins in Bevan's dispute with the government over the question of expenditure curbs in the National Health Service, and support for the Americans in the Korean War. However, there was never really a coherent Bevanite alternative strategy. Rather, the Bevanites were opposed to the Labour leadership's line on a specific narrow set of policies which were almost exclusively concerned with international and defence questions. Moreover, they broadly accepted the main features of Labour's post-war defence policies, differing only in detail. For example the Bevanite pamphlet *One Way Only* (Labour Party, 1952) accepted British membership of NATO, and the need for limited re-armament in the face of the Russian threat. Thus the Bevanite revolt never attempted to pose an alternative strategy for the Labour Party. As far as domestic policy was concerned the Bevanites advocated more socialism without being very specific about what this meant.

The main attempt to rethink the party's overall strategy in the 1950s was by the so-called revisionists. These were middle-class intellectuals such as Jay, Gaitskell and of course Crosland who sought a comprehensive restatement of Labour's aims in the light of changes which they perceived to have occurred in British society and capitalism. The most comprehensive statement of the revisionist case was made by Crosland in his book *The Future of Socialism* (1956). It is important to review this analysis before assessing its contribution to changing Labour's policy goals. Crosland started his analysis by posing the question 'Is Britain a Capitalist Society?', regarding this as the starting point of any rethinking of Labour's strategy. He concluded that capitalism in its traditional form had been completely transformed by developments in contemporary British society. He classified these developments into two broad types. Firstly, there were developments which had altered the role of the state in the management of the economy, and secondly, developments relating to the nature of the private capitalist firm.

In the context of the role of the state, Crosland argued, 'the State and the political authority have removed a wide, and strategically decisive segment of economic decisions out of the sphere of purely market influences, and made them subject to political control' (1956, pp. 29–30). State intervention, particularly public ownership had thus transformed *laissez faire* capitalism beyond all recognition. At the same time the nature of the private capitalist firm had been changed radically. Crosland noted an increasing divorce between ownership and control in the private corporation, with control being vested in a group of professional managers. This group were only marginally influenced in their behaviour by the shareholders who actually owned the company. In a parallel but later discussion of the same phenomenon, Galbraith (1978) described this group as the 'techno-structure'. Their power arose not from an ideological or political source but from the complex technical requirements for specialization and a division of Labour in the modern corporation. As Galbraith put it: 'The imperatives of technology and organisation, not the images of ideology, are what determine the shape of economic society' (p. 7). This meant that ownership was increasingly irrelevant to the question of control. The new business class or technostructure did, in Crosland's view, place major constraints on their power. Their freedom of action was constrained both by the state and by trade unions.

Crosland also discussed a number of other developments which he argued had transformed traditional capitalism: 'We noted a greater degree of equality in the distribution of income and wealth.' He felt that changes had taken place in 'capitalist ideology' which had previously insisted on the unconditional rights of property. This had been considerably modified by the arrival of the welfare state. He also argued that there had been a sharp decline in class conflict and class antagonism, making political conflicts between labour and capital much less violent than they had been in the nineteenth century.

Crosland concluded that although these changes had transformed the nature of capitalism there was still great scope for further socialist advance, but in the direction of greater equality rather than in the direction of more public ownership. In the area of social expenditure this would involve a 'generous, imaginative, long-term programme of social investment', although he did not accept the idea of universal benefits for all (p. 88). It would also involve an emphasis on greater equality of opportunity through educational advance, and the curbing of private privileges such as inherited wealth and private profits.

The key issue which underwrote this plan of greater social welfare and economic and social equality was a buoyant economy, characterized by high investment, full employment and above all economic growth. In Crosland's eyes socialism would achieve equality out of growth, rather than out of substantial redistribution between social classes. This was an attractive prospect politically since it held out the prospects of advances towards socialist goals without significant class conflict or political struggle. He wrote: 'Improved living standards, or any other economic claims, can now be met only by higher production per head; and questions of growth and efficiency more into the forefront of matters to be attended to' (p. 286).

Another important feature of the revisionist argument was scepticism about the need for more nationalization. This arose from two lines of reasoning. Firstly, there was the argument mentioned earlier that ownership in the modern corporation was divorced from control. The Keynesian macroeconomic management had given the government of the day an adequate means of controlling the private sector in order to promote investment and employment, and it was not necessary to own it. Secondly, though, there was the point that ownership did not necessarily bring control; the degree of government control over the nationalized industries had in practice been very limited. Crosland argued: 'In the crucial fuel and power industries, control was almost non-existent' (p. 317). This was partly because ministers had no clearly defined objectives for the nationalized industries, and so tended to take the line of least resistance by letting the boards do as they wished. But also it was because the structure of the nationalized industries with their independent public boards militated against detailed control. The result was no overall integrated policy, with for example the different industries within the fuel and power area competing with one another over investment, pricing and growth.

Revisionism received a boost by the election of Hugh Gaitskell to the leadership of the party in 1955, following the General Election defeat of that year. By the time of the 1959 election manifesto revisionism had clearly influenced the party policy. The manifestos for the elections in 1950 and 1951 had contained few new ideas, and were mainly concerned with defending the record of the 1945 Labour government and reiterating pledges made earlier on house building and full employment. The only noticeable change in these manifestos was the introduction of a special section on the cost of living, which was a sign of the increasing importance attached to inflation. The 1955 manifesto introduced the commitment to comprehensive education for the first time, but apart from this was rather similar to those at the earlier election.

In the case of the 1959 manifesto, revisionism influenced it in a number of ways. After pledging to re-nationalize steel it stated: 'we have no other plans for further nationalisation' (Craig, 1975, p. 227). Proposals for nationalizing particular industries had come and gone in the manifesto over the years, but this was the first time that the party had regarded the abandonment of nationalization as an electoral asset needing to be proclaimed in the manifesto. There was also a bigger emphasis than before on stimulating investment in industry, and economic growth. The instruments for doing this, however, all relied on indirect intervention through the tax system and the provision of financial incentives. It stated: 'our tax policy will be directed towards helping industry to mechanise, modernise and expand and make a maximum contribution to exports' (p. 228).

The social welfare commitments in the 1959 manifesto were also more extensively worked out than before. There was a pledge to introduce a long term superannuation scheme aimed at 'ending poverty in old age', a proposal for a widow's pension and for rent control. Finally the anti-capitalist rhetoric which, as we noted earlier, was a feature of prewar Labour policy statements and which had survived in a muted form in 1945 disappeared without trace. A comparison between the manifestos of 1945 and 1959 illustrates very clearly the influence of revisionism on the party's policy goals and political outlook.

Despite their influence in 1959 it was not until after the electoral defeat of that year that the revisionists led by Hugh Gaitskell went fully on the offensive with the aim of transforming the party constitution as well as party policy. Gaitskell's speech at the post-mortem conference in November 1959 was a comprehensive statement of the revisionist case (Labour Party, 1959, pp. 105–14). He began by asserting that the defeat was due to long term economic and social changes produced by a decline in traditional industries, long term full employment and greater affluence. In his view these all contributed to the declining Labour vote. His remedy for this was to get the party to revise its associations with class, and to abandon public ownership. He called for a revision of the party constitution, suggesting in particular an amendment to Clause 4, the famous section of the constitution which talks about promoting 'the common ownership of the means of production'. This speech initiated a major debate within the party, which centred around the party's future electoral prospects if it failed to modernize along revisionist lines (Abrams, Rose and Hinden, 1960). Ultimately the attempt to revise the constitution failed, although many in the party regarded the whole exercise as irrelevant, concerned as it was with symbols rather than policy.

This was however the only setback which the revisionists faced. Gaitskell met a challenge to the leadership on unilateral nuclear disarmament head on, and succeeded in overturning a conference resolution favouring unilateralism passed in 1960 at the conference the following year. He defeated a challenge to his leadership by Harold Wilson in the parliamentary party by 166 votes to 81. His early death prevented him from leading the party into the 1964 General Election, but the policy proposals put to the electorate at that election strongly reflected the revisionist case.

The election manifesto in 1964 was the first of the comprehensive 'modern' manifestos, in the sense that it covered the entire range of government functions in much more detail than before. The main innovation in 1964 was the emphasis on national planning as a means of stimulated investment and growth, stressing the importance of science and technology in this planning effort. However, none of the proposals involved a commitment to detailed microeconomic planning, but were macroeconomic in character, emphasizing the need to influence the fiscal and monetary environment in which industry worked. This can be seen in the proposals to introduce what later became known as the Department of Economic Affairs which stated: 'This Ministry will frame the broad strategy for increasing investment, expanding exports and replacing inessential imports. . . . (a) By using the tax system to encourage industries and firms to export more. (b) By providing better terms of credit where business justifies it . . .' (Craig, 1975, p. 259). This was essentially a 'hands-off' approach to intervention. Similarly there was a proposal to introduce a Ministry of Technology 'to bring advanced technology and new processes into industry' (p. 260) but no detailed suggestions of how this might be done by any methods of direct intervention.

The 1964 manifesto dropped all references to socialism in favour of a technocratic vision of the future which played on the fuddy-duddy, worn-out image of the Tories. There were no pledges to extend public ownership apart from the water supply industry which was already mostly owned by the community. It did make some solid proposals for extending welfare and employment protection, industrial retraining and education, health and housing provision. But in the key area of national economic planning the proposals did not differ all that much in substance from those of the Conservatives, who had stressed the importance of the National Economic Development Council which they had set up in 1961, and also the importance of science in industry.

The 1964 manifesto set the tone for the next six years of Labour government which provided comprehensive evidence of the effects of revisionism in practice. We shall examine the record of the 1964–70 Labour government in Chapter 6, but it is sufficient to note that after the debacle of the National Plan in 1965 the good intentions of implementing long term planning sank without trace. This was partly due to events in the economy, but also due to the fact that the proposals were not properly thought out in the first place.

In 1966 Labour reiterated many of the detailed proposals made earlier but also introduced for the first time proposals to modernize the government machine and Parliament. This was also the first year in which reference was made, albeit very brief, to the need for micro-economic intervention at the sectoral and industry levels; this was an interesting portent of things to come.

The defeat in the General Election of 1970 sparked off a debate in the party about what were seen as the failures of the Labour government. The post-mortem, though acrimonious at times, concentrated on broad policy goals, on the assumption that a change of aims would bring a change of strategy in office. The aims were significantly changed before the party again took office, but as events were to show, this did not change the strategy. However, for the moment we shall concentrate on the policy aims after 1970, a period which saw the resurgence of socialism.

The socialist resurgence after 1970

The debate following the election defeat in 1970 culminated in *Labour's Programme for Britain* which was accepted at the 1973 annual conference (Labour Party, 1973). This document represented a decisive break with revisionism, and represented a greater reorientation of Labour's policy goals than anything seen since 1918. It was much more comprehensive

and far-reaching in its objectives than anything the party had ever produced before. After the silence of the revisionist years the party's commitment to socialism was once again boldly asserted. Its opening sentence was
'we are a Democratic Socialist Party, and proud of it' (p. 7). In a frequently
quoted passage it asserted that the aim of the Labour Party was 'to bring
about a fundamental and irreversible shift in the balance of power and
wealth in favour of working people and their families' (ibid.).

The document covered all aspects of policy including health and
welfare, education, homes, transport and the environment, the Common
Market, food and agriculture, foreign policy and overseas development.
But the most important section which was also the most radical was on
economic strategy. This part of the document covered six sections, each
relating to different aspects of economic policy; the sections were demand
management, economic planning, price controls, the accountability of
economic power, the public sector and economic equality. The three
sections on economic planning, the accountability of economic power
and the public sector were the most radical and controversial.

The economic planning section contained three broad proposals.
Firstly, there was a proposal to establish a state holding company which
would acquire 'a major public stake in manufacturing industry' (p. 17).
Secondly, a proposal to establish planning agreements with the top 100
manufacturing firms, in effect the corporate sector. The agreements
aimed at monitoring the activities, influencing the policies and holding
these firms accountable to the country as a whole. Thirdly, there was the
proposal for a new Industry Act to give the government powers of selective intervention to operate if necessary at the level of the individual firm.
This was radically different from the 'hands-off' intervention envisaged
in 1964. For example, in the Industry Act it was proposed to take reserve
powers if need be to sack directors of firms with which the government
had a planning agreement, and to put in an 'Official Trustee' to control a
Company 'which fails to meet its responsibilities to its workers, to its
customers, or to the community as a whole' (p. 19).

These ideas arose out of a specific recognition of the changes which
had taken place in British industry associated with the growth of the
corporate sector. It stated 'the economy is now completely dominated by
a hundred or so giant companies. Fifty years ago the 100 largest manufacturing companies produced 15 per cent of the net manufacturing
output . . . and their share by 1970 had risen to as much as 50 per cent'
(p. 13). This analysis of corporate power and the threat to democracy
which it represents completely reversed the revisionist argument put by
Crosland, that the government had adequate controls over corporate
power through the normal instruments of macroeconomic management.
It was an analysis principally developed by Stuart Holland who had been
involved in the drafting of the document, and who later was to call for

controls over the 'mesoeconomic' (i.e. corporate) sector (Holland, 1975). The wide range of powers envisaged in the Industry Act included the compulsory disclosure of information, investment in, or outright purchase of companies, as well as the powers mentioned earlier. It was emphatic that these powers would apply 'to large multi-national companies' (p. 19).

The sections in *Labour's Programme for Britain* on the accountability of economic power were concerned with conciliation and arbitration in industry, trade union rights, consumer protection and industrial democracy, although they were less specific than the proposals on trade union rights. They envisaged the establishment of executive boards reporting to supervisory boards in major companies both containing representatives of workers. The 'programme of joint control' as it was called would be initiated by the workforce who would be given the legal right to initiate joint control committees in their companies. The proposals of trade union rights were also comprehensive and far-reaching and included protection against unfair dismissal, the statutory right to belong to a trade union, and statutory rights for information and recognition.

The section on public ownership envisaged the nationalization of North Sea oil, the docks, aircraft and shipbuilding, and all mineral rights. The most innovatory aspects of the public ownership proposals however concerned the National Enterprise Board. This was seen as a kind of state holding company which initially would include state corporations such as BP and Rolls-Royce, but would subsequently acquire 'a substantial addition of companies from the present private sector' (p. 33). The range of tasks envisaged for the NEB was vast including job creation, technological development, promoting prices policy, industrial democracy and tackling the spread of multinational companies.

The February 1974 manifesto broadly reflected the proposals on economic policy made in *Labour's Programme for Britain*. The introduction of planning agreements, the new Industry Act, and significant extensions of public enterprise were all included in the manifesto. The specific commitments to public ownership included shipbuilding, ship repairing, marine engineering, private ports and aerospace. The manifesto also stated:

> we shall not confine the extension of the public sector to loss making and subsidised industries. We shall also take over profitable sections or individual firms in these industries where a public holding is essential to enable the Government to control prices, stimulate investment, encourage exports, create employment, protect workers and consumers from the activities of irresponsible multi-national companies.   (Craig, 1975, p. 403)

Compared with the revisionist years of the 1950s and 1960s it was a remarkably radical restatement of Labour's socialist goals.

Within two years of the Labour victory at the February 1974 election, this radical economic strategy was abandoned and in ruins. We shall
discuss the reasons for this more fully in Chapter 6, but one of the main
reasons was the collapse of Keynesian macroeconomic demand management. By 1976 the government found itself in the same position as Philip
Snowden, the Labour Chancellor in 1929: it had radical pretensions but
these were destroyed on the altar of financial orthodoxy because the
leadership had no clear alternative strategy. But unlike the aftermath of
the 1931 debacle the party leadership did not try to formulate such an
alternative strategy. Instead, by the simple expedient of usurping the
decision-making institutions of the party they rewrote the manifesto so as
to eliminate the radical economic strategy altogether. Callaghan, the chief
instigator of this coup, increasingly became a kind of caricature of Stanley
Baldwin and his philosophy of 'safety first'. To be fair to the leadership,
there were grave risks to economic performance posed by the economic
strategy, at least in the short run, which its authors had not properly discussed (Gamble, 1981). But the end product was a manifesto in 1979
which in Geoff Bish's words was 'remarkably weak in terms of Party
Policy' (Bish, 1979, p. 201). He was the head of research at the Labour
Party headquarters in 1979, and was able to give a graphic account of how
Downing Street pre-empted the discussions on policy in 1979 by imposing its own manifesto on the party.

Apart from a cryptic reference to 'a major extension of industrial
democracy' (Bish 1979, p. 25) the radical economic strategy of 1974
disappeared from the 1979 manifesto virtually without trace. The party
had never before in its history adopted a far-reaching set of proposals like
the economic strategy of 1974 only to have these disappear completely in
the next manifesto. It was true that in the past specific ideas for public
ownership had been included in some years and dropped in others, but
the experience of 1979 was unique. The fact that the watered down
manifesto was associated with a massive electoral defeat made the post-
election crisis all the more acute. As we showed in Chapter 3 the electorate were voting on the record of the Labour government rather than
the manifesto proposals. But this did not stop many people linking the
policy programme and the electoral performance, and among most activists it discredited completely the revisionist argument that Labour only
wins votes when it is moderate in its aims.

It is also clear that the Callaghan coup played a key role in stimulating the campaign to revise the party constitution on the mandatory
reselection of MPs which was passed by four million votes to three
million at the annual conference of 1979 (Kogan and Kogan, 1982,
pp. 64–5). This conference produced a breakthrough for groups like the
Campaign for Labour Party Democracy which had been promoting the
idea of mandatory reselection for years. They were to win further successes

in the 1981 conference when the party adopted the electoral college for the election of the leader.

Fundamentally the changes in the party constitution after the 1979 election and the widening split between the Left and Right had its roots in the growing gap between Labour's policy goals and its performance in office. The rebirth of socialism in the early 1970s was largely a product of disillusionment inside the party with revisionism in practice, which failed in terms of its own professed goals of stimulating economic growth and greater equality, and even failed in terms of its key justification, electoral success. The disillusionment with the 1964–70 government had led to a reformulation of Labour's policy goals in a more radical socialist direction. When this proved insufficient to change party policies after 1974, attention was focused on internal party democracy, the selection of the leader and MPs and the writing of the manifesto. But were the reformers in the party right in concluding that revisionism in practice had failed? We turn to this question next.

6

The Labour Party and economic policy

In this and the subsequent chapter we review the implementation of Labour's policy goals in the areas of economic and social policy. For our purposes economic policy refers to the macroeconomic management of the economy which is concerned with influencing the behaviour of aggregates such as employment, inflation and growth. It also refers to intervention in the economy at the microeconomic level under the broad headings of regional and industrial policy. We are concerned with evaluating policy in relation to its objectives, as well as in relation to the performance of Conservative governments. Thus an inevitable normative component enters our discussion; we must ask how good or bad was the policy performance, as well as describing what actually happened.

There is a vast literature on economic policy in Britain. Some of it is purely theoretical or is concerned with technical questions such as economic forecasting (Peston, 1974; Ormerod, 1979; Ball, 1982). Some of it is concerned with analysing the economic history of post-war Britain (Shonfield, 1958; Dow, 1964; Brittan, 1964; Stewart, 1978), or with different aspects of economic management, such as economic growth (Beckerman, 1979), demand management (Posner, 1978), incomes policy (Clegg, 1971; Jones, 1973) and inflation (Hirsch and Goldthorpe, 1978). We shall be focusing particularly on the performance of the economy when Labour was in power, and a few writers have concentrated on this question alone (Lapping, 1970; Beckerman, 1972; Bosanquet and Townsend, 1980).

Despite this variety of literature there are some common themes which emerge in discussions of Britain's economic performance and these provide a background against which we can review Labour in office. We start by examining the main features of economic policy making in Britain since the war. There are recurrent problems which have taxed policy makers on both sides of the political spectrum, and we must examine these as a prelude to evaluating Labour in power.

The main features of economic policy since the war

Britain's economic performance since the Second World War is a story of persistent decline relative to our major competitors in Europe and elsewhere. This decline was less apparent in the 1950s and early 1960s, but became glaringly obvious by the 1970s. A team from the Brookings Institute did a detailed assessment of Britain's economic performance in the 1960s and 1970s, and their report throws much light on this relative decline (Caves and Krause, 1980). They showed that between 1957 and 1967 the average annual growth rate of gross domestic product in the UK was 3.1 per cent compared with 4.8 per cent for members of the Organization of Economic Co-operation and Development, that is the advanced industrialized western countries, as a whole. Between 1973 and 1978 growth averaged 1.1 per cent for the UK and 2.5 per cent for the OECD as a whole. Thus the percentage gap between Britain's growth rates, and those of our OECD competitors had widened. In 1967 the gross domestic product *per capita* for the UK was 86 per cent of the average for the OECD, but by 1971 this had fallen to 71 per cent. The average rate of inflation in the UK between 1967 and 1978 was 10.5 per cent, compared with 7.1 per cent for the OECD, although both figures were increased significantly by the inflationary explosion of 1974–5, following the quadrupling of the price of oil. The mean unemployment rate in Britain between 1955 and 1975 was 2.3 per cent of the working population, and was 3 per cent for the OECD. But by 1978 the position was reversed; the unemployment rate for Britain was 5.6 per cent of the working population and 5.2 per cent for the seven largest OECD countries. Thus all the aggregate indicators point to an increasing decline in Britain's economic performance compared with the rest of the industrial world.

Time series data on the main economic aggregates appear in Table 6.1, and these confirm the picture of economic decline. During the twenty years from 1959 to 1979 there was a trend decline in the growth rate in real terms and a trend increase in unemployment, inflation with a peak in the mid-1970s, and in strikes. During this period the balance of payments became more and more of a constraint on expansion.

The background to economic policy making during this period was the use of techniques of demand management derived from Keynes' *General Theory of Employment, Interest and Money* (1936), coupled with a sporadic but increasing emphasis on industrial or supply policy as time went on. The postwar Labour government was the first to employ the new techniques of stabilization policy developed by Keynes and embodied

Table 6.1 The main economic indicators, 1959–79

	Change in GDP (constant price) (%)	Unemployment (%)	Change in retail prices (%)	Balance of payments, current (£m)	Days lost in strikes (m)	Public expenditure as % GDP
1959	3.3	2.0	0.6	+172	5.3	33.4
1960	4.6	1.5	1.0	−228	3.0	33.2
1961	3.7	1.3	3.4	+47	3.0	33.8
1962	0.9	1.8	2.6	+155	5.8	34.2
1963	4.2	2.2	2.1	+125	1.8	34.0
1964	5.4	1.6	3.3	−362	2.3	34.1
1965	2.7	1.3	4.8	−43	2.9	35.2
1966	2.1	1.4	3.9	+113	2.4	35.7
1967	2.6	2.2	2.5	−289	2.8	39.0
1968	4.4	2.3	4.7	−273	4.7	39.4
1969	1.8	2.3	5.4	+471	6.8	37.8
1970	1.9	2.5	6.4	+781	11.0	37.6
1971	2.5	3.3	9.4	+1,076	13.6	37.5
1972	1.3	3.6	7.1	+176	23.9	38.5
1973	7.7	2.6	9.2	−1,056	7.2	39.0
1974	−1.1	2.5	16.1	−3,379	14.8	44.2
1975	−0.6	3.9	24.3	−1,674	6.0	46.2
1976	4.3	5.2	16.5	−1,116	3.3	44.1
1977	1.1	5.7	15.8	−284	10.1	40.2
1978	2.9	5.6	8.2	+620	9.4	40.9
1979	0.6	5.3	13.4	−1,863	29.1	41.3

Sources: 1 Percentage change in GDP at constant prices: calculated from *Economic Trends 1981*, Annual Supplement 5.
2 Unemployment in Great Britain, excluding school leavers: *British Labour Statistics Historical Abstracts* and the *Department of Employment Gazette*.
3 Percentage change in retail prices: *Economic Trends 1980*, Annual Supplement, p. 114.
4 Balance of payments: *Economic Trends 1981*, Annual Supplement, p. 124.
5 Days lost in strikes: *British Labour Statistics Historical Abstracts* and the *Department of Employment Gazette*.
6 Public expenditure as % GDP: Appendix 1 (Pliatzky, 1982).

in the 1944 White Paper on employment policy (HMSO, 1944a). As we argued in Chapter 5 Keynes' analysis was concerned with maintaining adequate demand in the economy in order to sustain full employment. Keynes' analysis was essentially an inversion of the classical economic relation known as 'Says Law' which held that 'supply creates its own demand'. Thus, in essence Keynes argued that 'demand creates its own supply' (Skidelsky, 1979). In this view if demand was right supply could look after itself. Thus macroeconomic policy for more than fifteen years following the Second World War was wholly concerned with demand management, and virtually ignored supply policy altogether.

The perennial problem of the postwar British economy was that the domestic economy could never fully respond to demand stimulus which tended to encourage imports as much as home production. Moreover, this problem became progressively worse as time went on. Although relatively full employment existed in the 1950s and early 1960s, policy makers were unable to stimulate production and economic growth at a rate comparable to Britain's competitors without producing a balance of payments crisis, which in turn led to deflationary action. Attempts to do this produced a policy of 'stop–go', or the alternate expansion and contraction of the economy by government action.

The sequence of events in the 'stop–go' cycle was roughly as follows: the Chancellor stimulated consumption and accompanied this with exhortations to industry to invest. Investment duly occurred as demand expanded but this increased imports and caused a balance of payments deficit. The deteriorating balance of payments sparked off speculative attacks on the pound, which had been fixed at $2.80 since 1949. To protect the exchange rate and restore 'confidence' the Chancellor then deflated the economy which reduced imports and restored the balance of payments. In the short run deflation worked but in the long run it damaged investment, slowed technical change and caused unemployment. The repeated disruption of investment caused by this policy made businessmen more and more reluctant to invest in the 'go' part of the cycle, and the resulting low rate of technological progress produced low productivity and ultimately a failure to compete in prices and quality in domestic and export markets. This dynamic process of industrial decline produced greater import penetration into British markets and in the absence of import controls the economy hit the balance of payments constraint earlier in the 'go' part of the cycle. At the height of the consumer boom in 1955 the deficit on the current account had been £150 million. In 1960 it was £228 million, and by 1964 it was £362 million. Moreover, if the deficits on capital account were included, the overall balance of payments problems were even larger than this. Each phase of the 'stop–go' cycle produced greater import penetration and a bigger deficit than the previous phase.

In a searing attack on the post-war management of the economy Pollard exposes the faulty logic at the heart of the 'stop–go' policy:

Consider the framework, Keynesian or otherwise, within which the Treasury and other policy-makers operated. They believed that in Britain (unlike other countries where high growth rates were proved to be sustainable almost indefinitely) there is something in the internal relationships which ensures that as the economy gets into higher gear the foreign balance of payments will turn adverse. In other words, at full blast, call it 100, there is inherently a deficit. This can be cured by going down to less than full employment, call it 95. At 95, the balance is restored and may even become positive. After a suitable interval, the policy is then to go back to 100.

(1982, p. 54)

Pollard explains the economic decline as an inevitable outcome of repeated deflations and cuts in investment imposed by policy makers with a 'contempt for production'. Keynesian policies were regarded very favourably by decision makers both in Britain and abroad throughout the postwar era; but they had two major defects. Firstly, they emphasized the short run and played down the long run. Keynes' famous dictum was that 'in the long run we are all dead', so that policy makers routinely ignored the long-term consequences of short-term policies. This was one of the most telling criticisms of demand management made by Friedman (1968) in his discussion of the long-run effects of short-term stabilization policies on inflation. The long-run effects of 'stop–go' on growth were, if anything, more serious than the effects on inflation. Secondly, Keynesian policies ignored the supply side of the economy. Paradoxically countries which did not accept Keynesian policies in the immediate postwar era, such as Germany and France, benefited from this, because they paid much greater attention to supply side questions than did decision makers in Britain (Shonfield, 1969). The first elements of an industrial policy in Britain did not appear until 1961 when the Chancellor, Selwyn Lloyd, established the National Economic Development Council. Later attempts by the Labour government to introduce the National Plan aimed at extending industrial intervention further.

We shall examine the record of Labour in industrial policy below, but the main thing to note at this stage is that such a policy has on the whole been ineffective. This is true for two broad reasons. Firstly, industrial policy was never properly co-ordinated with demand management which frequently produced situations in which the policies were in conflict. For example, attempts were being made to stimulate industrial investment in depressed areas on the one hand, as the economy was being drastically deflated to deal with the latest balance of payments crisis on the other. Secondly, it is broadly true that successive governments have had few effective policy instruments with which to implement industrial policy at the level of the firm. Policy instruments have usually taken the form of grants of various kinds, many of them not in the least cost-effective (Grant, 1982). As we noted in Chapter 5 in connection with the National Plan of 1965, too often governments have adopted a 'hands-off' approach to intervention believing that the announcement of targets in Whitehall would produce the necessary action on the ground.

Another important feature of economic policy in the postwar period has been the autonomous influence of economic theory on policy, with monetarism being only the most recent example. Apart from the background provided by Keynesianism there have been a number of occasions when developments in economics have directly influenced policy making. A clear example of this was the policy of 'fine tuning' the economy which came into vogue in the early 1960s and was strongly influenced by the discovery of the Phillips curve (Phillips, 1958). This was the stable relationship between unemployment and the rate of change of money wages. Phillips discovered that an apparently stable inverse relationship existed between these variables over the period 1861 to 1957. Since the largest component of incomes is wages and the change in incomes was closely related to inflation, the curve demonstrated an apparently stable relationship between unemployment and inflation. It was argued that the Phillips curve provided a 'menu' of alternative policy choices, enabling the policy maker to select a given rate of inflation in exchange for a given level of unemployment (Rees, 1970). This was 'fine tuning'.

In practice 'fine tuning' had the unfortunate effect of legitimizing the policies of deflation which were pursued by the Labour government with increasing vigour after 1965. This was because 'fine tuning' implied that deflation and reflation were somehow equivalent, and that deflation now could easily be followed by reflation later. In fact they are not equivalent at all as we argued earlier; deflation produces a permanent loss of production, a reduction in investment, increased unemployment and a loss of competitiveness. This cannot easily be put right, so that although 'fine tuning' was initially seen as a means of avoiding 'stop–go', in practice it made things worse. The Phillips curve relationship began to break down in the late 1960s so that by 1970 wage inflation was some 12 per cent higher than the rate predicted by the curve (Kennedy, 1976, p. 44). Unfortunately by then policy makers began to acquire new theoretical justifications for deflation as monetarism gained ground.

The experience of monetarism is an excellent example of how theoretical doctrines can be used to justify policies which are highly damaging to the real economy, and which are ultimately self-defeating. The theoretical and empirical weaknesses of monetarism have been thoroughly explored by a number of writers (Hahn, 1980; Desai, 1981; Kaldor, 1982). The essence of monetarism is the doctrine that monetary and fiscal policy cannot influence the state of the real economy or employment and the rate of growth of productivity, in the long run. In this view if a government attempts to stimulate the economy by monetary or fiscal means this will not influence employment, but instead will stimulate inflation. Moreover, it is argued by some theorists that any short-run influences of monetary policy on employment are due entirely to the fact that individuals do not correctly anticipate the inflationary consequences of government action. If they had 'rational expectations' (Muth, 1961; Lucas, 1972) – that is correctly anticipate the results of monetary policy – then a financial stimulus to the economy would be translated into inflation almost immediately and employment would remain unaffected. These arguments have prompted monetarists to assert that governments should not attempt to stabilize the economy, or stimulate demand during a recession but simply try to keep the supply of money in line with the underlying growth of the real economy. In other words governments should respond to the real economy, but not try to stimulate it. These views have been very influential in the period of the Thatcher government, but they are largely fallacious. They can only be sustained by ignoring important theoretical links between a monetary and fiscal policy and the real economy (Buiter, 1980) by ignoring the empirical evidence that stabilization policy has improved the state of the real economy (Modigliani, 1977) and finally by denying the growing evidence that the link between the money supply and inflation is extremely tenuous and unstable (Kaldor, 1982). Moreover, even if such a relationship was stable the supply of money could not be used to control inflation in a modern credit economy which has many money substitutes (Balogh, 1982). The doctrine that a single monetary aggregate can be used to control inflation without adverse effects on employment has been aptly described as the 'unmeasurable in pursuit of the uncontrollable'. Although perhaps we should add that inflation can be controlled, but not by monetary policy. Given that the Radcliffe Committee on the workings of the monetary system (HMSO, 1959) had argued that monetary policy could, at best, play only a subordinate role in economic management, it is a puzzle as to why such ideas should have gained so much credence by the mid-1970s. Kaldor attributes this to the pervasive role of the city in economic policy making and the growing influence of the financial press both in Britain and the US. Whatever the reason, by 1979 these ideas had become a dogma amongst leading Conservatives. Kaldor writes:

> when Mrs Thatcher's government came to power bold assertions were made in official publications, as well as in ministerial speeches which marked a sharp break with past traditions. . . . They set themselves precise targets in terms of the PSBR, the money supply, the reduction in the tax burden, and the reduction of inflation. . . . So far they have failed on every count.   (1982, pp. xi–xii)

Undoubtedly, the theoretical arguments of Friedman and his supporters in Britain, like Laidler (1976) and Ball and Burns (1976) of the London Business School, played an important role in promoting these ideas. Economic theory is abstract and complex, and econometric evidence is difficult to interpret even for the expert, and so politicians who lack any clear perspective of their own can be persuaded to accept doctrines that are little more than ideological dogma. Perhaps the best epitaph on monetarism in Britain is provided by Friedman himself who in his evidence to the House of Commons Treasury and Civil Service Committee confidently predicted that 'only a modest reduction in output and employment will be a side effect of reducing inflation to single figures by 1982' (House of Commons, 1980–1). The contrast between this statement and the reality of a huge number of redundancies and bankruptcies caused by monetarism applied to Britain in 1982 could not be more stark.

A further feature of postwar economic policy has been the episodic use of incomes policies as a means of controlling inflation. In the ten years alone between 1965 and 1975 there were no less than twenty different types of incomes policy varying from the voluntary restraint of 1965–6 to the statutory policy of 1972–3 (Metcalf and Richardson, 1976, p. 287). The original White Paper on employment policy (HMSO, 1944a) recognized a basic conflict between full employment, stable prices and free collective bargaining in the long run. This conflict arises from the fact that labour supply shortages tend to drive up wages in full employment, and in the absence of any restraint this produces inflation. The inflation then creates a set of expectations which encourage bargainers to raise their demands above the inflation rate thereby accelerating it even further. If the government tries to accommodate this by stimulating demand then the result could be hyper-inflation (Meade, 1982). If the government does not accommodate it the result is unemployment as bargainers price themselves out of jobs. In this situation incomes policy has the role of reconciling full employment and price stability.

Unfortunately, incomes policy is extremely difficult to sustain. If it is voluntary each union involved finds itself locked in one of the paradoxes of collective action referred to earlier (Olson, 1965). It is in the interests of all unions to co-operate in restraining wages, in order to reduce inflation. However, it is in the interests of any one union to 'free-ride' and not co-operate when the others are doing so, in order to get a larger settlement. If a few unions refuse to co-operate it makes co-operation for the remainder extremely difficult. Thus there is a tendency for such co-operation not to take place, or for it to break down rapidly if there is a single breach. In game theoretic terms a voluntary incomes policy is a prisoner's dilemma game (Rapoport, 1960).

There are only two ways out of the dilemma described above. The first is for government to attempt to enforce a statutory policy or some sort of 'voluntary' policy with teeth, involving perhaps enforcement by the TUC. There are two major difficulties with this approach. First, it tends to politicize all wage negotiations, putting the prestige of the government at risk every time there is a wage dispute. A corollary of this is that wage settlements tend to be decided on arbitrary political grounds, instead of on economic grounds. Secondly, in practice it is very difficult to enforce a compulsory wages policy in a democracy since it is impossible to deter breaches by, for example, threatening the imprisonment of recalcitrants. In a real sense all incomes policies are voluntary policies.

The second way out of the dilemma is for the government to allow unemployment to rise, as markets are lost with inflationary price rises. Eventually this increased unemployment reduces trade union bargaining power and the competitive bidding up of wages becomes extremely difficult. This is of course the policy of deflation which we have criticized for undermining the long-term growth of the economy.

The other disadvantage of incomes policy apart from these problems of enforcement, is that it tends to distort differentials, and in effect it 'freezes' labour markets. Incomes policies have tended to compress differentials, causing much discontent amongst skilled workers, and they slow down the reallocation of labour from declining to profitable industries. The record of incomes policies in restraining wage inflation is somewhat mixed. Recent econometric evidence shows that incomes policies in the 1960s and 1970s succeeded in bringing down wage inflation, but wages caught up rapidly when the policies were relaxed (Henry, 1981). The two common characteristics of successful postwar policies are that they have only been successful in the short run, and secondly, a key element of this success has been the attitude of the trade unions; when the unions have not co-operated incomes policies have inevitably collapsed.

Despite the disadvantages of incomes policies it remains broadly true that full employment, stable prices and free collective bargaining are fundamentally irreconcilable. This suggests the need for a permanent incomes policy. Considerable experience has been gained in operating incomes policies in Britain, which can be put to use in designing a long term policy (Jones, 1973; Clegg, 1971), and such policies have worked for long periods in other countries, notably Sweden (Robinson, 1974). It seems clear that such a policy will be an inevitable requirement of industrial reconstruction.

A third feature of economic policy in Britain is the long term growth of public expenditure. In a Keynesian world public expenditure should operate counter-cyclically, that is it should increase in a depression and decrease in a boom. Taxation and expenditure policy should be co-ordinated to ensure an adequate level of aggregate demand. In practice neither of these conditions have been met. Public expenditure as a percentage of gross domestic product has risen inexorably over the years as the figures in Table 6.1 demonstrate. Moreover, rapid increases which occurred from time to time have had little to do with the state of aggregate demand. By the same token Leo Pliatzky, the senior civil servant in charge of public expenditure in the Treasury during the 1970s, noted that 'The divorce between the collective decision making process on public expenditure and the Treasury's budget-making processes remained total' (Pliatzky, 1982, p. 131).

There has been a certain amount of academic work aimed at explaining the nature of the budgeting process (Wildavsky, 1975; Cameron, 1978). The work on expenditure in Britain explains the growth in terms of a number of factors, including the ratchet effect of wars and social upheavals which bring rises in public expenditure that are never subsequently reduced (Peacock and Wiseman, 1961), the processes of party competition and the 'bidding' for votes (Tufte, 1978; Klein, 1976), the role of the bureaucracy and the British political system which gives political prestige to spending Ministers (Niskanen, 1971; Heclo and Wildavsky, 1974). There are also the problems of controlling expenditure. The PESC system of five-year rolling expenditure plans was eminently sensible, but it did tend to increase expenditure simply by the way it operated. Calculations were done in real terms, not in money terms, and although this was sensible from a planning point of view it automatically meant that expenditure kept ahead of inflation. Some argued that it actually underwrote inflation (Pliatzky, 1982, p. 137). Similarly, after 1965 expenditure plans were made on the basis of unrealistic assumptions about the future growth of the economy built into the National Plan. The growth failed to materialize, but the expenditure continued regardless.

In the data on public expenditure in Table 6.1 there is clear evidence of political influences at work. In 1966–7 expenditure rose from 35.7 per cent to 39 per cent of GDP, and in 1973–4 it rose from 39 per cent to 44.2 per cent. Both were election years, and were followed by years in which cuts were imposed. This pattern is consistent with a political cycle in which an incoming Labour government enthusiastically embarks on social expenditure planned in opposition, only to find that the economic problems which this creates entail cutbacks in subsequent years. There is similar evidence for this in 1972 during the Heath administration. Public expenditure as a percentage of GDP is not usually high in the UK compared with other industrial countries (OECD, 1978; Castles and McKinlay, 1979). But undoubtedly rapid increases of the sort observed in Table 6.1 have a disruptive effect on the economy. A more controlled expansion in expenditure would have helped to avoid speculative attacks on the pound, particularly after 1974. Whether cuts in expenditure reduce inflation is more doubtful. Cuts after 1968 coincided with rising inflation, and with falling inflation after 1975. So the link between these two variables is somewhat tenuous. But it is generally true that large abrupt shocks to the economy are bad for investment and growth and on these grounds large shifts in expenditure should have been avoided.

A final feature of the British economy which has attracted the attention of policy makers is the decline of manufacturing industry, or de-industrialization (Blackaby, 1979). Employment in manufacturing industry showed a relative expansion in the ten years following the Second World War, but since the mid-1960s it has been contracting at an accelerating rate. Between 1966 and 1974 the annual percentage rate of change of employment in manufacturing industry was −1.1 per cent; from 1974 to 1976 it was −3.8 per cent (Cairncross, 1979, p. 6). An influential book which first drew attention to this phenomenon was written by Bacon and Eltis (1976). They argued that the root cause of de-industrialization was the growth of public sector employment. In their view rising taxation to finance expenditure reduced profits and savings, and stimulated wage increases as workers resisted the fall in private consumption required to accommodate increased public spending. They distinguished between the market sector of the economy which is concerned with producing saleable goods and services, and the non-market sector which includes social welfare, health and education and also some private sector activities. They write (Bacon and Eltis, 1976, p. 93): 'The claims on marketed output from outside the market sector increased from 41.4 per cent of marketed output in 1961 to 60.3 per cent in 1974, thus apparently reducing the proportion of output that market-sector producers could themselves invest and consume by nearly one third.'

This book was very influential in buttressing the case for cuts in public expenditure after 1976. The main problem with the thesis concerns the cause and effect of the growth in public sector employment, and also the nature of this employment. Cairncross (1979) points out that much of the growth in employment in the 1970s was due to increased female participation in the workforce, rather than a direct transfer of labour from manufacturing to the public sector. Moreover, the decline of the manufacturing sector predates the rise of public sector employment, which suggests that the latter absorbed surplus labour rather than crowded out the market sector. In other words the increase in the public sector is more an effect of de-industrialization than a cause.

The team at the Cambridge Department of Applied Economics have put a different interpretation on de-industrialization. In their view the decline in the manufacturing base has produced a failure by British industry to maintain its share of international and domestic markets. They argue: 'Stagnation and inflation have been caused by determining "supply side" conditions. . . . We assert that in the medium term the foreign trade performance of the economy is the main determinant of the level of domestic spending, output and income' (*Cambridge Economic Policy Review*, 1981, p. 10). Inflation and unemployment together tend to produce 'stagflation' because workers try to maintain real incomes in the face of recession. This problem is made worse by mounting costs of social security and unemployment relief, and attempts by manufacturers to raise prices in order to offset increased costs. Such income maintenance pressure can be suppressed by a deep enough recession, but only in terms of hugely reduced investment, employment and output. Once reflation is attempted, the problems recur.

The Cambridge analysis does not give an account of the causes of the underlying supply side problem, but it is important in focusing on foreign trade as the main constraint on remedial action. Reflation by traditional Keynesian methods is ruled out without import controls, because the balance of payments position prevents it. The problem is not made much easier by devaluation of the pound. Devaluation gives British exports a price advantage and makes imports more expensive, but the rising cost of imports itself gives an impetus to inflation which in turn reduces the original price advantage. Moreover there is convincing evidence that non-price factors such as quality, reliability and delivery times are significantly more important than prices in export markets (Posner and Steer, 1979; Stout, 1977; Kravis and Lipsey, 1977). Sterling was devalued from $2.5 in the fourth quarter of 1971 to $1.65 in the fourth quarter of 1976. During this period exports increased in real terms by 51 per cent, and imports by 76 per cent. Thus devaluation may help to stimulate exports, but it does not reduce imports. Another study shows that the UK increasingly tends to export at the cheap end of the market, and import at the expensive end, in sharp contrast with West Germany. It appears that much of the increased imports can be explained by the superior technical quality of imports compared with domestic products (Rothwell and Zegveld, 1981, pp. 23–45). The fact that Britain is moving 'down market' in international trade can be traced back to low investment, and low expenditure on research and development (Freeman, 1979) and the dynamic of industrial decline referred to earlier.

In this brief review we have examined some of the major recurring features of economic policy making, and in particular looked at the major problems faced by both parties in power. But are there any distinctive features of Labour administrations? Has Labour made a difference in influencing economic policy outcomes? To answer these questions we begin by reviewing the economic policies of Labour administrations before deriving some quantitative estimates of the effects of Labour incumbency.

Economic policy and Labour in office

Our main focus in assessing the economic performance of Labour in office is the record of the 1964–70 and 1974–9 governments. But there are some preliminary points to make about the record of the 1945–51 government which have implications for policy later on.

The 1945 Labour government faced the enormous problems of trying to rebuild a wartime economy which had been starved of investment, and was dominated by the production of arms. It made solid achievements like increasing the gross domestic product by more than 3.8 per cent per annum after 1948, and increasing industrial production by 7 per cent per annum (Dow, 1964, p. 39). Between 1948 and 1950 exports increased from $1.6 billion to $2.25 billion, inflation fell from 5.9 per cent to 3 per cent and unemployment remained static at the historically very low level of 1.5 per cent.

However, between 1947 and 1950 fixed investment fell from £250 million to £75 million, which had ominous implications for the future. This came about largely as a result of government action in deflating the economy which thereby initiated the policy of 'stop–go'. The first occasion this happened was in 1947 when the government cut investment by £200 million, largely because of concern over inflation. The second occasion was in 1949 after the devaluation of the pound. One of the main reasons for devaluation was the mishandling of a loan negotiated from the United States following the abrupt ending of lend-lease in 1946. The loan was negotiated on very adverse terms and one of the conditions, that Britain should restore full convertibility to the pound within a year, was simply impossible to meet. Britain had huge war debts and had no prospects of paying them off for several years until the economy recovered. This could not be achieved within a year. The result was that when convertibility was restored at the rate of $4.03 there was a massive run on the pound, and the loan was rapidly used up defending the currency. Britain was forced into a large devaluation, and the government deflated the economy with the aim of channelling production into exports. The convertibility crisis would have had much worse economic consequences had not the Marshall Aid programme subsequently begun to benefit the economy.

Thus the major mistake of the 1945 to 1951 Labour government was to initiate the policy of deflating the economy and cutting investment for reasons of short term stabilization. It made another major blunder in the last few months of the administration when it embarked on a huge programme of rearmament, with a plan to increase defence spending from 7 per cent to 10.5 per cent of the gross national product between 1948 and 1952. This produced the legacy which remains to this day of excessively high defence spending, compared with our European allies. Apart from diverting scarce resources to unproductive uses, the excessive burden of defence spending has badly distorted the country's research and development programmes (Rothwell and Zegveld, 1981, p. 27). Large amounts have been wasted on unprofitable aerospace projects like the TSR2 bomber, the Blue Streak Missile and, of course, Concorde. If these resources had been put into commercial projects as they were in Germany and Japan, the economic history of the post-war period might have been very different.

With these two points in mind, we can go on to examine the record of the Labour party in government after 1964.

The Wilson years, 1964–70

The Labour government of 1964 took office with the intention of revitalizing the economy and stimulating growth after what were seen as 'thirteen wasted years' of Conservative government. These objectives which as we have seen were prominent in the manifesto, were underlined forcefully in the Joint Statement of Intent signed by the government, the TUC and representatives of industry and the city in December 1964. The document stated:

> Much greater emphasis will be given to increasing productivity. The Government will encourage and develop policies designed to promote technological advance in industry, and to get rid of restrictive practices and prevent the abuse of monopoly power, and so improve efficiency, cut out waste, and reduce excessive prices.
>
> (Brittan, 1971, p. 316)

Despite these brave words by 1970 full employment had been abandoned, growth and productivity forgotten in a rapid series of deflationary cuts, which ultimately laid the basis of the 'stagflation' or stagnation and inflation of the 1970s. As can be seen from Table 6.1, between 1965 and 1970 the unemployment percentage nearly doubled, inflation increased by a third, economic growth fell substantially, and the days lost in strikes rose dramatically. The only measure which improved was the balance of payments, which went from a large deficit to a substantial surplus.

There are specific decisions one can point to, such as the refusal to devalue the pound in 1965 which played a key role in explaining this economic performance. But ultimately it came about because the government had no real alternative to the financial orthodoxy of the treasury. It had talked about national planning and industrial intervention but as we argued earlier, it failed to arm itself with the necessary policy instruments to make this effective. When the crunch came these policies were quickly abandoned in favour of orthodox deflation. In other words the industrial policy was largely rhetoric rather than substance.

The new government had inherited what was then an unprecedentedly large balance of payments deficit of £800 million on current and capital account, which had been produced largely by the Conservatives' attempts to engineer a pre-election boom. In the first few days of the administration the government took the fateful decision not to devalue, which set in train a series of events which destroyed the industrial strategy, and ultimately led to the electoral defeat of 1970. Wilson has been blamed personally for this decision (Stewart, 1978, p. 27). He was allegedly opposed to devaluation on political grounds, feeling that it would tar Labour with the brush of being the 'devaluation party'. However, he was also influenced by the belief that growth could eliminate the need for devaluation were the industrial strategy to be successful.

Just over a month after the election the government faced a run on the pound. It reacted by raising bank rate to 7 per cent, and arranged a standby credit of $3 billion. It also imposed a surcharge of 15 per cent on all imports of manufactured and semi-manufactured goods. The basic cause of the crisis was the balance of payments deficit, but there is no doubt that the hostility of the city to the new government, and from this the suspicion of bankers throughout the world, played a significant role. This hostility was exemplified by Lord Cromer, the Governor of the Bank of England, who made a thinly veiled attack on the new government in a speech at the Mansion House in November 1964. When the run on the pound gathered force Cromer went to see Wilson and demanded cuts in public expenditure and an across the board reversal of Labour policies as the price of restoring confidence (Wilson, 1974, pp. 64–6). By his own account Wilson met this challenge head on by threatening to float the pound, dissolve Parliament and hold an election on the theme of 'the people versus the bankers'. Cromer backed down and within twenty-four hours had organized $3 billion support from central banks in the US and the EEC. Ironically in retrospect it would have been better for the economy if Cromer had not backed down, and the pound had been floated. This would have removed at a stroke the need to defend the parity of the pound which rapidly became the sole objective of policy.

Keynesian economists sympathetic to the Labour government (Stewart, 1978; Beckerman, 1972) have made much of the decision not to devalue in 1964, and there is no doubt that it was a mistake. But there is an important sense in which devaluation was a side issue, the main issue being to stimulate productivity and growth. Devaluation would have eliminated the constraints imposed on the supply side of the economy by the need to defend the pound and was a necessary, but not sufficient, condition for success. Floating on its own could not ensure success as many enthusiasts for this policy found out after 1972 when the pound was floated. The problem as we have seen is that a floating pound acts only on the demand side of the economy by reducing the cost of exports and raising the cost of imports. Since it is not true that demand creates its own supply as far as the domestic economy is concerned this cannot be the whole solution. It has to be part of a wider policy of stimulating investment, research and development and productivity. However, in retrospect there was a real chance that floating the pound in 1965 would have allowed the strategy of growth to work, and in this sense a great opportunity was missed.

The strategy of growth was to be undertaken by the Department of Economic Affairs, a new ministry headed by George Brown, the Deputy Leader of the party. Brown saw incomes policy as the prerequisite of any attempts to stimulate growth. The government introduced what was initially a voluntary policy with a norm or target percentage increase of 3.5 per cent *per annum* (Metcalf and Richardson, 1976, p. 287) and it established the Prices and Incomes Board chaired by a former Conservative, Aubrey Jones, to enforce the norm. The government planned to refer pay claims to the board which would then review their conformity with the policy. Criteria for rises above the norm were set out, in order to try and avoid the rigidities associated with incomes policies. However, there were no sanctions for making employers or unions conform with the norm, and thus the whole policy lacked teeth. In 1966 the government was forced to abandon this voluntary policy and introduce a statutory wage freeze.

After the initial run on the pound, at the start of 1965 the pressure on sterling eased somewhat, and the government began to take action on the massive long term export of capital. Half the balance of payments deficit of £800 million in 1964 was caused by the export of capital – money which went in effect to boost the productivity of our competitors. The government had some success in curbing this; in 1964 net private investment overseas was £266 million, and this was reduced progressively so that by 1970 there was a surplus of net investment of £25 million (CSO, 1981, p. 140).

The lull in the speculation against the pound in early 1965 was, however, short lived. The $3 billion credit was renewed for the three months up to May, but it became clear that after that expired additional foreign support was needed. The Johnson administration in the US urged heavy cuts in home demand as a condition of further support, and in July 1965 the Chancellor announced a set of severe restrictions on capital investment and local authority spending amounting to cuts of £200 million in a full year. Brittan comments on these measures as follows:

> It was as a result of the July 1965 package – a full year before the more famous 1966 measures – that many close students became finally convinced that the Government had abandoned its growth and employment objectives, and would be prepared to deflate to the extent necessary to maintain the exchange rate. Thus the National Plan was written off by many people two months before it was published.   (1971, p. 309)

The strategy of indicative planning and growth had lasted just nine months. The government had another eight months to go before a general election victory gave it a substantial majority. But the hope that we would break out of the cycle of 'stop–go' was already dead, and though no-one knew it at the time, the countdown to the election defeat of 1970 had begun.

The economic history of the remaining years of the Labour government is a story of continuing 'stop–go' with longer and longer periods of 'stop', interspersed with shorter periods of 'go'. The election victory in March 1966 solved the immediate problems of governing with a tiny majority but it did nothing for the balance of payments. In May and June speculation against the pound began to build up and the same scenario of cuts and deflation was repeated all over again in July. The package of cuts on this occasion aimed at reducing demand by £500 million, with cuts of £150 million in public investment, tax increases and a wage freeze. The package of cuts on this occasion has a certain historical significance since in retrospect they represent the abandonment of full employment, a principle which had been maintained by successive governments since 1945. The rate of unemployment in 1966 was 1.4 per cent of the working population, which is as close to full employment as a modern economy can get. From this year onwards it rose continuously until it peaked in 1972 at 3.6 per cent, before climbing again after 1975.

Despite the series of cuts, the pound came under speculative attack again in 1967, and by November of that year the government was forced to devalue by 40 cents in the pound. Between the July measures of 1965 and the final devaluation there had been one long war of attrition. Labour's ambitions in opposition were ground into the dust of financial orthodoxy. When devaluation finally came many Labour MPs were relieved, since a group of seventy of them had signed a motion in November deploring the deflationary policies. But devaluation went down very badly in the city. Stewart remarks: 'Devaluation was seen not as a belated and essentially technical adjustment to changed economic conditions, but as a crushing blow to the City's self-esteem' (1978, p. 83).

After devaluation James Callaghan was replaced by Roy Jenkins as Chancellor. In this role Jenkins redoubled efforts to deflate the economy. Between 1967 and 1969 he presided over five separate deflationary exercises. First, the bank rate was raised to 8 per cent, then in January 1968 drastic cuts in public expenditure were made; purchase tax and selective employment tax was raised in March, hire purchase controls and restrictions on bank advances were imposed in November and finally in the budget of April 1969 demand was again reduced by £250 million.

The net result of all this was that by 1970 the government had succeeded in achieving a balance of payments surplus, but it had done this at the cost of abandoning all other objectives, in particular the objective of full employment which the Labour Party had first proclaimed in 1918.

The new Heath administration pursued a radical free market philosophy involving the abolition of the Prices and Incomes Board, the Industrial Reorganization Corporation and the Land Commission, the latter being remnants of Labour's original interventionist policy. They phased out the regional employment premium, which had in any case been undermined by deflation, and advocated a policy of allowing 'lame duck' industries to collapse. However, the *laissez faire* philosophy was abandoned in 1972 after the twin crises of upper Clyde shipbuilders and the bankruptcy of Rolls-Royce. The rapid 'U'-turn after 1972 involved a statutory incomes policy, a highly interventionist Industry Act, floating the pound, and the 'Barber boom' in which a huge reflation was undertaken. This was the last time a Keynesian expansion of demand was used to try and promote growth, and it stoked up huge inflationary problems which hit the economy after Labour took office in February 1974.

The Wilson–Callaghan government, 1974–9

The outstanding features of the early years of the Labour government were the runaway inflation which reached the unprecedented rate of 24 per cent per annum in 1975, the very rapid rise in public expenditure in 1974 and 1975 and the more gradual but inexorable rise in unemployment. The world economy had been plunged into recession by the rapid rise in oil prices after the Arab–Israeli war of 1973, and this affected the immediate problem of inflation. But a great deal of the inflation in 1974 was attributable to the attempt by the Conservatives to go for growth after 1972. Labour inherited an economic situation which was very much worse than 1964.

In this situation an immediate wage and price freeze should have been imposed in order to bring the situation under some sort of control. However, Labour was a minority government which in opposition had pledged itself to free collective bargaining. So this was ruled out on political grounds. However, in his post-election budget, the new Chancellor, Denis Healey, did not revert to the classic Keynesian strategy of reflation even though considerable unemployed resources existed in the economy with the unemployment rate at 2.5 per cent. Instead he adopted a mildly deflationary budget which was considerably influenced by some new ideas from the Cambridge Applied Economics Department.

Although Keynesianism was discredited by the experience of the Barber boom and stagflation, economic theory still continued to play an important role in influencing policy. The new Cambridge School, as it was called, argued that the public sector deficit, or the difference between government income and expenditure, determined the balance of payments deficit, which had always been the main constraint on growth. Cripps, Godley and Featherstone, economists from Cambridge, had explained their theory to the Expenditure Committee of the House of Commons in 1974 (House of Commons, 1974) and it had gained credence in government circles. In practice it meant that for the first time, serious attention was paid by policy makers to the public sector borrowing requirement, which up till then had been a minor concern. The new Cambridge analysis was rapidly discredited (Bispham, 1975) when it predicted a balance of payments deficit of £11 billion at a time when the deficit was £3.3 billion. But the legacy of concern about the PSBR continued, as it rose dramatically with public expenditure.

We have referred to the analysis of the causes of public expenditure growth earlier, but none of those theories fully explain the quantum jump in public expenditure which took place in 1974. There were a number of factors which explain it. The Barber boom had involved large increases in public expenditure, many of which did not come through until 1974; the PSBR in 1974 was £6.4 billion and this involved large debt servicing which of course itself increased public expenditure; there was the reorganization of the Health Service and local government which enormously increased public spending in these areas. The magnitude of the increases in local authority spending can be seen from the figures relating to the contribution of local government to the public sector borrowing requirement; in 1972 it had been £0.5 billion or some 25 per cent of the total PSBR. In 1974 it was £2.2 billion or some 34 per cent of the total (CSO, 1981, p. 154). Local government spending was virtually out of control. One of the main causes of inflated expenditure was the rapid rise in public sector pay, a substantial amount of which was caused by automatic increases resulting from the index linking of pay by the Conservative government. Essentially, public sector workers were attempting to catch up, and more, in the pay stakes following the restraint imposed on them by the Heath policy. The pressure built up during the Heath period, together with the miners' successful breach of the policy in early 1974 which opened a floodgate. Finally, the government introduced new food and housing subsidies which also inflated expenditure.

Between the post-election budget and the second election of October 1974 no significant macroeconomic policy decisions were taken. The Cabinet was aware that it needed a majority and the major feeling was 'don't rock the boat' until a new election. However, there was a battle going on in Whitehall over the new industrial policy which we reviewed in Chapter 5. The political campaign to develop an industry policy along the lines set out in the manifesto was led by Tony Benn, the Minister for Industry, with the opposition to the proposals being led by Wilson himself. The argument was conducted with some rancour. Wilson referred to a draft White Paper on industrial policy as 'a sloppy and half-baked document, polemical, indeed menacing in tone, redolent, more of an NEC Home Policy Committee document than a Command Paper' (1979, p. 33).

Benn and his supporters were heavily defeated as the White Paper on the regeneration of British industry published in August 1974 shows (HMSO, 1974d). The contrast between the White Paper and *Labour's Programme for Britain* (Labour Party, 1973) could not be sharper. Firstly, it made planning agreements voluntary rather than compulsory, and even removed the one incentive which companies might have had to conclude such agreements by stating:

> Financial assistance under the Industry Act 1972, including regional development grants, will of course continue to be available for companies not covered by Planning Agreements.
>
> (HMSO, 1974d, p. 3)

As a result the planning agreements were a non-starter. Secondly, it envisaged the National Enterprise Board as a kind of expanded version of the old Industrial Reorganization Corporation which had promoted mergers between private companies in the Wilson government of 1964–70. The White Paper did suggest that the NEB, unlike the IRC, would generally retain any shareholdings which it might acquire. It was also given the task of creating employment in depressed regions, the power to create new ventures and participate in joint ventures, and to extend public ownership to profitable manufacturing industry. However, this provision which was a key element of the original manifesto proposals was more or less nullified by the statement: 'The intention is that all holdings in companies, whether 100 per cent or in part, should be acquired by agreement' (HMSO, 1974d, p. 8). Needless to say, there were not many profitable manufacturing industries eager to be taken over by the NEB.

The third element of the industrial strategy set out in *Labour's Programme for Britain, 1973* was a new Industry Act. The White Paper had nothing directly to say about this, although it did speak of extending the provisions of the Industry Act of 1972 which had included wide powers of intervention.

After the defeat of the Left in the Common Market referendum of 1975, Tony Benn was moved to the Department of Energy and Eric Varley, a long-time Wilson loyalist, was given the job in the Department of Trade and Industry. He entered into a series of consultations with industry and eventually produced a new White Paper (HMSO, 1975) which further diluted the original proposals. In fact this document more or less abandoned the idea of an interventionist industrial strategy. It states: 'The Government must take the initiative in developing the industrial strategy, but the main task of seeing that it brings higher productivity in British industry must fall on unions and management' (p. 6). This was a move back towards the ineffective 'hands-off' intervention of earlier years. In the White Paper there was much discussion about the need to be flexible, to collect statistical information and to hold tripartite discussions, but the document cannot be said to set out a strategy in any sense of the word.

In his review of industry policy in the 1970s Grant concludes: 'The period 1972–9 in industrial policy was characterised by a complex series of selective assistance schemes, largely under the terms of the 1972 Act' (1982, p. 51). In other words the Conservatives had considerably more influence on shaping industry policy in the 1970s than Labour did, even though Labour had worked out an elaborate strategy in opposition and regarded this as the centrepiece of its manifesto.

In explaining the reason for this it is important to remember the basic dilemma facing the party. An interventionist industrial strategy along the lines set out in the manifesto was an anathema to industrialists and bankers. If the strategy had been applied it would have involved enormous conflict with industry and the city. Moreover, if it really had set out to confront the multinationals in Britain it would have put large numbers of jobs at risk. In addition the strategy was schizophrenic about its objectives; on the one hand it wanted to regenerate industry making it profitable again, and on the other it wanted to fulfil worthy social goals which potentially conflict with this, such as reducing unemployment, introducing democracy and improving trade union bargaining rights. Labour in office chose to work with industry rather than in conflict with it, and so it abandoned the original strategy. The only thing new which developed out of the policy was the National Enterprise Board, but this operated along commercial lines as a public sector merchant bank (Grant, 1982, pp. 101–9) and for that reason was retained by the Conservatives after 1979. Ultimately, the manifesto had no influence on the industrial policy because it was felt by the Labour leadership to be either irrelevant or damaging to the regeneration of industry.

To return to the macroeconomic policy, the major problem facing the newly elected government from October 1974 was undoubtedly inflation. It chose to confront this with an incomes policy. When the mid-June figures were published they showed inflation running at 26 per cent, and wage agreements in the pipeline would have increased this further. The pound began to slide and the prospects for the economy looked more and more alarming. The government and the TUC had been working close together on the TUC/Labour Party Liaison Committee, and in the face of the economic crisis Jack Jones proposed a £6 a week incomes policy for everyone except people on high incomes, which was adopted in July and helped to stabilize the pound. The magnitude of the crisis had alarmed the TUC leaders. Hugh Scanlon spoke about it at the TUC Congress in 1976 saying: 'We honestly believed then – and still do – that no agreement would have meant a catastrophic run on the pound' (Keegan and Pennant-Rea, 1979, pp. 124–5).

The incomes policy held and ultimately it was primarily responsible for bringing down the rate of inflation to just over 8 per cent in 1978. But a new threat to the pound arose from the burgeoning growth in public expenditure. The unprecedented rise in expenditure had attracted the attention of decision makers and Britain's foreign creditors to the question of public spending as never before. Leo Pliatzky captured the mood very well when he wrote: 'All in all, the first year or so of the new administration was a period of frenetic activity. It was also in some ways a period of collective madness. Public expenditure, after rising 8.5 per cent in real terms in the last year of the Conservative Government, rose by no less than 12.2 per cent in Labour's first year' (1982, p. 130).

To make matters worse, at the end of 1975 the Treasury was accused of losing £5 billion between 1970–1 and 1974–5. Expenditure had risen by this amount more than could be accounted for by policy changes (Godley, 1975). To Britain's foreign creditors it appeared that there was little or no control over the system, which further served to undermine their confidence. All this was background to the IMF crisis of 1976, the worst crisis that any government had faced since the war.

The incomes policy had given the economy a respite from foreign exchange pressure, and plans were underway to impose a new system of cash limits on public expenditure. The new system, though harsh, had the virtue of no longer underwriting inflation, which the PESC system of planning expenditure in real terms had done. It was outlined in a White Paper in 1976 (HMSO, 1976a). Just at the time when both incomes and expenditure appeared to be coming under control the currency crisis hit with full force. It was triggered by an inept attempt to devalue the pound, which was thought to be overvalued after the inflation of the previous two years. According to Fay and Young (1978) the devaluation strategy was suggested by Sir Douglas Wass, the Permanent Secretary of the Treasury. In March 1976 the Bank of England began to sell sterling on a falling market, which was a clear signal to international financiers that the government wanted to devalue. This triggered a speculative attack on the pound, and it rapidly fell through the psychological barrier of $2, and despite heavy Bank of England support kept falling further. Harold Lever the Labour minister and financial expert, urged the government to arrange a large loan in order to stabilize the pound. Preliminary consultations were held with the IMF in May, but their view was that the PSBR and the money supply were rising too rapidly and needed cutting. The head of the US Treasury, Wilham Simon, and his colleague, the head of the Federal Reserve, Arthur Burns, were both hard-line monetarists, and, to quote one account, 'wanted to use the fall in the sterling balances to ensnare the British Government' (Keegan and Pennant-Rea, 1979, p. 163). After considerable negotiations the US central bank allocated a credit of $5.3 billion, with various strings attached. Chancellor Healey introduced further deflationary measures in July which, among other things, increased employers' national insurance contributions by £1 billion, which further served to undermine the industrial policy.

The measures however were insufficient and the pound continued to slide. By September the government was forced to go to the IMF. The final deal negotiated with the IMF involved reducing the PSBR by £3 billion to be achieved by massive cuts in public expenditure.

In retrospect there was no real economic justification for the IMF crisis of 1976, and it illustrates the irrationality of financial markets. If the crisis had occurred in late 1974 or 1975 it would have been more understandable, but by 1976 the government had begun to turn around a difficult situation. The crisis was a product of a hostile financial community at home and abroad, coupled with a determination by monetarist ideologues in the US Treasury and the IMF, to cut down to size what they saw as a profligate socialist government. They took such a hard line to begin with that President Ford intervened personally to soften the terms, fearing the consequences for the alliance of a political collapse of the British government (Keegan and Pennant-Rea, 1979, p. 165). In fact the British government could have stood up to the IMF, since there was a large element of bluff in its position. If the government had suspended payments and introduced a centrally managed system of foreign currency allocations, it would have been bad for British trade, but it would have had a devastating effect on the international financial system, and put the dollar under immediate pressure. The US Treasury would have been hoist by its own petard. However, the government chose instead to accept unnecessarily restrictive financial terms in exchange for a loan. The essentially psychological nature of the crisis was confirmed when the pound rapidly recovered. As Pliatzky put it: 'We were ourselves astonished by the speed with which, following the relatively limited though politically difficult adjustments agreed with the IMF, confidence was resurrected, the adverse financial trends were reversed, and we sailed suddenly from the eye of the storm into unusually calm waters' (1982, p. 159).

The final irony of the crisis is that there were large surpluses of planned budgets in 1976–7 caused by underspending (Pliatzky, 1982, p. 160). In that year there was a shortfall in spending of about £2 billion, or twice the amount of the agreed IMF cuts in that financial year. In short the whole exercise was unnecessary, although this was not known until later.

The effect of the IMF crisis of 1976 was to impose a quasi-monetarist strategy on the government. As the figures in Table 6.1 show, this rapidly reduced public expenditure from 44 per cent of GDP in 1976 to 40 per cent in 1977. This put the government through a very damaging political period, and ultimately it undermined the incomes policy which was the real cause of the reduction in inflation after 1977. Public sector workers in particular became very discontented by the consequences of cuts in the public sector, and this produced the industrial crisis of 1978 which led to the election defeat. Once again the vitality of the real economy had been undermined for short-term financial reasons.

After 1976 there were no more major crises; North Sea oil began to come on stream in increasing amounts, and the large deficits of the early 1970s turned into a balance of payments surplus. By January 1978 official reserves stood at $20.6 billion, the highest ever. In September 1977, the TUC agreed to support the so-called twelve month rule in stage 3 of the incomes policy. This limited wage negotiations to a twelve month cycle. But this was the last time that TUC support was forthcoming for incomes policy.

This concludes our review of the events surrounding the economic performance of Labour in office. This still leaves open the question: Did Labour make a difference? That is, has Britain's economic performance been significantly influenced by Labour incumbency? We examine this next.

The impact of Labour on the economy

In an analysis of annual economic data Rose (1980) concluded that economic series such as inflation and unemployment were dominated by secular trends, which did not differ greatly between Labour and Conservative governments. He found some short-term changes but these did not conform to the conventional adversary model of politics which holds that incoming administrations attempt to undo everything done by their predecessors (Finer, 1980). Instead Rose found cycles within the life of an administration, so that policy changes within an administration appear to be more significant than policy changes between administrations. Thus the IMF crisis of 1976 produced a bigger shift in policy than the change of government in 1974, and the U-turn by the Heath administration in 1972 represented a bigger change than occurred in 1970, and so on.

Rose's analysis is based on a relatively unsophisticated technique. Essentially he correlated the various economic series with time, and interpreted a high linear correlation as evidence for a strong secular trend which dominated any trends within particular administrations. But this approach leaves trends within a particular administration unmeasured as part of the unexplained variation in a model. To assess trends within a particular administration it is necessary to model them explicitly. By failing to do this Rose cannot really assert that such trends are unimportant.

Accordingly, we shall repeat Rose's analysis, but this time using the more sophisticated technique of multiple interrupted time series analysis (Campbell, 1969; Campbell and Cook, 1979; Lewis-Beck and Alford, 1980) with quarterly data of various economic indicators. The MITS approach applied to our problem involves estimating models of the following type (see Appendix I):

$$Y_t = b_0 + b_1X_{1t} + b_2X_{2t} + b_3X_{3t} + b_4X_{4t} + b_5X_{5t} + e_t$$

where the variables are defined as follows:

Y_t quarterly observations on the economic series

X_{1t} a counter for quarters from 1 to N, the number of observations

X_{2t} a dummy variable scoring 0 before the 1964 Labour government, 1 during it, and 0 after

X_{3t} a counter scoring 0 before the 1964 Labour government 1, 2, 3 . . . and so on during it, 0 after

X_{4t} a dummy variable scoring 0 before the 1974 Labour government and 1 during it

X_{5t} a counter scoring 0 before the 1974 Labour government and 1, 2, 3 . . . during it

e_t an error term

The rationale behind this model can be seen in Figure 6.1. The parameters b_0 and b_1 indicate respectively the level and slope of the hypothetical series before the Labour government. In our example there is no long term trend in the series and thus $b_1 = 0$, although the series fluctuates around a positive level and therefore $b_0 \neq 0$. To evaluate if this was changed by the arrival of a Labour government we must examine b_2 and b_3. If $b_2 \neq 0$ this implies that the mean value of the series has changed during that government, though if $b_3 = 0$ there is no cumulative change over time. Finally, if b_4 and $b_5 \neq 0$ this implies a change in the mean level, and a cumulative change in the series after 1974. Obviously, a third possibility is a cumulative change with no mean change. With this type of model we can assess the effect of Labour incumbency on various economic time series.

The results of an MITS time series analysis on thirteen economic series between 1955 and 1979 appear in Table 6.2. Some of the series refer to shorter periods of time because earlier data are not available. Each of the regression models in this table were calculated using generalized least squares, with the Cochrane–Orcutt procedure. Ordinary least squares estimates were inadequate because of autocorrelation in the residuals.[1]

It is common to divide economic series into targets or series which are the objectives of policy, and instruments or series which can be manipulated directly by the government (Peston, 1974). The distinction between these is not exact but roughly speaking the first six series in Table 6.2 could be influenced directly by government action, whereas the remaining seven series can only be influenced indirectly via other measures. To consider the instruments first, in the case of bank rate and the public sector borrowing requirement there are trend increases present in the data which are not affected by Labour incumbency. In the case of the money supply, which Pliatzky makes clear was not a serious objective of policy before 1970 (Pliatzky, 1982, p. 80), Labour achieved a

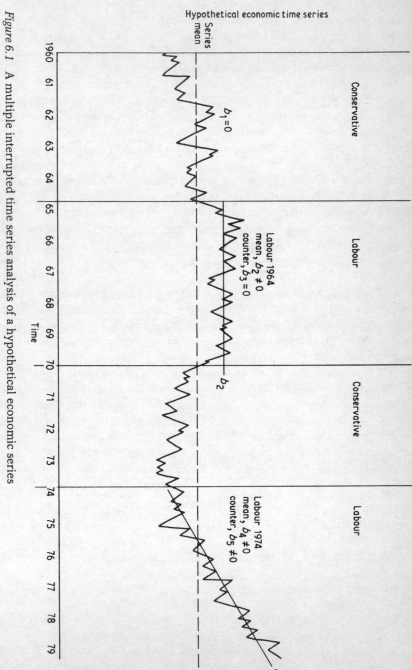

Figure 6.1   A multiple interrupted time series analysis of a hypothetical economic series

Table 6.2 Generalized least squares estimates of the influence of Labour incumbency on economic time series

Dependent variable	Constant term	Trend	I64	S64	I74	S74	R²	DWS	Interpretation
1 Bank rate 1955–79	3.65 (2.87)	0.06 (2.25)	1.37 (1.23)	−0.04 (0.63)	0.25 (0.22)	0.08 (0.75)	0.82	1.74	Trend increase. Labour incumbency makes no difference
2 Change in M3 money supply 1963–79	−1195.5 (2.68)	34.47 (4.77)	50.24 (0.17)	−35.14 (1.91)	−660.1 (2.39)	−0.08 (0.0)	0.54	1.81	Trend increase. Cumulative decrease 1964–70. Mean decrease 1974–79
3 Public sector borrowing 1963–79	−1100 (1.07)	26.67 (1.62)	22.11 (0.07)	0.89 (0.04)	416.56 (1.32)	13.6 (0.38)	0.89	2.18	Small trend increase. Labour incumbency makes no difference
4 Taxes and national insurance 1961–79	30.34 (7.63) (10.8)	0.79 (0.74)	−2.74 (0.74)	0.56 (2.11)	3.02 (0.74)	−0.55 (2.10)	0.75	2.20	Trend increase, cumulative increase 1964–70, cumulative decrease 1974–9
5 Public expenditure as per cent GDP 1961–79	31.75 (31.88) (7.53)	0.14 (0.28)	−0.26 (0.28)	0.13 (1.98)	7.70 (7.42)	−0.44 (6.71)	0.73	1.72	Trend increase, cumulative increase 1964–70. Mean increase and cumulative decline 1974–9
6 Expenditure tax as per cent GDP 1955–79	13.6 (0.98)	0.02 (0.55)	0.58 (1.60)	−0.02 (0.73)	0.20 (0.36)	0.01 (0.10)	0.90	2.06	No trend increase, mean increase 1964–70, otherwise no effect
7 Change in index retail prices	2.43 (0.07)	1.59 (2.31)	−4.47 (0.19)	−0.16 (0.11)	23.35 (0.86)	−6.43 (2.41)	0.82	1.86	Trend increase, cumulative reduction 1974–9

(cont. overleaf)

Table 6.2—cont.

Dependent variable	Constant term	Trend	I64	S64	I74	S74	R²	DWS	Interpretation
8 Change in unemployment 1955–79	10.87 (0.39)	1.47 (2.54)	−7.20 (0.30)	−0.14 (0.09)	33.74 (1.35)	−7.16 (2.95)	0.80	2.02	Trend increase, cumulative decrease but mean increase 1974–9
9 GDP per capita in constant prices 1955–79	258.8 (71.25)	2.06 (25.8)	1.05 (0.22)	−0.20 (0.60)	−4.36 (0.85)	0.07 (0.19)	0.99	2.03	Trend increase, Labour incumbency makes no difference
10 Gross domestic capital formation as percentage GDP 1955–79	15.24 (69.31)	0.05 (10.73)	0.66 (2.06)	−0.02 (0.95)	1.45 (4.18)	−0.20 (7.70)	0.93	1.94	Trend increase, mean increase 1964–70, mean increase and cumulative decline 1974–9
11 Balance of payments 1955–79	0.91 (0.82)	−0.01 (0.41)	−1.27 (0.70)	0.11 (0.82)	−8.45 (4.28)	0.39 (2.90)	0.55	1.98	No trend, mean increase in deficits with cumulative reduction 1974–9
12 Index of real wages 1955–79	1.09 (10.0)	0.007 (3.66)	−0.006 (0.25)	−0.003 (0.19)	−0.02 (0.77)	0.003 (0.62)	0.98	1.59	Trend increase, Labour incumbency makes no difference
13 Output per man	20.2 (10.09)	1.20 (3.45)	1.53 (0.22)	−0.07 (0.15)	−4.41 (0.63)	−1.05 (0.98)	0.96	1.96	Trend increase, Labour incumbency makes no difference

Sources: All data are taken from *Economic Trends 1981*, Annual Supplement no. 6 (HMSO, 1981), from the following tables:

1 Bank rate [minimum lending rate after May 1978] 192
2 Change in M3 seasonally adjusted (£m) 146–7
3 Public sector borrowing requirement, seasonally adjusted total (£m) 154–5
4 Taxes and national insurance contributions in current prices (£m) 152–3
5 Public expenditure as a percentage of GDP calculated from total government expenditure in current prices (£m) 152–3 and gross domestic product in market prices 10–12
6 Taxes on expenditure as percentage of GDP at market prices calculated from 10–12
7 Change in all item index of retail prices (1975 = 100) calculated from 115–17
8 Change in unemployment in thousands, seasonally adjusted excluding school leavers calculated from 103–5
9 Gross domestic product *per capita* at 1975 prices, seasonally adjusted 45–7
10 Gross domestic capital fixed formation as a percentage of GDP at market prices calculated from 10–12
11 Balance of payments in current prices, unadjusted 131–5
12 Index of basic weekly wages of manual workers, unadjusted (1972 = 100) in all industries and services 11–113
13 Output per person employed, seasonally adjusted (1975 = 100) whole economy 97–9.

Notes:

I64: mean changes 1964–70
S64: cumulative changes 1964–70
I74: mean changes 1974–9
S74: cumulative changes 1974–9

t statistics are in parenthesis below the coefficients
R^2 is the percentage of variance explained in the dependent variable
DWS is the Durbin–Watson statistic to test autocorrelation in the residuals.

cumulative reduction in the rate of increase during 1964–70, a clear by-product of the deflationary policies. It achieved a mean reduction in 1974–9, when money supply was a conscious object of policy, but this was partly a stabilization of increases in the money supply after the rapid increases of the Barber chancellorship, and partly a reflection of the IMF cuts.

On the expenditure and taxation side, Labour achieved a cumulative increase in public expenditure in 1964–70 which was over and above the trend increase. The picture in 1974–9 is more mixed with an overall mean increase in expenditure for the period as a whole, and a cumulative decrease after 1976. Essentially expenditure was out of control at the start of the period and was gradually brought back under control and reduced as time went on, but the net result was still above the long-term trend. The two measures of taxation provide interesting insights into the results of Labour policies. In the case of taxes and national insurance contributions in current prices there was, of course, the inevitable trend increase due to inflation but there was also a cumulative increase in 1964–70, and a cumulative decrease in 1974–9. Given a commitment to redistribution we might expect to see taxes rise under a Labour government; clearly this was not the case in 1974–9. Another expectation is that indirect taxes or taxes on expenditure should fall under a Labour government since these place an unequal burden on the poor compared with direct taxation. In fact indirect taxation as a percentage of GDP rose under the Labour government between 1964 and 1970, and did not fall after 1974. Thus in practice Labour did not help the poor by changes in the burden of taxation, although of course thresholds were raised from time to time; even then thresholds did not rise in line with inflation.

The three most important target variables are inflation, growth and unemployment. On inflation Labour succeeded in bringing the rate down against the long term trend increase after 1974. As far as growth of gross domestic product *per capita* was concerned Labour incumbency made no difference to the trend increase. In the case of unemployment the mean rate of change increased under Labour after 1974, but this increase cumulatively declined over time. In other words Labour presided over faster increases in unemployment, but it managed to slow this down. If, as some writers argue (Hibbs, 1977), governments of the Left favour low unemployment and high inflation, and governments of the Right the opposite, then the Labour government of 1974–9 did not behave like a government of the Left. Its number one priority was inflation, and unemployment was sacrificed to bring down the inflation rate. As far as the balance of payments was concerned, no long term trend was evident in the data, although the deficit significantly increased after 1974 and it gradually improved as time went on. In the case of gross investment or gross domestic capital formation, the 1964–70 government could claim a success in increasing the long-term trend; the 1974–9 government also achieved an increase which was progressively reduced as time went on. In the case of real wages and productivity or output per man, Labour incumbency made no difference.

Conclusions

Looking back at the economic performance of Labour in power over more than two decades one can point to certain successes, such as the reduction in inflation after 1976, albeit at a cost of rising unemployment. But the major impression is that Labour achieved little in dealing with the underlying problems of the real economy, the question of productivity and real growth. Successive British governments have devoted enormous attention to the management of the economy but all this has achieved is a long term decline *vis-à-vis* our competitors, which has turned into an absolute decline in the 1980s. Labour has less excuse for this than the Conservatives because it promised much more both in 1964 and later. If we examine the policy outcomes there was very little which was distinctively socialist about Labour in office, just as there was little that was really successful in terms of influencing the real economy.

In general policy has been too concerned with short-term expediency which has served to make the underlying long-term problems worse. The strongest criticism of Labour in office is that it failed to achieve a coherent and positive industrial policy to fill the political vacuum opened up by the demise of Keynesian demand management policies and the arrival of stagflation. In the comparatively good years of the 1960s it abandoned the growth strategy in favour of an irrational and ultimately unsuccessful policy of defending the exchange rate. It then approached the 1974 election with an industrial strategy which posed great problems for its relations with industry and the city, but which the leadership cynically abandoned within months of being elected. It achieved an incomes policy at great political cost which ultimately brought down inflation, but then threw away the long-term benefits of this by indulging in a series of unnecessary cuts in public expenditure forced on it by the monetarist ideologues of the IMF and the US Treasury. The weak monetarism adopted after 1976 proved to be a stalking horse for the full-blooded version under Margaret Thatcher, which has proved so disastrous for the state of the real economy. In the absence of the unnecessary cuts of 1976 the results of the election of 1979 might have been different. As it was the electorate passed what, at the time, could only be described as a fair judgement on a dismal economic performance.

If the getting of wisdom involves recognizing the failures of the past then we should use the experience of Labour in office to develop a strategy for the future. We discuss this in Chapter 8, but before that we examine Labour's record in social policy.

Notes

1 Autocorrelation refers to a positive association between successive residuals over time. The coefficients of the regression model are unbiased when autocorrelation is present, but the test statistics are unreliable. For a discussion of this problem, and generalized least squares as a solution to it, see Maddala (1977, Chapter 12).

7

Labour's social policy –
the case of poverty

The scope of social policy is very wide and can be thought of as including all aspects of welfare such as social security, education, health and housing (Titmuss, 1974, pp. 23–32; Marshall, 1975, pp. 11–18). To limit the scope of the discussion we shall concentrate on one area, that of income maintenance or social security. This refers to central government programmes for income support, and is the cornerstone of policy against poverty.

Social security is the most important area of social policy. This is true for two reasons: firstly, it is the largest item in the public expenditure budget. In 1982–3 £32.0 billion was planned to be spent on social security, which was more than twice as much as the next largest area of expenditure, defence at £14.1 billion (HMSO, 1982). Altogether social security spending represented some 28 per cent of all public expenditure in that year. The second reason why social security is important is that it is central to the Labour Party's image of itself as a party of redistribution and social justice. Within the Labour tradition writers as politically different as Anthony Crosland (1956, pp. 81–101) and Aneurin Bevan (1961, pp. 21–31) have stressed the central importance of redistribution through social security. This makes it particularly appropriate to examine Labour's record in this area.

Social security consists of two types of programmes: firstly, there are national insurance benefits such as retirement pensions and war and disablement pensions which are not means-tested and constitute about 70 per cent of the total budget; then there are means-tested benefits such as supplementary benefits and family income supplement. The main elements of the social security budget in 1982–3 are set out in Table 7.1. It can be seen in this table that the largest item of expenditure was retirement pensions, which were more than three times larger than the next highest item, supplementary allowances. Family allowances were received by nearly thirteen million people and were the third largest item in the budget. The most complicated category contained the sickness and disablement benefits, which were made up of several items, none of which was means-tested, although eligibility requirements of varying complexities were imposed.

Social security policy is still strongly influenced by the legacy of the Beveridge Report on social insurance and allied services (HMSO, 1942), which laid down the framework for Labour's postwar social security

Table 7.1   The social security budget in 1982–3 – the main elements

Benefits	Total expenditure (£ million at current prices)	Average numbers receiving benefits (thousands)
Old persons' benefits		
Retirement pensions	13,496	9,040
Old persons' pensions	38	40
Sickness and disablement benefits		
Invalidity benefit	1,401	610
Industrial disablement benefit	356	195
Sickness and injury benefit and maternity allowance	718	530
War disablement pension	510	250
Attendance allowance and invalid care allowance	325	310
Non-contributory invalidity pensions	141	180
Mobility allowance	205	230
Mothers'/widows' benefits		
Widows' allowance, maternity/death grants	102	165
Widows' pension and industrial death benefit	724	450
Family benefits		
Family allowance/child benefit	3,778	12,900
Family income supplement	70	130
Unemployment benefit	1,991	1,440
Supplementary benefits		
Supplementary pensions	1,578	1,700
Supplementary allowances	4,486	2,210

Source: HMSO (1982, Tables 2.12 and 2.12.2).

legislation. We begin by examining the Beveridge Report, and the main debates on social security arising from it, before looking at the record of Labour in office.

The Beveridge Report and its implementation

The Beveridge proposals aimed at providing a comprehensive and coherent framework for social security, to replace the fragmented and often inconsistent system which had existed before the war. The report was based on 'three guiding principles'. The first principle was that the new system should be a complete departure from previous practices. As Beveridge put it: 'Now, when the war is abolishing landmarks of every kind, is the opportunity for using experience in a clear field. A revolutionary moment in the world's history is a time for revolution, not for patching' (HMSO, 1942, p. 6). The second principle was that the social security plan should be seen only as a part of a comprehensive plan of social welfare. The other, and in his view essential, components of this plan were the introduction of the National Health Service, and the implementation of full employment. He argued that without these the social security plans could not be implemented. The third principle was that social security should involve the co-operation of the state and the individual; neither could carry the whole burden on its own. He wrote: 'The state should offer security for service and contribution. The state in organising security should not stifle incentive, opportunity, responsibility; in establishing a national minimum, it should leave room and encouragement for voluntary action by each individual to provide more than that minimum for himself and his family' (HMSO, 1942, pp. 6–7).

In the plan flat rate benefits financed by flat rate contributions would provide a minimum level of subsistence, and private pensions and insurance could be used by individuals to supplement these. Beveridge placed particular emphasis on social insurance 'as a right', arguing that the principle of individual contribution legitimized the idea of universal provision of benefits. He also felt strongly that benefits should be adequate to provide a basic minimum, and should be paid as long as they were actually needed. He wrote: 'Unemployment benefit, disability benefit, basic retirement pension after a transition period, and training benefit will be at the same rate irrespective of earnings. The rate will provide by itself the income necessary for subsistence in all normal cases' (HMSO, 1942, p. 10).

In addition, he noted the need for a 'safety-net' of a means tested system of national assistance 'for the limited number of cases of need not covered by social insurance' (HMSO, 1942, p. 11). In the 1930s means tests had become very stigmatized, a point which he recognized, but he felt that under the scheme national assistance would be very much a residual element for individuals who could not build up a record of national insurance contributions.

The Labour government of 1945–51 implemented the Beveridge proposals with some significant amendments in a series of Acts passed after 1945. The first of these was the Family Allowance Act of 1945 which provided a flat rate benefit for the second and subsequent children at a rather lower rate of benefit than Beveridge wanted (Ashford, 1981, p. 205). It was, however, a universal benefit provided without a means test. The second and more comprehensive National Insurance Act of 1946 enacted most of the proposals on social insurance in the report. Under this Act flat rate benefits were provided for the unemployed, the sick, the industrially disabled, widows and the retired. Finally, the 1948 National Assistance Act provided the means-tested 'safety-net' element, with the establishment of the National Assistance Board. From the start national assistance benefits were less generous than national insurance benefits, which accorded with Beveridge's own preferences. The shadow of the old Poor Law was cast over the National Assistance Board by the operation of the 'wage stop' rule. This rule ensured that means-tested benefits were less than those a claimant received in full time employment. This was the 'less eligibility' rule originally embodied in nineteenth century legislation. There were also a number of other rules for limiting payments, which ensured that significant numbers of people received less than the minimum or 'poverty line' level of benefits.

The most important departures from the Beveridge principles in the postwar legislation related to the adequacy and duration of payments under the scheme. The flat rate benefits payable under the National Insurance scheme were never adequate on their own to raise an individual's income above the poverty line. Beveridge calculated the minimum income needed to avoid poverty from social research carried out before the war, notably Rowntree's survey of poverty in York (Rowntree, 1941). His proposals were less generous than those calculated for the subsistence poverty line by Rowntree, and in turn the proposals implemented by the Labour government were less generous than those set out by Beveridge. This meant that individuals with no other source of income had to claim national assistance in order to stay out of poverty. The other major departure from the Beveridge principles was the refusal by successive governments to pay benefits as long as need lasted. The White Paper on social insurance of 1944 (HMSO, 1944b) rejected this principle, and it has never subsequently been accepted. Thus restrictions on the time periods over which rates of sickness and unemployment benefits can be paid have always been in force.

In some important respects the Beveridge proposals were inadequate in their provision for certain types of need. For example, provisions for the disabled concentrated almost exclusively on those disabled by industrial injuries and ignored the needs of those disabled from birth who could not build up a contribution record (Field, 1982, p. 76). Another problem concerned single parent families. The report proposed a benefit to cover 'marriage needs' for widows and the divorced. But at the same time Beveridge argued that the benefit should not be paid if the break-up of the marriage was the woman's own 'fault'. The problems of trying to define fault in each case were so great that the proposals were never implemented. Thus there was an important gap in the provisions for the needs of women in general and single parent families in particular. A third major problem concerned the inadequate provision for rent in the calculations of benefit levels. Beveridge opted for a flat rate element for rent in the benefit provisions, even though some people paid much higher rents than others.

Despite these problems in the years immediately following the implementation of the Beveridge proposals, it was widely believed that poverty in Britain had been abolished. This belief was reinforced by the publication in 1951 of the last of the classic poverty surveys by Rowntree. In this survey Rowntree showed that the proportion of the working class in poverty in York had fallen from 31.1 per cent to 2.8 per cent between 1936 and 1951 (Rowntree and Lavers, 1951, p. 50). This used an absolute or subsistence measure of poverty. During the 1950s poverty was effectively off the political agenda, and no significant legislative action was taken on this issue until the mid-1960s.

Poverty was placed on the political agenda again largely as a result of academic work in the 1960s. In the 1950s writers like Titmuss and Townsend had begun to argue in favour of a relative conception of poverty (Townsend, 1954, 1962; Titmuss, 1963). At its most general Townsend defines relative poverty: 'Individuals, families and groups in the population can be said to be in poverty when they lack the resources to obtain the types of diet, participate in the activities and have the living conditions and amenities which are customary, or at least widely encouraged or approved in the societies to which they belong' (1979, p. 31). Thus at the centre of this definition of poverty is the notion of relative deprivation (Runciman, 1966). To apply a relative definition of poverty, a standard measure of the poverty line was needed which would be widely accepted by policy makers. This proved to be the 'safety-net' level of benefits paid by the National Assistance Board, renamed the Supplementary Benefits Commission in 1966. Discussions of poverty in social policy now centre on the supplementary benefits levels.

The most influential book in re-opening the question of poverty was the *Poor and the Poorest* by Abel-Smith and Townsend (1965). They re-analysed existing data on family expenditure in 1954 and 1960, and showed that poverty had actually increased between those years. Defining the poverty line as the basic national assistance scale some 4.7 per cent of households, and 3.8 per cent of the population, were in poverty in 1960. However, as we saw earlier, the national assistance rates were originally set at a very low level, below those recommended by Beveridge. Accordingly Abel-Smith and Townsend took the more realistic level of 140 per cent of the basic national assistance level of benefit. When this standard was used some 14 per cent of the population, or 7.5 million people, were in poverty and some 2.25 million of these were children (Abel-Smith and Townsend, 1965, p. 65).

It is perhaps useful at this stage to examine the various types of people who are likely to be in poverty. In his report Beveridge had drawn on social surveys carried out in the inter-war period and he concluded from these that 'of all the want shown by the surveys, from three-quarters to five-sixths, according to the precise standard chosen for want, was due to interruption or loss of earning power. Practically the whole of the remaining one-quarter to one-sixth was due to failure to relate income during earning to the size of the family' (HMSO, 1942, p. 7). Thus interruptions in earning caused by sickness, unemployment or retirement, and inadequate means in relation to family size, were the main factors in explaining poverty. The Beveridge analysis was based on an absolute standard of poverty, and since his time more sophisticated work has been done using a relative standard. One of the best examples of this is Townsend's classic survey of poverty carried out in the late 1960s (Townsend, 1979). But to get a more recent overview of poverty in Britain we can use the data provided by Layard and his associates in their analysis for the Royal Commission on the Distribution of Income and Wealth (Layard *et al.*, 1978), which used the General Household Survey. Their estimates of the numbers of people in the various categories of need in the population appear in Table 7.2. They defined the poverty line as the long-term rate of supplementary benefits, net of housing costs (Layard *et al.*, 1978, pp. 6–12). The same data expressed in percentages of the various groups in poverty appear in Table 7.3.

The elderly made up 16 per cent of the population of the country in 1975, according to Layard's figures, and 48 per cent of those were on the poverty line (100 per cent or less of the supplementary benefits level). Single parent families were 4 per cent of the population and 15 per cent of households in poverty. Thirdly, couples with five or more children were 2 per cent of the population and 5 per cent of those in poverty. These figures are not significantly altered by defining poverty as an income up to 140 per cent of the supplementary benefits line. The disabled are not distinguished in these tables, but the evidence showed that 50 per cent of all couples where the man was disabled were on or below 140 per cent of the poverty line (Layard *et al.*, 1978, p. 29); and in the case of the long-term sick or unemployed no less than 71 per cent who had not worked the previous year were on the poverty line (Layard *et al.*, 1978, p. 28). Thus

Table 7.2 The distribution of individuals, by household income relative to the supplementary benefits line and type of family, 1975

Type of family	Household income as a percentage of SB level							
	100 or less	100–	120–	140–	200–	250–	over 500	all
Elderly couple	620	860	710	1,090	350	320	40	3,990
Elderly man	200	160	110	180	70	50	10	770
Elderly woman	1,370	680	410	620	230	160	10	3,490
Couple, no children	230	160	310	1,840	1,950	4,720	400	9,590
Couple, 1 child	120	280	450	2,660	1,900	1,820	110	7,330
Couple, 2 children	350	590	980	4,960	2,860	2,040	140	11,920
Couple, 3 children	280	440	780	2,340	980	730	40	5,600
Couple, 4 children	230	360	280	880	130	160	10	2,040
Couple, 5+ children	220	280	260	340	—	20	—	1,120
Single parent	670	340	210	410	140	130	—	1,910
Single man	140	110	140	870	790	760	30	2,840
Single woman	160	160	230	750	500	390	20	2,210
	4,580	4,410	4,890	16,930	9,880	11,270	810	52,790

Source: Layard *et al.* (1978, p. 14).

Table 7.3 The distribution of individuals, type of family by household income relative to the supplementary benefits line

Type of family	Household income as a percentage of SB level							
	100 or less	100–	120–	140–	200–	250–	over 500	all
Elderly couple	14	20	14	6	3	3	5	8
Elderly man	4	4	2	1	1	—	1	1
Elderly woman	30	15	8	4	2	1	1	7
Couple, no children	5	4	6	11	20	42	49	18
Couple, 1 child	3	6	9	16	19	16	13	14
Couple, 2 children	8	13	20	29	29	18	18	23
Couple, 3 children	6	10	16	14	10	7	4	11
Couple, 4 children	5	8	6	5	1	1	2	4
Couple, 5+ children	5	6	5	2	—	—	—	2
Single parent	15	8	4	2	1	1	—	4
Single man	3	2	3	5	8	8	4	5
Single woman	3	4	5	4	5	3	3	4
	100	100	100	100	100	100	100	100

Source: Layard *et al.* (1978, p. 14).

the poor are disproportionately the old, single parent families, the disabled, the long-term sick or unemployed, and couples with large families.

In the light of this we can examine the main debates about social security policy in relation to the poor since the rediscovery of poverty, before examining Labour's record in office.

The main debates over income maintenance policy for the poor

Since Beveridge social, economic and demographic changes have increased the numbers of people dependent on social security. In Table 7.4 we can examine the numbers of people receiving certain types of benefits over the period 1960 to 1979. The perennial economic crisis which has faced the country over this period has produced a secular trend increase in the number of people receiving unemployment benefits. The number of recipients of unemployment benefit has increased more than $2\frac{1}{2}$ times over this period. The most important demographic trend has been the increase in the number of retired people. People are living much longer than they did before the war and this has greatly increased the number of recipients of retirement pensions. This trend is likely to continue in the future, and led to the introduction of a special increased level of benefit in 1971 for those retired over the age of 80. There was a slight increase in the number of families receiving child benefit, or family allowance as it was before 1977. The extension of benefit to the first child in that year accounts for the big rise in numbers in 1977. Within the figures relating to child benefit, single parent families are becoming a larger category of those in poverty. The Finer Report on single parent families estimated, for example, that illegitimate births as a proportion of all live births had increased from 5.1 per cent to 8.6 per cent between 1950 and 1972, and the divorce rate had increased by a factor of nearly three over the same period (HMSO, 1974c, pp. 41 and 60). Both developments have helped to increase the number of single parent families.

However, the most striking trend which can be observed in Table 7.4 is the rise in the number of people receiving supplementary benefits over this period. This reflects political decisions by successive governments to increase means testing and selectivity, contrary to the principle of universality outlined in the Beveridge Report. National insurance benefits are inadequate for increasing numbers of people, so that more and more are obliged to claim means-tested benefits. The debate between supporters and opponents of means testing is probably the most important debate in social security policy.

To some extent this debate has followed party lines. Conservatives have tended to favour means testing as a device for concentrating help on those who really need it, whereas Labour politicians (with some notable

Table 7.4   Changes in numbers of beneficiaries, 1960–79 (thousands)

Year	Unemployment benefit	Retirement pensions	Supplementary benefits	Child benefit (families)
1960	213	5,676	1,903	3,659
1961	209	5,793	1,880	3,712
1962	281	5,935	2,037	3,724
1963	390	6,107	1,994	3,806
1964	220	6,286	1,980	3,877
1965	188	6,493	2,012	3,958
1966	208	6,677	2,495	4,038
1967	362	6,913	2,559	4,168
1968	331	7,122	2,637	4,257
1969	309	7,343	2,688	4,323
1970	327	7,568	2,738	4,387
1971	438	7,677	3,013	4,463
1972	451	7,834	3,033	4,502
1973	261	7,993	2,772	4,595
1974	272	8,144	2,778	4,606
1975	464	8,324	2,897	4,603
1976	617	8,510	3,049	4,592
1977	589	8,637	3,106	7,506[a]
1978	561	8,785	3,048	7,390
1979	503	8,936	2,970	7,410

[a] Child benefit replaced family allowance.

Sources: Annual Abstract of Statistics, 1971, Tables 43, 47, 50; *1982,* Table 3.16.

exceptions) have tended to oppose means testing. Thus, when Keith Joseph, the Social Services Secretary, introduced the means-tested family income supplement in 1971 he justified it in the following terms (Field, 1982, p. 40): 'An increase in family allowances at the level which has been discussed, whether taxed or tax-free, could not provide the scale of help the very poorest of wage earning households desperately need.' By contrast, in 1968 Douglas Houghton and Margaret Herbison, the Labour ministers responsible for social security, had opposed a scheme very similar to family income supplement because it was means tested (Banting, 1979, p. 89). They chose to raise the levels of child benefit instead.

At first sight the argument that means testing concentrates help where it is most needed seems plausible. But means-tested benefits suffer from two grave defects which have led many people in the poverty lobby to oppose them strongly. The first of these defects is the problem of take-up. For a variety of reasons individuals who are eligible for benefits do not claim them, and this makes them ineffective in combating poverty. The reasons for this are diverse and include ignorance of benefits available, pride at being independent, and the shame of claiming what are often seen as stigmatized payments. But, whatever the reason, according to the state's own figures only 50 per cent of those eligible claimed family income supplement, and only 75 per cent claimed supplementary benefit in 1978–9 (HMSO, 1981, p. 253). This evidence makes the purely theoretical argument about concentrating benefits where there is need look rather less plausible.

But there is another reason why means-tested benefits are a bad way of helping the poor. This is the problem of the 'poverty trap', or situation where a combination of increased taxation and loss of benefits robs the claimant of any increases in his or her earnings. In some cases the effective marginal rate of taxation can exceed 100 per cent, which traps the individual in permanent poverty. In 1979 a family with two children, with the head of the household in full employment, would have gained less than 10p in the pound over a range of earnings from £35 up to £48 per week (HMSO, 1980c, pp. 143–4). A DHSS analysis of the Family Expenditure Survey showed that at the end of 1977 about 50,000 families with children would receive no increase at all from a rise in net earnings of £1; a further 60,000 families would receive less than 25p (HMSO, 1980c, p. 145). Obviously any means-tested benefit will suffer from this problem to varying extents.

For these reasons the main pressure group in the area of family poverty, the Child Poverty Action Group, has consistently opposed the extension of means testing in social security and advocated raising child benefit as the best means of alleviating family poverty (Field, 1982, pp. 94–103). Moreover, there is evidence that this message has penetrated to civil servants in Whitehall, if not to their political masters (Whiteley and Winyard, 1983).

Another major debate in social security concerns the adequacy of benefits. In the case of supplementary benefits, although basic scales are the same for all, there are wide variations in payments made because of the discretionary powers of the board. In particular the discretionary power to award extra benefits in cases of 'exceptional circumstances' has been increasingly used over time, particularly for pensioners. Between 1970 and 1978 the number of pensioners receiving exceptional needs payments went from 18 per cent to 75 per cent of claimants (Berthoud *et al.*, 1981, p. 161). These payments mainly include allowances for heating and food, and clearly constitute an essential item in household budgets.

To help those in long-term poverty the Labour government in 1966 introduced a long-term additional payment for claimants who had received benefits for more than two years. This became a separate long-term benefits scale in 1973. For reasons which cannot easily be justified on grounds of objective needs long-term claimants have a higher income level than short-term claimants, and since then the gap between these has been growing. In general the growth of exceptional needs payments, and the distinction between the long- and short-term rates, are clear indications that the state regards basic rates as inadequate.

Definitions of 'adequate' are to some extent arbitrary, but we can compare the growth in the value of benefits over time with the general level of prices, and with increases in average earnings. Both provide a convenient yardstick for measuring adequacy. In Table 7.5 we compare the value of the four major benefits expressed as a percentage of their 1951 values in real terms over the period 1964 to 1979. There have been substantial increases in real terms in the value of these benefits over this period but marked differences in these increases between types of benefits. The contributory retirement and unemployment benefits have increased substantially more than the non-contributory supplementary benefits. Family allowances have barely increased at all, and for practically the whole period were below their value in real terms in 1951. Essentially these data indicate that successive governments have given

Table 7.5   The changes in real terms in social security benefits, 1964–79 (in 1981 prices, 1951 = 100)

Year	Sup-plementary benefits[a]	Sickness/ unemploy-ment benefit[b]	Retirement pensions[c]	Family allowance/ child benefit[d]	Notes
1964	146	176	149	85	Tory last increase
1965	166	199	168	85	
1966	165	199	168	82	Earnings related
1967	173	318	173	80	unemployment sickness
1968	173	318	173	77	benefit introduced
1969	172	329	172	72	Labour last increase
1970	173	329	172	69	Different rates for over
1971	178	354	177	80	and under 80 years of
1972	187	356	183	75	age for pensions
1973	186	342	191	68	Tory last increase
1974	191	345	216	78	
1975	187	327	215	69	
1976	189	323	219	72	
1977	190	326	221	69	Child benefit introduced
1978	189	321	228	82	Labour last increase
1979	190	308	232	102	

a Refers to married couple.
b Refers to man plus dependent wife.
c Refers to man plus wife on his insurance. After 1971 refers to recipients under 80 years old.
d Includes family allowance and tax allowance combined for second child up to 1977, when these were unified into the child benefit.

Source: Social Security Statistics, 1982, calculated from Tables 46.07, and 46.09 to 46.11.

family support a much lower priority than other types of social security, and have given contributory benefits a higher priority than means tested benefits. Clearly, by 1979, if retirement pensions were considered adequate supplementary benefits were not adequate in terms of a relative standard of living.

In Table 7.6 we examine the value of these benefits in relation to average earnings for selected years. Using this standard, sickness/unemployment benefits and pensions have increased as a percentage of the average earnings of manual workers between 1951 and 1979; supplementary benefits have remained about the same and family support has fallen substantially. The second column in Table 7.5 refers to unemployment benefits plus the earnings related supplement introduced by Labour in 1967. Claimants received ERS for up to six months after becoming unemployed. This produced a substantial increase in the value of unemployment benefit, but this was not maintained over time. The value of ERS as a percentage of average earnings declined over time until it was phased out completely by the Conservatives in 1982.

If poverty is defined in terms of the relationship between the individual's income and average earnings, clearly it has increased over this period. The people who relied on supplementary benefits were not significantly better off in 1979 than they were in 1951 and there were

Table 7.6 Social security benefits as a percentage of average earnings for last increases of various governments, 1951–79

Year	Sickness/ unemploy- ment benefit[a]	[a]plus earnings related supplement[b]	Retirement pensions[c]	Supplemen- tary benefits[d]	Family allowance/ child benefit[e]
1951 (Labour)	25.7	25.7	30.4	30.4	8.0
1963 (Tory)	33.8	33.8	33.0	31.6	5.3
1969 (Labour)	32.4	52.3	32.4	31.4	3.8
1973 (Tory)	29.1	46.2	30.5	28.5	3.0
1978 (Labour)	30.5	44.4	37.4	30.2	3.7

a,b Man plus dependent wife.

  c Man plus dependent wife on his insurance.

  d Married couple.

  e For 1 child.

Source: Social Security Statistics, 1982, Tables 46.07 to 46.11.

more of them; equally people with large families were worse off because of the falling value of child benefit. In this sense policy towards poverty could be said to have failed. In 1978 the Supplementary Benefits Commission was itself arguing that benefits were too low in its annual report (HMSO, 1979, pp. 2–3). This argument is further reinforced since 1979 by the decision of the Conservative government to reduce the value of benefits in real terms (Walker, 1982). Clearly a debate about the adequacy of benefits inevitably involves value judgements; but there is much substance to the view that benefits are inadequate in relation to needs, and the state has implicitly recognized this by the actions it has taken on supplementary benefits in the 1970s.

A third debate concerns the relationship between social security and taxation. There are two aspects to this: the first concerns the distribution of the burden of taxation and the second the question of tax allowances and tax relief. If we examine the question of tax burdens, it is a commonly held view that Britain is heavily overtaxed compared with other industrial countries. This is quite wrong: in 1976 Britain ranked tenth out of twenty-one OECD countries in the percentage of gross domestic product taken in taxes (OECD, 1978, p. 43); clearly this was not excessive compared with other OECD countries. Altogether thirteen countries had larger increases in the burden of taxation than Britain over this period. But the burden of taxation in Britain has been more and more concentrated on personal incomes. Unlike other countries, private wealth is virtually exempt from taxation because death duties have been successfully evaded by large numbers of people; and the corporate sector has had to bear a smaller burden of taxation as time went on, through the action of successive governments in giving tax subsidies to industry. The decline of corporate taxation is particularly striking. According to one estimate, the ratio of taxes to company profits fell from 37 per cent to 14 per cent between 1950 and 1973 (King, 1975).

This has meant that the tax threshold, or the minimum income at which tax is paid, has continuously declined over the years. In other words, tax concessions to the wealthy and to industry have been financed by increasing the burden of income tax, particularly for those with low incomes. The income tax threshold as a percentage of median earnings fell from 61 per cent in 1971–2 to 47 per cent in 1978–9. During this period the percentage of income taken in direct taxation increased from 4 per cent to 10 per cent for the lowest decile of earnings (HMSO, 1980c, p. 142). This produced the ridiculous situation where the state was taxing individuals with incomes below the official poverty line; in November 1980 the supplementary benefits rate for a married couple with two children was £60.03 per week, and the tax threshold was £50.75 per week (Pond, 1982, p. 54). Thus low pay and an increasing burden of taxation is forcing more and more people into poverty, even when the head of the household is employed.

Another feature of the burden of taxation in Britain is the high marginal rates of taxation for low income families. Pond points out:

> The tax system with which we are left is hardly recognisable as a 'progressive' system at all. The same marginal rate of tax (30p in the £ in 1980–1981) is payable by a married wage earner on £45 a week (below the Supplementary Benefit level) as by someone with the same family circumstances earning more than five times that amount. Indeed if we take account of national insurance contributions, the marginal rate faced by those on £45 a week exceeds that payable on £250 a week.   (1982, p. 55)

These facts taken together mean that the changes in the distribution of taxation over time have tended to make the poor worse off.

The second feature of taxation is the growth in the system of tax allowances, which in most cases act as an inegalitarian form of transfer payment. Titmuss was the first to draw attention to tax allowances as a type of transfer payment comparable to direct payments such as supplementary benefits. He argued: 'In their primary objectives and their effects on individual purchasing power there are no differences in these two ways by which collective provision is made for dependencies' (1963, p. 45). There is, however, one key difference between direct transfer payments and tax allowances: the former are clearly related to need in a way that the latter are not. For example, owner occupation is supported by three different tax benefits: mortgage interest relief, the exemption from capital gains tax, and the abolition of Schedule A, which was a tax on the imputed rent from a property. In each case the benefits are in no way related to need.

The growth of tax relief as an inegalitarian form of transfer payment has prompted writers like Field to talk about the 'hidden welfare state' (Field, 1981). He argues that there are actually five 'welfare states' operating in Britain: the tax allowance system; the company welfare state which includes perks such as subsidized cars, private pensions and health schemes; inherited wealth and power which gives access to unearned income from investments and capital gains; the private market system in education and health which give advantages of privilege and which are subsidized by tax allowances; and, finally, the national insurance and supplementary benefits system, or the 'visible' welfare state.

Whether one agrees with Field's analysis or not, there is an enormous amount of money returned to taxpayers in the form of tax benefits. In a comprehensive analysis of tax expenditures (i.e. public expenditure on tax relief) Willis and Hardwick (1978) estimated that in 1973–4 over £11 billion was relieved from income tax through exemptions of various kinds. The main exemptions are the single and married persons' allowances, wives' earned income allowance and the age allowance. There is also tax relief on life assurance and on mortgage payments. The Inland Revenue Statistics for 1979 gave details of total incomes liable to tax, and the extent to which this was reduced by exemptions. In 1976–7 the Inland Revenue calculated that total net personal income was £80.8 billion, and exemptions or tax free income was £30.9 billion. From the £49.9 billion liable for tax, the total raised was £18.3 billion (HMSO, 1980b, Table 1.8). The inegalitarian distribution of such exemptions can be seen from Field's calculations that the value of personal allowances for a married person paying a marginal rate of 30 per cent in 1980–1 was £642.24; for a person paying a marginal rate of 60 per cent with a much higher income the value of allowances was £1287.0 (Field, 1981, p. 132).

The main thing which emerges from this brief discussion of the relationship between social security and taxation is that large subsidies are being given to those who do not really need them in the sense of having a standard of living well above the poverty line, and a significant amount of this is being paid for by individuals who do need support because their income is at or below the poverty line. Clearly discussions of social security policy cannot be confined merely to the direct transfer payments, whether contributory or not, but must consider the whole field of transfer payments. As long as benefits and taxes are discussed separately the picture which emerges of redistribution is likely to be misleading.

This concludes our discussion of the main debates in the area of social security policy in Britain. As we have seen, they centre around the question of means testing, the issue of the adequacy of benefits, and the growth of the 'hidden' or private welfare system. We turn now to an examination of Labour's record in office.

The Wilson years, 1964–70

The starting point of an evaluation of Labour in office is an examination of changes in the major social security benefits set out in Tables 7.5 and 7.6. We can see in Table 7.5 that in the thirteen years of Conservative government supplementary benefits rose by 46 percentage points in real terms, sickness and unemployment benefits by 76 per cent, pensions by 49 and family allowances fell by 15 percentage points. In the five years from 1964 up to the last increases made by the Labour government in 1969 supplementary benefits rose by 26 percentage points, sickness and unemployment by 153 per cent, largely due to the introduction of earnings related benefits in 1967, pensions rose by 23 per cent and family allowances fell by 13 percentage points despite the first increases in money terms in 1968 for sixteen years.

To compare the Conservative period of office with the Labour period, we can use the changes in benefits per year as a rough estimate of comparative performance. For the Conservatives and Labour respectively increases in supplementary benefits per year were 3.5 and 5.2 percentage points, for sickness and unemployment benefits 5.8 and 30.6 percentage points, for pensions 3.8 and 4.6, and for family allowances −1.2 and −2.6. Thus the poor, the retired, the sick and the unemployed did better in real terms under Labour than they did under Conservatives, and families did worse.

If we repeat the comparison by examining benefits in relation to average earnings in Table 7.6, the picture is rather different. During the Conservative years all the benefits (apart from family allowances) rose as a percentage of the average earnings of manual workers. During the Labour years the value of benefits in relation to earnings fell in the case of pensions and family allowances, were more or less maintained in the case of supplementary benefits and rose in the case of earnings related benefits. Thus Labour did better than the Conservatives in increasing benefits in real terms, but not in increasing their value in relation to earnings − with the notable exception of sickness and unemployment benefits.

An alternative way of evaluating Labour's performance is to examine the record in relation to objectives in the social security field. In this case the answer is fairly unequivocal: Labour failed to meet any of its major objectives except in relation to earnings related benefits. We shall examine this in detail, and begin by looking at the plans formulated in Opposition before 1964.

Labour had become sensitive to the question of poverty during the 1950s, before the academic rediscovery of poverty took place. However, at that stage it was exclusively concerned with poverty in old age and did not recognize other categories of poverty. In 1957 the party published a policy document called *National Superannuation, Labour's Policy for Security in Old Age* (Labour Party, 1957b). The document had arisen from the recognition that the flat rate retirement pensions introduced under the Beveridge scheme were inadequate, and left many pensioners in poverty. In the debate on the proposals in this document at the 1957 annual conference Crossman had said: 'Just as unemployment was the great social disgrace of the 1930s, poverty in old age is the great social disgrace and the great challenge of the 1950s' (Labour Party, 1957b, p. 124). The proposals marked a sharp break with the Beveridge principles, since they advocated an earnings related pension which in the long run would provide benefits at a high level, in exchange for earnings related contributions. The scheme required a long period of transition during which a fund of contributions could be built up, and so it proposed an interim increase in pensions to meet immediate need. The plan was to raise the basic pension from £2 to £3 a week in 1957. In the event the party did not get the chance to implement these proposals since it was defeated in the 1959 General Election.

The basic framework set out in the 1957 document was retained in subsequent work on social security after 1959, but by then the party had become aware of other categories of poverty as well as the pensioners. In 1963 a document called *New Frontiers for Social Security* (Labour Party, 1963) was published which extended the principle of earnings related benefits to the unemployed, sick and widows. The transitional period was to be filled by an income guarantee which aimed at supplementing incomes without a means test. The plan was to get information on incomes from the Inland Revenue, and to pay benefits on the basis of this information without people having to apply and take a means test. In view of the problems of take-up referred to earlier, this was an attractive feature of the scheme. The document further proposed to abolish the National Assistance Board, and the entire apparatus of means testing. Unfortunately *New Frontiers* was vague about the detailed implementation of the scheme. There was no information about the scope, timing, costs, rates of benefit and the administrative machinery of the scheme. This was a major error, since the details of social security policy are crucial if underlying principles are to be maintained. The error was understandable, however, since the party had been in opposition for twelve years and did not have access to the relevant data.

The section on social security in the 1964 manifesto included the proposal for the minimum income guarantee. It stated: 'Those whose incomes fall below the new minimum will receive as of right, and without recourse to National Assistance, an income supplement (Craig, 1975, p. 265). In addition the manifesto contained proposals for linking national insurance benefits to earnings. This applied to sickness, unemployment and retirement pensions. It stated: 'The objective is half-pay benefits for the worker on average pay' (ibid.). In addition, there were other proposals in the manifesto for a scheme of redundancy pay, and for improved widows' benefits. Altogether these proposals were as revolutionary as the original Beveridge scheme in their impact on social security.

In the Queen's Speech following the election victory there was no mention of the minimum income guarantee, but only a proposal to review existing schemes. The only immediate proposals were for increases in existing benefits. In fact, the minimum income guarantee was subsequently postponed, and finally abandoned altogether. In a debate on the government's social security record in 1965 Harold Wilson explained this failure as partly a product of the economic situation, and partly a product of administrative difficulties (Webb, 1975, p. 441). In some ways this admission was typical of the entire Wilson government. Labour made ambitious and radical policies in opposition but had feet of clay when it came to their implementation in government. The argument that the party could not anticipate the economic situation was valid up to a point, but it was not difficult to see in opposition that with nearly 6.5 million pensioners in 1965 that the minimum income guarantee was going to be very costly. This could have been anticipated, at least in outline. Similarly, the 'administrative difficulties' which Wilson referred to were largely a product of the refusal of the Inland Revenue to co-operate in implementing the new system. It saw its role as one of revenue raising and refused to be involved in questions of redistribution. As we shall see below, the same problem appeared again in 1976 over the introduction of child benefit and was only overcome by a vigorous political campaign. Thus 'administrative difficulties' primarily meant civil service traditionalism which Wilson was either unwilling or unable to overcome. The truth was that a revolutionary set of proposals like these needed an administration with enough political courage to put them through, assuming it thought they were sound in the first place. The Wilson government did not have that courage.

The same fate befell the pension scheme as did the minimum income guarantee. The proposals were initially delayed pending the review, were subsequently changed and finally overtaken by the 1970 Election. To be fair to Crossman, who was the main architect of the earnings related pension scheme, a number of important changes had taken place in the area of pensions since the initial proposals were made in 1957. The major difficulty for the Crossman scheme was what to do about the occupational pensions, which had grown significantly by 1965. The pension plan needed to be re-examined in the light of these changes. But instead it was effectively shelved.

Instead of implementing the original proposals, Labour undertook a rather cosmetic reform of the National Assistance Board, which involved integrating national insurance and national assistance into one overall ministry. The reform was cosmetic because the two parts of the social security system remained organizationally distinct within the new department and retained their separate traditions. The aim was to try to eliminate the stigma associated with the means tested side of social security by linking it with national insurance, but it was in fact unworkable given the very different traditions of the two parts of the system. National insurance worked within a tradition of legal entitlement quite separate from any discretionary notion of need. National assistance, on the other hand, worked within a tradition in which officials had wide powers to grant and to withdraw discretionary benefits, and were enjoined to enforce rules like the wage stop designed to introduce stigma into the system. In a real sense these were incompatible and, given no basic change in the system, would not be greatly affected by a minor reorganization.

The 1966 Social Security Act, which implemented the re-organization, gave a number of specific entitlements to benefits which did increase take-up rates amongst the elderly poor in particular. This was an improvement, but it was a far cry from the original plans. Moreover, the government characteristically exaggerated the impact of the measure. Douglas Houghton, the Labour minister in charge of the review of social security, claimed that by 1967 the Social Security Act had practically solved the problems of take-up, since it had encouraged some half a million extra people to apply for benefits (Houghton, 1967, p. 12). But Atkinson showed that up to two-thirds of this increase in the number of claimants was caused by the rise in the assistance scales which accompanied the Act; thus as benefits increased so more people became eligible to receive assistance (Atkinson, 1970, p. 76).

The Supplementary Benefits Commission continued to operate a number of rules which in some cases severely limited entitlements. Atkinson showed that by the end of 1966 some 25,000 households were subject to 'wage stop', and by late 1967 this had increased to over 32,000 (Atkinson, 1970, p. 93). Another restriction was the 'four week rule', which involved ending benefits for unemployed claimants after four weeks unless they could give 'good reasons' why they had not found work. This was applied in areas of high unemployment and caused real hardship. A third was the 'cohabitation rule', which reduced the benefit received by a single woman who was cohabiting to the same level as that received by a wife living with her husband. On the face of it, this seemed reasonable, but it did involve social security 'snooping' into the lives of claimants in a way likely to increase stigma, and thus reduce take-up rates.

The only substantial beneficiaries from Labour's social security plans were the unemployed and the sick, who received earnings related benefits after 1966. The Social Security Act of 1966 also included extra benefits for widows. The earnings related scheme involved an initial large increase in benefits, as we can see in Table 7.4, but the value of ERS was eroded by inflation as time went on.

The worst aspect of Labour's social security record was family allowances, despite the fact that in 1968 Labour increased them by 75p for the second child. Banting (1979) has provided a detailed case study of the political battle waged inside the Cabinet to increase family allowances, following the policy from the initial outlining of options to the final decision. He describes how the policy options for tackling family poverty were developed as follows:

> This process was a remarkably closed bureaucratic one. . . . The Social Security ministers did not involve themselves as deeply in the initial structuring of options as did Crossman; outside experts were not brought in at senior levels, and there was virtually no consultation with outside groups. (p. 86)

The effective policy options for dealing with family poverty were reduced to two: a universal benefit on the one hand and a means tested benefit on the other. The Labour ministers, Douglas Houghton and Margaret Herbison, were very much against means testing, but they faced strong opposition from the Treasury and the Chancellor of the Exchequer, Callaghan.

The opposition to increasing family allowances as an alternative to means testing was based on two arguments. The first was that the increase in family allowances would mean the reduction in child tax allowances for the average wage earner, if it were not to be prohibitively expensive. This was known as 'clawback' and in effect meant that an increase in family allowance for those on average incomes was merely a transfer from the pay packet to the purse. There was concern too about the likely unpopularity of this in the male dominated trade unions. The second reason, which has been referred to earlier, was the objection of the Board of Inland Revenue to participating in schemes of redistribution. They took the wholly ideological view that the tax system was for revenue raising only, despite the fact that the progressive nature of the system already meant that it redistributed income. Callaghan agreed with this traditionalist view (Banting, 1979, p. 95).

The Social Services ministers successfully achieved important outside support for the increase in family allowances. The Child Poverty Action Group provided support in the media and a wealth of case study material, and when the General Council of the TUC came out against means testing this effectively destroyed Callaghan's most potent argument; it could no longer be said that trade unions objected to family allowances. Despite this, the final vote in Cabinet on family allowances was fairly close; according to Banting, the vote was thirteen for the increase and eleven against, taken after an acrimonious debate.

When examining Labour's record on family allowances it is important to remember that many ministers and backbench MPs thought the proposal was unpopular in the country. The left-wing member, Eric Heffer, summed up this feeling in the debate on the proposals when he said: 'Throughout the country in all our constituencies there are many people who are opposed to the idea of extending family allowances. . . . The Government have acted very courageously' (House of Commons, 1967, pp. 240–1). Furthermore, many supporters of measures to help the poor were ignorant of the problems of take-up which affected means tested schemes. But, even allowing for this, the position of families considerably worsened under Labour, when it prided itself on being the party which represents the poor. Labour's record prompted the Child Poverty Action Group to publish a controversial pamphlet immediately prior to the election, which attacked the government's record. It stated: 'Of all the groups to benefit from this Government's measures, low income families have benefited least – if at all' (Field, 1982, p. 98). This severely embarrassed some ministers.

After the general election victory the Conservatives introduced the means-tested family income supplement, which was basically the same plan supported by Callaghan and the Treasury in 1968 in opposition to family allowances. In the debate on the new scheme Crossman described FIS as 'an old friend of ours' (House of Commons, 1971–2, p. 253). Retrospectively FIS was a great failure since it had a very low take-up rate. Increases in benefits under the Heath government were significantly lower than under Labour in the case of supplementary benefits and sickness/unemployment benefits, but higher in the case of pensions. Similarly, the fall in the value of family allowances and tax allowances combined was rather less than it had been under Labour.

The Wilson and Callaghan years, 1974–9

Labour fought the election of February 1974 with four specific policy commitments on social security. These were increased pensions, a new scheme for the disabled, a new system of child benefits to replace family allowances and price controls, particularly on food. Compared with 1964 this was an extremely limited set of policy objectives. The only commitment which involved large scale public expenditure was the promise to raise pensions by nearly 30 per cent.

The performance of Labour in power from 1974 to 1979 in social security was considerably worse than in 1964 to 1970, with the exception of pensions. The value of supplementary benefits and sickness/unemployment benefits fell in real terms; child benefit was increased in real terms but when Labour left office it was still at a lower level than it had been in 1964. Pensioners did quite well, with the value of their benefits increasing by 43 percentage points, or an average of 8.6 per cent per annum. If we compare benefits with average earnings Labour did better than the Conservatives, except in the case of earnings related unemployment and sickness benefits which declined in value in relation to average earnings. However, with the exception of pensions all these benefits had lower values in relation to earnings in 1979 than they did in 1969, the previous Labour government's last year of office.

Turning to the details of policy implementation, perhaps the most far reaching reform enacted by the Labour government in social security was the Pensions Act of 1975. We saw earlier that the Crossman plan for an earnings related pension had never got off the ground by the time Labour left office. In 1973 the Conservatives had enacted legislation in the pensions area which was largely designed to encourage occupational pensions. This did very little for the poor, who for the most part did not participate in occupational pension schemes. Labour opposed the 1973 legislation for this reason.

The Labour proposals for the reform of pensions were published in a White Paper in September 1974 (HMSO, 1974a). This was enacted with a small number of changes and finally came into force in 1978. The scheme contained two parts: firstly, a flat rate pensions element and, secondly, an earnings related element. Under the scheme the value of the final pension is based on the twenty best earning years, and the pension is index linked to protect its value in real terms. Full entitlement builds up over twenty years with the full scheme coming into operation in the late 1990s. The scheme allows individuals in an approved occupational pension scheme to contract out of the state system, and in other respects provides favourable treatment to occupational pensions. In developing the scheme the Labour government sought all-party support so that it would be protected from further changes by a future Conservative government. The new system does bring potential benefits to the poor; for example, the twenty best years' provision and the formula for calculating the flat rate element hold out the possibility of redistribution in favour of the low paid. In this respect the scheme is an improvement on its Conservative predecessor. However, it has been criticized by representatives of pensioners. They pointed out that it failed to improve the incomes of existing pensioners, many of whom rely on supplementary benefits. It also does little to improve the position of those who will retire before the 1990s, when the full scheme comes into operation. However, in the long run it holds out the hope that fewer pensioners will be dependent on means tested benefits in the future.

The second of Labour's commitments – the proposal to provide a new scheme of help for the disabled – grew out of dissatisfaction with the complex, inconsistent pattern of benefits for the disabled (Simkins and Tickner, 1978). We mentioned earlier that Beveridge had neglected the needs of people disabled from birth, and in 1970 the only non-means tested benefits for the disabled were for war veterans and for workers disabled by industrial accidents or work related diseases. This meant that a person disabled in an industrial injury would receive more than a person in similar circumstances disabled in, say, a car accident; this made little sense in practice. The first change in benefits for the disabled was the introduction in 1971 of a flat rate invalidity pension which replaced sickness benefit when the earnings related element of that ran out. But this was not paid if the disabled person were employed, so that individuals suffering from a partial loss of earnings through a downgrading of employment following an industrial injury would receive nothing. Another measure introduced in 1971 was the attendance allowance paid to the severely disabled who needed constant attendance. This was non-means tested and represented an important new principle because it was not dependent on the payment of contributions and was paid strictly according to need.

In the mid-1970s groups representing the disabled (like the Disability Alliance and the Disablement Income Group) started to campaign for the introduction of a comprehensive disability income to be paid solely according to need (Disability Alliance, 1975). The Chronically Sick and Disabled Persons Act of 1970, which was largely the work of the Labour minister, Alf Morris, put the needs of the disabled on the political agenda. In July 1974 the new government published a White Paper on social security and the disabled (HMSO, 1974b). This proposed a new non-contributory invalidity pension and an invalid care allowance, and these were introduced in 1975. The former is aimed at the long term disabled who have not built up a contribution record, and the latter at relatives who are unable to work when they are caring for a disabled person. Initially married women were excluded from both benefits but a Labour backbench revolt in 1975 ensured that they received the invalidity pension. In addition, Labour introduced a mobility allowance in 1976 to provide help towards the transport costs of the severely disabled. In general the Labour government met its commitments in the manifesto to the disabled, but it did not introduce the comprehensive disability benefit favoured by some.

The third of Labour's commitments concerned with child benefit was designed to 'help the low paid and other families in poverty' (Craig, 1975, p. 402). After the election the new Secretary of State, Barbara Castle, immediately began to retreat from this commitment (Land, 1977), arguing that the benefit could not be extended to the first child until 1976. Following considerable pressure, family allowances were extended to the first child in single parent families as an interim measure, but not for families in general.

James Callaghan was elected party leader in March 1976 and in May the government announced its intention of abandoning the child benefit scheme. It argued, much as Callaghan had done in 1968, that increases in family benefits would involve an 'unacceptable' reduction in take-home pay due to the reduction in child tax allowance. As an alternative, the government promised to introduce a £1 a week benefit for first children, but this would have been subject to clawback. The announcement of this change angered and shocked many Labour backbenchers, not to mention the influential poverty pressure groups. The Cabinet minutes on the entire child benefit issue were leaked to Frank Field, the director of the Child Poverty Action Group, and they were published in *New Society* (1976), much to the embarrassment of the government. This leak gives us unique insights into the decision making process in the Labour government.

The battle over child benefit involved the Social Services minister, David Ennals, and Barbara Castle, who had been sacked by Callaghan, on the one hand, and Denis Healey and Jim Callaghan on the other. Ennals declared in a confidential Cabinet memo: 'If we continue to let child support be eroded by inflation, the whole scheme would be condemned as a trick to give children less, not more' (Field, 1982, p. 110). Callaghan argued at the Cabinet meeting of 6 May that the Labour backbenchers were increasingly worried about the political consequences of the scheme. He said that he had been informed of this by the Chief Whip. However, on 24 May the TUC/Labour Party Liaison Committee, which was highly influential, made a firm commitment to child benefit. Denis Healey called a small group of senior trade union leaders together after this meeting and persuaded them that the cut in child allowances would be unacceptable to their members. It was then put to the Cabinet that both the backbench party and senior trade union leaders were against child benefit and the Cabinet agreed to abandon the proposal. The decision was taken as a result of backstairs lobbying, coupled with deliberate misinformation, since it was fairly clear that a majority of both the parliamentary party and the TUC/Labour Party Liaison Committee favoured child benefit.

The opposition to the decision, much of it sustained by the CPAG, kept the issue alive even after the announcement of the decision. In early 1978 the CPAG published a polemical pamphlet called *All Children Worse Off under Labour* (1978). This was designed to influence the budget, and it caused considerable concern amongst backbenchers and trade unionists. At the same time, David Donnison, the Chairman of the Supplementary Benefits Commission, had come out in support of child benefit, and so a good deal of opinion was building up in favour of a restoration of the scheme. The threat of a backbench revolt led by Barbara Castle during the debate on the budget proved decisive and the government gave way. As a result, the budget of 1978 produced the largest increases in family support since the introduction of family allowances. In a post-mortem on the original decision to cancel child benefit, Field sums up the entire episode as follows: 'It is a clear example of a potentially radical government becoming managers rather than reformers' (1982, pp. 112–13).

The fourth element in the manifesto, related to the question of poverty, was the commitment to introduce price controls. These were totally ineffective, and when the control of inflation became the sole priority of the government after 1976 it was achieved partly at the expense of the poor by increasing unemployment. To be fair to the government, though, the incomes policy of 1975 did help to improve the relative position of the low paid, although this did not help the increasing numbers of unemployed.

With the exception of price controls, the Labour government of 1974 to 1979 succeeded in implementing its manifesto commitments on social security. But the only group actually to benefit significantly in real terms from Labour's policies were the pensioners. Poor families also received limited benefits, except that at the end of 1978 family support was at a lower level than it had been when Labour left office in 1951.

Conclusions

We began this chapter by examining the main debates on social security policy since Beveridge: that is, the question of selectivity, the adequacy of benefits and the issue of taxation and benefits. On all three issues Labour's performance in office was poor. The number of individuals dependent on means tested benefits grew significantly in both Labour terms. As we saw in Table 7.4, the number of people dependent on supplementary benefits grew by 750,000 between 1964 and 1970, and by 270,000 between 1974 and 1978. The growth in exceptional needs payments, particularly for pensioners, during the 1970s was an admission by the state that benefits were inadequate; and no attention was paid to reforming the increasingly regressive tax system, with its lower and lower tax thresholds. By 1979 large transfer payments were being made both to industry and to the affluent, who had successfully evaded a wealth tax promised by Labour in 1974. A significant amount of money to fund those transfer payments came from the low paid; and, as earnings related benefits declined in value over time, from the unemployed. In terms of manifesto commitments fulfilled, the 1974–9 government was more successful than the 1964–70 government, but this was only because it set its sights at a much lower level. Even then the government reneged on one commitment in 1976, the child benefit proposal, and presumably would have done nothing more about it were it not for a backbench revolt in 1978. As in the case of economic policy, it is difficult to argue that the 1979 election was a grossly unjust verdict on Labour in office.

8

The future of the Labour Party

The starting point of an assessment of the future of the Labour Party must be the basic thesis of this book: that failures in policy have eroded the support base of the party. The internal faction fighting of recent years has contributed to this decline; but this too is largely a reflection of the underlying policy failure. We have reviewed the nature of this failure in two key areas: economic and social security policy. But a similar point could be made about other policy areas such as health and housing. Ultimately most of the problems derive from policy failures in the key area of economic management; if the economy could be turned around, there would be a much better prospect of achieving objectives in other areas of policy.

In this final chapter we examine the future prospects for the party, in particular by evaluating the plans which have been developed in opposition to bring about a regeneration of the economy. The essential argument will be that if Labour can achieve electoral success, and if it can then implement a successful economic strategy, then it can reverse the decline in its support base. There is of course a paradox in this argument, namely that the party needs success at the next election if it is to achieve success in the long run. If it continues to fail to win electoral success and remains in opposition for an extended period of time, the faction fighting is likely to be renewed with greater force, and the link between the trade union movement and the party is likely to be further weakened as the trade unions seek an accommodation with whatever political forces make up the government. In the medium term there is always the possibility of a change in the electoral system designed to benefit the Liberals and Social Democrats. This will make the task of winning future elections and forming a government not dependent on the centre–right even more difficult. For reasons discussed below a coalition between the Alliance and Labour would be unable to implement the policies needed to regenerate British industry, and so if Labour were trapped in such a coalition its support would continue to haemorrhage away. For all these reasons Labour needs electoral success.

But achieving power is only a starting point in the task of regenerating the Labour Party. If the economic performance of a future Labour government is the same as that of 1974 to 1979 this could prove disastrous for the long-term survival of the party. Accordingly, we begin by examining the economic strategy worked out by Labour in opposition, and then we evaluate the prospects for the strategy in turning round the economy. We then briefly examine Labour's plans for social security before considering finally long-term electoral prospects.

Labour's economic policy plans, 1982

Following the defeat in the General Election of 1979 the party began to formulate future policies. The core of Labour's proposals for economic policy were set out in *Labour's Plan for Expansion* (Labour Party, 1981), a policy document which was elaborated at length in the report of the National Executive Committee to the annual conference of 1981. The proposals were revised and worked out in more detail for inclusion in *Labour's Programme, 1982* (Labour Party, 1982b), which is a general statement about future party policy across the whole field of government. This was accepted by the 1982 annual conference. The 1982 programme is more comprehensive and far-reaching than ever before, containing some 280 pages of detailed proposals on all aspects of policy.

The economic policy proposals in the 1982 programme are set out in the first section entitled 'Labour's Plan for Jobs' (pp. 15–66) and fall under three broad headings: the Socialist Strategy; Employment and Training Policy; and the Industrial Strategy. We shall briefly outline these proposals.

To consider the 'Socialist Strategy' first, the aim is:

> to rebuild our industrial base, to reconquer our domestic markets, to restore Britain to full employment. But, equally, we intend to introduce greater democracy and accountability throughout the economy; to bring about greater equality in the distribution of income and wealth; to extend common ownership; and to provide new rights for workers and consumers and ethnic minorities.   (p. 5)

Thus, as they stand, the proposals are very ambitious. Most of the discussion in the 'Socialist Strategy' is concerned with economic policy and focuses on macroeconomic management. The key proposal concerns employment. The programme states:

> We restate our commitment to the principle set out in the 1944
> Employment White Paper. . . . As a first step towards meeting this
> commitment, the central aim of our economic strategy will be to
> reduce unemployment to below a million within five years of taking
> office. (p. 17)

The package of proposals designed to bring this about contains a number
of elements. Firstly, there is the expansion of demand involving additional
public spending, selective tax reductions and increases in the PSBR or
government borrowing. The main emphasis here is on additional public
spending. Secondly, there is an extensive programme of public investment which includes house building, railway electrification, the modern-
ization of telecommunications and urban renewal. Thirdly, there is
monetary policy, which involves the abandonment of the largely discredited Conservative system of targets for monetary expansion; there
are proposals for the control of bank lending and the introduction of a
differential interest rate structure for different types of investment.
Overall, this part of the programme follows a fairly traditional policy of
Keynesian demand expansion.

The departure from Keynesian orthodoxy comes in the section of
the programme which discusses the balance of payments. The programme recognizes that the balance of payments is the main problem in
ensuring a sustained expansion of the economy, and argues:

> We will therefore set import penetration ceilings on an industry-by-
> industry basis across a broad range of sectors. Our aim will be to
> prevent the growth of imports overall outstripping the growth of
> exports, and to cut import penetration in certain sectors. (p. 21)

The clauses in the General Agreement on Tariffs and Trade which provide for trade controls are cited as a means of doing this without breach-
ing international agreements. The document also uses the argument
originally put by the Cambridge Group, that trade controls are compatible with absolute increases in the volume of imports. The point made
here is that economic expansion increases GDP, and this is compatible
with a relative decline but an absolute increase in imports provided that
trade volumes grow more slowly than GDP. The document notes that this
makes retaliation much less likely than is true when imports are being
reduced in absolute terms.

Alongside import controls the programme proposes to set up a
special export promotion division of a new Department of Economic and
Industrial Planning. Other measures to deal with the balance of payments
constraint include a new system of exchange controls, 'so that capital

flows are regulated with regard to their industrial implications as well as their immediate financial impact' (p. 22). The aim is also to manage the exchange rate to avoid the over-valuing of the pound experienced in 1980–1 when exports were severely damaged. There is a recognition that devaluation may be necessary, but also that it can go too far and boost inflation by raising import prices. The objective is to ensure that exchange rates are consistent with economic expansion.

The section of the programme dealing with inflation opens with the phrase: 'In four successive general elections the electorate has judged the major parties on the credibility of their policies to control inflation' (p. 23). This is a fairly stark recognition of the importance of controlling inflation. The proposals call for price controls both directly on public sector charges, such as nationalized industry prices, and indirectly by cuts in VAT and national insurance charges. There is a commitment to establish a Price Commission to enforce these controls. The major omission is any discussion of incomes policy. In fact, the programme appears to rule this out completely when it states: 'We have also made clear our opposition to any policies of wage restraint' (p. 24). Clearly if nationalized industry prices are to be controlled, but there is to be no control over pay, this is a recipe for open-ended losses in the public sector.

The chapter on employment and training is very detailed and comprehensive, and represents a real innovation compared with the earlier programmes of the party. The growth of unemployment in the 1960s and 1970s has led to a series of *ad hoc* manpower training and work experience programmes which have grown enormously in size. The proposals aim to co-ordinate and extend these various programmes. There is a short term 'emergency programme' which involves subsidies to firms to promote short-time working as an alternative to redundancy, a system of job-creating employment subsidies targeted on particular groups, such as the long term unemployed and youth, and a system of allowances to promote the formation and growth of new enterprises. The long term or 'training programme' is more ambitious and aims to ensure that: 'All young people should have the opportunity of further education or planned training as a preparation for working life' (p. 29). The plan is to develop the existing adult training opportunities schemes in skill centres and colleges of further education, to give training opportunities to all young people who need them. The training schemes will be developed by the Manpower Services Commission, alongside a new system of plant level training committees, an idea originally proposed by the TUC. In addition, there are sections in the chapter on training which deal with the special needs of women, the disabled and black workers.

The proposals for a new industrial strategy are again more comprehensive than those made before in 1974. Unlike the earlier proposals, there is a much bigger emphasis on democratic participation in industry.

The programme states: 'Our challenge is to reconcile a planned approach to the regeneration of industry with the full democratic participation at enterprise, sector and national levels' (p. 39). There is a discussion of an earlier failure in industrial policy, the National Plan of 1965. Its failure is attributed to the fact that 'key macroeconomic decisions were not geared into the Plan's objectives and remained under separate control of the Treasury' (p. 40). This is an important point, since, as we have argued earlier, industrial policy and macroeconomic policy have often operated in conflict with one another.

The machinery for implementing the new Industrial Strategy and ensuring that it is consistent with macroeconomic management will be quite formidable:

> At the centre of the framework are a new Department of Economic and Industrial Planning and an independent National Planning Council. These will co-ordinate the work of government departments, develop sectoral plans and provide formal machinery for consultation with those working in industry. They will have direct responsibility for a number of other new and existing institutions such as the Price Commission, the National Investment Bank, and the National Enterprise Board. (p. 41)

The aim is to introduce a system of indicative five year plans aimed at the industrial sector levels. Statutory powers will be taken, and companies will be given a variety of incentives to ensure that they participate in the system. The incentives will include price controls, which will be 'tightened where a company refuses to co-operate' (p. 43); a system of long term credits at low interest rates operating through the proposed National Investment Bank; an import control package used to help co-operative sectors; and finally discretionary financial support.

The section on the control of multinationals is toned down considerably in comparison with 1974, where they were frequently depicted as the villains of the piece. But the programme includes a proposal to introduce selective public ownership where necessary, which will include subsidiaries of foreign-owned multinationals. It suggests the establishment of a 'Foreign Investment Unit' to monitor the inward and outward flow of investment. Public ownership will play a fairly important role in the entire strategy. The programme states: 'To plan effectively we shall in particular need public ownership in electronics; pharmaceuticals and health equipment; the construction industry and building materials; the private road haulage industry; major ports; forestry and timber' (p. 49). In addition, there is a commitment to take a majority stake in existing and future North Sea oil fields, and to nationalize one of the major banks. The rationale for the public ownership of this rather heterogeneous group of industries is not developed, other than the point that there is a need to promote new technology like micro-chips and electronics. These proposals follow a pattern previously established in party manifestos of including candidates for nationalization on an *ad hoc* basis, only to exclude them subsequently.

The proposals for a National Planning Council are designed to replace the National Economic Development Council with a new body having greater powers and more resources. The National Investment Bank will be a conduit for channelling funds from the long-term saving institutions, such as the Pension Funds and Life Assurance Companies, into industrial investment.

Altogether Labour's economic strategy represents a comprehensive set of proposals for the regeneration of British industry. We turn next to an evaluation of the likelihood of these proposals working if Labour wins power in the future.

Evaluating the economic strategy

The starting point for evaluating Labour's economic strategy is a consideration of the economic situation immediately following a Labour victory, assuming this occurs within the next five years. Unless there is a dramatic change in government policy, unemployment will be at historically very high levels and de-industrialization, which has been made considerably worse by monetarism, will have laid waste whole areas of productive industry; it is very likely that investment will have been stagnant for several years, and research and development will be at a very low ebb. The task of reconstruction will be as great as that following the Second World War. For this reason industrial reconstruction should be the central aim of the government, which it should pursue almost to the exclusion of everything else. Just as defence of the currency was the sole objective of the Wilson government before 1967, and reducing inflation was the sole objective of the Callaghan government after 1976, then economic reconstruction should be the sole objective of a future Labour government. All other objectives which might conflict with this should be abandoned or postponed, such is the magnitude of the task.

In view of this the most immediate, and most dangerous, obstacle in the way of the economic strategy is that either it will get diverted into the pursuit of the wrong objectives, or it will lose sight of the main objective by trying to do too much. Surprising as it may seem, a government which pursues a growth strategy to the exclusion of everything else will be doing something revolutionary in terms of British postwar economic policy. A concern with the state of the underlying real economy, to the exclusion of financial aggregates, would be a fundamental change of course.

Successive governments have started out with the intention of promoting real growth and jobs, but have been diverted into questions of financial management which have produced policies that have actively encouraged de-industrialization. This concern with finance comes about for a number of reasons. Firstly, financial markets, particularly the exchange rate, change much more rapidly than the underlying real economy and can do so in perverse ways. The IMF crisis of 1976 is a good illustration of this. Such rapid changes in the behaviour of these markets mean that they impose themselves on politicians and senior officials. Policy makers are obliged to take fast action, if the ever ubiquitous 'confidence' is to be restored. At a time of instability in the foreign exchange markets economic ministers can become almost obsessed by the state of thē currency, to the exclusion of everything else. Another factor is the short-term planning horizon of most politicians, which has been legitimized, as we have seen, by the legacy of Keynesianism. Changes in the real economy take years to bring about, so there is an inherent bias in the system against pursuing policies which take several years to come to fruition. Another factor related to these is the style of decision making in government. If decision makers behaved according to the classic tenets of rational behaviour they would follow their most preferred course of action consistently until they achieved their objectives (Simon, 1959). However, decision making in government is not at all like that. Some writers have pointed out that policy making is inherently too complex, uncertain and value laden to be anything other than a process of incrementalism, involving small adjustments to the *status quo* (Lindblom, 1959; Braybrooke and Lindblom, 1963); others see decision making as almost chaotic (Cohen, March and Olsen, 1972). Clearly in the case of economic management, policy making does not appear to approximate classical notions of rationality at all.

We might describe the decision making process in economic policy as 'crisis-offset' decision making. In other words, policy makers pursue a series of objectives, often mutually inconsistent, and the objective which currently occupies them most is the one which is causing the biggest crisis. They are continually trying to offset the most immediate crisis, whether it is in the exchange markets, in industrial relations or in the nationalized industries. The current crisis thus becomes overtaken by another, which in turn is overtaken by a third, and so on. In this situation it is very difficult for a coherent strategy of any sort to emerge by the conscious decision of the political leadership. Policy is easily diverted in pursuit of the wrong objectives, or indeed no coherent objectives at all.

For these reasons it will be difficult for a future Labour government actually to implement the economic strategy when it is in office, and concentrate on reviving the real economy. This problem is, of course, something to bear in mind when it achieves office, but there is something which can be done before then. As set out in the programme, the economic strategy is clearly trying to do too much. It is a programme which could take a Labour government two or three terms of office to fulfil. For example, the proposals for industrial democracy are perhaps desirable in themselves, but they are a diversion from the main task. There is, of course, a school of thought within the party which holds that industrial democracy is the key to a more efficient management in British industry. But this is largely an illusion, since industrial democracy can throw up as many problems as it solves. There are, for example, wide differences of interest between low-paid unskilled workers and skilled workers. The former are interested in narrowing differentials and the latter in widening them, and these conflicts can potentially be made worse by workers' participation. By the same token, workers on the board can easily become divorced from the rank and file, leading to real problems in industrial relations. It is not necessary to review all the arguments for and against industrial democracy to make the point that the industrial strategy should concentrate on revitalizing industry and not get diverted into issues of marginal relevance to this objective. The same point could be made about one or two other proposals in the strategy. The party in power needs to concentrate its efforts on questions which really matter and ignore the rest.

One element of the economic strategy which is essential to industrial reconstruction is the proposals for planning trade. In some ways Britain is in the position of a country which is embarking on industrialization and which needs to protect domestic markets in order to promote fledgling industries. Free trade once brought great advantages to Britain, and indeed the country became the workshop of the world by pursuing it. But now free trade has become the engine of de-industrialization. In pursuing the strategy of trade planning the Labour government will face a formidable array of ideological barriers reinforced by vested interests, largely though not exclusively in the City. The main ideological barrier lies in the economics profession, which is now very influential in the policy making process. This comes about because the discipline of economics has chiefly been concerned with market allocation, rather than the real world of production and technological progress. Most economists, socialized in the neo-classical school, would argue that if the market is allowed to operate freely then industrial production and innovation can be left to itself. This belief explains why much of the so-called theory of economic growth is an exercise in pure mathematics rather than an analysis of growth in the real world economy (Whiteley, 1983). This produces a curious blind spot in the case of the issue of free trade. Economists who pride themselves on their willingness to evaluate policy in terms of costs and benefits completely abandon this position when it comes to the question of free trade, which they elevate to the level of a sacrosanct principle. Massive deflation of the economy for the purpose of reducing imports is seen as quite acceptable, whereas import controls which achieve the same objective far more cost-effectively are regarded as an anathema. Wynne Godley, one of the few British economists to take a dispassionate view of trade planning, was bewildered by his own profession's refusal to examine this issue. He wrote:

> I am disconcerted and distressed to find myself, together with the group of people with whom I work in Cambridge, in such an isolated position. For we seem to be the only professional group of economists who entertain the possibility that control of international trade may be the only way of recovering and maintaining the prosperity of this country.   (1979, p. 226)

The truth is, of course, that international trade markets are not the stable, self-equilibrating systems of classical theory which maximize welfare when they are left to themselves. Kindelberger (1976), an eminent international economist, has argued that free trade has always required a hegemonic power to underwrite it, providing liquidity and coping with the periodic crises which occur. In the nineteenth century this was Britain, and after the Second World War until the mid-1970s it was the United States. Since the demise of the Bretton Woods system of fixed exchange rates, there is no dominant power in a position to underwrite world trade and the system has increasingly become subject to wild commodity and currency fluctuations. Things have been made much worse by the recession which has increasingly turned trade into a zero-sum game, in which one country's gains from trade are another country's losses. Even at the level of abstract economic theory it is becoming increasingly evident that markets are in a deep sense chaotic (Schofield, 1978a and b, 1982) and subject to manipulation for private gain by small groups of actors (Satterthwaite and Sonnenschein, 1981). All this implies that for Britain free trade increasingly means the wholesale export of jobs. Import controls are quite simply inevitable if Britain is ever going to climb out of the recession (Neild, 1979). In Britain's present economic position free trade is highly damaging. Historically there are no examples of countries in the modern era who have achieved advanced developed status without extensive trade planning. This was certainly true of three leading western industrial economies: Germany, Japan and the United States. The most successful of these countries in achieving high growth, Japan, only did it with the help of extensive government intervention in the economy as well as trade planning (Johnson, 1982). Re-industrialization in Britain is going to require similar policies. It is a testament to the influence of ideology in modern economic theory, that most economists still advocate free trade as a means to maximizing efficiency and welfare when the empirical evidence clearly shows that in the modern world growth and development require trade planning.

The intellectual argument against free trade may be easier to win than the battle against vested interests. The chief vested interest is the City of London, whose concerns frequently diverge from those of productive industry. To illustrate this point with a couple of examples, the high interest rates produced by monetarism have done enormous damage to the real economy and productive investment. The city has, however, prospered on high interest rates, since they have produced very high returns on securities. In the long run, of course, they will wipe out the productive base upon which finance capital is constructed; but the city is only really interested in quick returns, which explains its preference for investment in unproductive areas like property rather than in the real economy. Another example concerns the export of capital; when the Conservatives abolished exchange controls in 1981, huge amounts of money flowed abroad, much of it to improve the productivity of our competitors. It is easy to see why the city has a vested interest in free trade.

In a real sense economic planning in the postwar era has been dominated by the interests of the city and finance capital in general (Longstreth, 1979). In the final analysis successive governments have been willing to sacrifice the real economy in the interests of short-term financial gain. It is important to remember, though, that this has come about largely because there was no serious opposition to the orthodoxy supported by the city, the Treasury and the Bank of England (Blank, 1977). Industrial capital has not been at all well represented in the policy making process (Grant and Marsh, 1977) and, even when it has, the interests of corporate and multinational capital have tended to dominate. It is fairly clear that a future Labour government will face an enormous task overcoming the vested interests represented by finance capital. It should develop plans for downgrading the Treasury to make it into a Ministry of Finance along the lines of those in continental countries. Responsibility for all economic planning, short term and long term, should be placed in the new Department of Economic and Industrial Planning if the position of the latter is not to be undermined in the same way as the Department of Economic Affairs was in 1965.

Apart from the problem of overcoming obsolete ideology and vested interests, there is an additional question raised by trade planning which is not discussed in the party programme. This is the question of retaliation in response to import controls. As we have seen in Labour's programme, the argument is used that relative trade volumes can be held static even when absolute volumes increase, and this will discourage retaliation. However, there is no simple mechanism which will ensure that this occurs, other than the impossibly cumbersome policy of fixing quotas on all goods and services which are traded. If we place a tariff on a particular commodity, say, cars, there is no way of ensuring that this will prevent imports from countries in surplus with Britain, rather than countries in deficit. Obviously, if the exports of a country in deficit to Britain were reduced by a tariff, the risk of retaliation and a net loss to Britain at the end of the day is much greater than if a country were in surplus to Britain. This is because a country in surplus has more to lose from a trade war with Britain than a country in deficit. It is also the case that import penetration is far too high in many areas, for example cars, where 60 per cent of those sold are imports. In this case there is going to have to be a reduction in absolute volume as well as relative volumes if the British car industry is to survive; this risks retaliation in other areas, if not in cars.

The point about this discussion is that there are real risks of retaliation if Britain takes unilateral action. Trade planning is going to require bilateral negotiations with trade partners to avoid a trade war in which Britain could emerge as a net loser. In such negotiations our bargaining power is directly related to the size of our trade deficit with a given country. If a country has a huge surplus with respect to Britain, such as Japan, we can afford to place very tight quotas, or high tariffs, on its goods. In fact, no real negotiations are necessary in the case of Japan, so large is its surplus. In its case we can simply impose trade quotas, and if they retaliate increase the barriers even more. At the end of the day Japan will lose much more in a trade war than Britain, and this will deter it from retaliating. But, in the case of a country with an approximate balance of trade with Britain, we will have to be much more circumspect to avoid ending up a net loser in any trade war. This reasoning suggests that in the future we will have to move away from multilateral trade towards a system of planned bilateral trade, negotiated with individual countries. The socialist government in France would be sympathetic towards such a planning system, since it actively seeks trade planning itself (Petit, 1982, p. 32). In a limited sense such planning has already occurred at the EEC level with the multifibre agreement and the negotiations on steel, so there are precedents. But a new Labour government should rapidly impose tariffs and quotas on Japanese goods as a symbolic act, to show that things have changed, and thereafter it should seek to negotiate trade levels with all our major partners with a view to establishing parity.

This suggests that the proposals to set up a specialist export division in the new Department of Economic and Industrial Planning are inadequate. What is needed is a trade planning division concerned with promoting exports and import substitutes, but perhaps most importantly preparing briefs for trade negotiations, and supervising the enforcement of agreed quotas. There is also much which can be done to introduce covert trade controls, or complex legal and technical regulations aimed at curbing imports. The Japanese have been particularly adept at using these in the past (Allen, 1978). Trade planning is essentially a political question concerned with balancing the loss of consumer choice and the risks of retaliation, on the one hand, against saving jobs and promoting growth in the domestic economy on the other. If it is to be successful Labour needs to think out its trade planning strategy more thoroughly than it has already.

Another weakness of the trade strategy is that inadequate attention has been paid to the management of exchange rates. The programme states: 'As well as reintroducing exchange controls to prevent massive outflows of domestic capital, Labour will take further action to defend the pound against heavy selling by foreign holders of sterling' (p. 22). Unfortunately there is no mention of how this will be achieved and so, as it stands, this is little more than a pious hope. The major question facing a future Labour government would be the question of the speed and extent of demand reflation. As we have seen, the major constraint on this is the balance of payments and the parity of the pound. The pound will continue to float but it cannot be allowed to float down without limit, since this boosts domestic inflation via rising import prices. Of course, if trade were comprehensively planned there would be no need to worry about rapidly rising imports resulting from reflation. But it is going to take time, at least several years, to negotiate planned trade and in the meantime there is an urgent need to reflate the economy. Thus there is an immediate danger that recovery will be cut short by a balance of payments crisis.

We have seen that the programme sets out the objective of reducing unemployment to below one million within five years. If that is to be achieved, the reflationary stimulus needed is going to be very large indeed. In the programme there are no figures provided on the extent of reflation required to achieve this objective. One suggestion, by the Cambridge Group, is that Labour could reflate the economy by as much as £7 to £8 billion a year for three or four years (CEPR, 1982, p. 2). But even then, in their view, reflation on this scale would still leave unemployment at 1.9 million by 1990 (CEPR, 1982, p. 17). An alternative suggestion comes from the TUC in its annual economic review (TUC, 1982), or 'Programme for Recovery'. In this report the TUC calls for an expansion of £8.3 billion, or 4 per cent of GDP (TUC, 1982, p. 13). It tested out this plan on the Treasury econometric model, and the model forecast a modest rise in inflation, a fall in unemployment by 574,000 and a 3.9 per cent fall in the exchange rate (TUC, 1982, p. 15). It is doubtful how relevant the Treasury model is in accurately estimating the behaviour of the economy in such an unprecedented recession. The model parameters are estimated from many years of data, applicable to a situation quite unlike the present one. Spare capacity undoubtedly exists to support such a reflation, but given the irrationality of currency markets there is likely to be a run on the pound and a currency crisis if reflation on this scale were attempted.

A useful lesson about reflation can be learned from the experience of the Mitterrand government in France. After winning office in 1981 the new government began to reflate the economy by a very modest expansion of demand amounting to 20 billion francs, or 0.7 per cent of GDP (Petit, 1982, p. 29). As a result, it avoided currency problems in its first year of office almost completely. However, the 1982 budget was much more ambitious, combining an expansionary increase in the budget deficit with increased public spending aiming to achieve a growth in GDP of 3 per cent (Petit, 1982, p. 29). Despite a wage freeze and a new austerity programme as well as devaluation, it rapidly began to run into currency problems, and it is now doubtful if France will remain a member of the European Monetary System of fixed exchanges. The major problem facing the French government in 1983–4 is the defence of the franc, despite its willingness to devalue.

If a new Labour government really meant to achieve a reduction of unemployment by 2.5 million in five years, it would have to reflate the economy at a faster rate than that suggested by the TUC and the Cambridge Group, perhaps to the tune of £10 or £12 billion a year. Historically a reduction in unemployment of 500,000 in a year has only been achieved twice this century. This was in 1933, when unemployment fell by 548,000, and again in 1948, when it fell by 1.5 million (Butler and Sloman, 1980, pp. 340–1); the latter figure was artificially boosted by the temporary registration of demobilized troops from the forces. Thus it appears most unlikely that Labour can achieve this goal without a damaging currency crisis leading to another round of deflation. It took more than six years for unemployment to rise from 1 to 3.5 million, and it is going to take longer for it to fall below 1 million again, given the weak state of the British economy.

The Labour government should initiate economic expansion very slowly at first, with an initial package of expansionary measures adding up to perhaps no more than 1 per cent of GDP. It should then proceed faster only when the trade planning strategy provides a guarantee that a flood of imports will not abort the expansion. Trade planning and demand management have to be kept co-ordinated, and the government should proceed carefully on both if expansion is to be sustained in the long run. A return to 'stop–go' would be disastrous.

Unfortunately the Labour government may not be in a position to control the speed of reflation. After years of wage control, primarily achieved via unemployment, there is a real risk of a wages explosion once reflation is attempted. The most fundamental weakness of the entire economic strategy is the failure to plan for an incomes policy to cover the interim period whilst the domestic economy expands and trade planning is implemented. If there is a wage explosion in the first year or so of the new government this will undoubtedly ruin economic recovery. We have seen earlier that the programme specifically rules out wage restraint, but it does contain a very cryptic reference to 'a need for a national economic assessment of the prospects for the growth of the economy, involving such key issues as the use of resources between personal consumption, public and private investment, public services and the balance of trade' (p. 24). It appears that the aim is to try to get some sort of incomes policy by stealth. The great problem with this approach is that it takes a massive crisis of the magnitude of 1975 to frighten the trade union leadership into accepting such a policy. Instead of using an incomes policy to avert the crisis, it can only be used in an attempt to recover from it. Labour should have the courage in opposition to argue the case for an incomes policy, and attack the fundamentally dishonest argument that Labour can plan the economy and trade without planning incomes. It goes without saying, of course, that an incomes policy should include all incomes as well as profits and dividends and it should be managed in conjunction with price restraint. But without it there is a real danger that the growth strategy will collapse in the first year.

There is a line of argument developed by some economists (Meade, 1982; Layard, 1982) which holds that an incomes policy can be imposed through the tax system without the agreement of industry and the trade union movement. For example, Layard's scheme would operate by imposing a tax on firms related to the size of the wage claims they concede. He writes: 'Under the tax any firm that gives a £1 wage increase will lose not only the pound, but also £1 times the tax rate. If the tax rate were 100 per cent, it would lose £2; if the tax rate were infinite, it would lose everything' (p. 225). There are two major problems with this approach. The first is that it places the entire burden of enforcement on industry, at a time when industry has been severely weakened by the recession, and by monetarism. In this situation the tax is as likely to produce additional unemployment as it is to produce lower wage settlements. A related point is that industry is likely to oppose such a scheme for this reason, which would undermine any support the government might achieve amongst industrialists for the economic strategy. The second problem is that the scheme is likely to politicize the tax system. One can envisage unions calling for a collective withdrawal from the PAYE system; it will give an enormous stimulus to the black economy by making taxes seem illegitimate in the eyes of many people; and it might even provoke tax strikes. The truth is that incomes policies cannot be made effective without the acquiescence, if not the agreement, of the trade union movement. There are no clever technical devices or short-cuts which will get round what is basically a political problem. It is true that incomes policies have never been successful for longer than about three years in Britain. But such a policy is only required to fill the interim before expansion and trade planning allow increases in real incomes. The fundamental need is to avoid a wages explosion which will abort the expansion before it can get under way.

We have argued that a future Labour government should avoid a currency crisis by slow reflation coupled with an incomes policy and trade planning. However, such is the instability and irrationality of international financial markets that this may not be enough to prevent a currency crisis similar to the one of 1976. Such a crisis is quite capable of occurring totally independently of the state of the real economy, as international speculators seek to promote and profit from a devaluation. A Labour government should prepare plans well in advance for dealing with this – plans which specifically rule out the traditional policy of deflation. It should be prepared to suspend all currency transactions for a temporary period and introduce a centralized system of currency allocations. In other words, market allocation should be replaced by bureaucratic allocation for a period until it is safe to restore the market. This is not an easy option and it would undoubtedly disrupt trade, but it is essential that a Labour government should be prepared to sacrifice the market for sterling in order to protect the growth strategy. The central currency exchange agency would buy or sell sterling according to a predetermined system of priorities. Some type of end-user certification would be needed to ensure that currency was being put to the use specified. Trade and the financing of exports would be given the highest priority, and anyone attempting to convert sterling purely for speculative purposes would be refused. This system would have the additional advantage of providing an excellent policy instrument for enforcing import controls. Once it had been imposed it would have to be removed very gradually if currency speculation were not to be resumed again at a level damaging to the growth strategy. The system should be used as a last resort to deal with the problem of the exchange rate. It would have to be imposed in the teeth of opposition from the City and the Bank of England. But it would be essential in such a crisis to protect the real economy.

The key problems in the economic strategy concern macroeconomic policy. The employment and training policies are, however, an important part of the growth strategy, but they will take a long time to implement. The same is true of the industrial strategy. The ideas for a National Planning Council, a strengthened National Enterprise Board and a new investment bank are essential for long-term growth. But in the case of the industrial strategy a future Labour government will face the same dilemma as it did in 1974: should it co-operate with or confront industry? In view of the possibility of unrelenting hostility from the City to the alternative strategy, it would be wise for Labour to try to build alliances with industrial capitalism. This means doing one important thing: it should drop the proposals in the industrial strategy which are strongly opposed by industry and which are not central to the question of industrial regeneration. We have already mentioned the question of industrial democracy. Industry will probably not baulk at measures to increase rights of disclosure and employee access to certain kinds of information. But it would bitterly oppose anything like the Bullock proposals for full scale employee representation on company boards. Given that the TUC was distinctly lukewarm in its reaction to Bullock, any proposals on these lines should be dropped. For the same reason, the party should drop unnecessary proposals for the public ownership of existing firms unless there is a clear rationale for doing so. There is such a rationale in the case of pharmaceuticals, whose profiteering from the National Health Service has become something of a scandal. But what is the reason for nationalizing the construction industry or road haulage? It is unlikely that public ownership will improve efficiency or create jobs in these industries. Public ownership should be used to establish new industries under the aegis of the National Enterprise Board, where possible in conjunction with the private sector. It is in the stimulation of 'sunrise' industries, like micro-electronics and computers, that public ownership can make the greatest contribution. The virtue of this approach is that it not only fills an important gap in stimulating new enterprise and providing risk capital, it is politically uncontroversial. Industry will not oppose joint enterprises, or even wholly state-owned enterprises in new areas, in the same way as it will oppose the public ownership of existing firms. Thus INMOS, the micro-chip manufacturer, was established with a grant from the NEB without any political controversy. This would not be the case if Labour attempted to nationalize GEC; if this were done it would poison relationships with industry for no good purpose. This means that the political aim behind the industrial strategy should be to try to recruit industrial capital as an ally against finance capital, which is the real enemy of the alternative economic strategy. The Labour government should be prepared to confront industry only in those matters which are absolutely central to reconstruction, such as curbs on the export of capital. On other questions which are peripheral to the main strategy it should seek co-operation. Given that industry will benefit enormously from an economic policy based on stimulating the real economy, the possibilities for building alliances with industrial capital are immense, after the years of monetarist destruction.

To summarize our discussion, we have argued that Labour's economic strategy represents an important new departure in economic management, and it gives real hope for industrial reconstruction. But there are important flaws in the strategy, particularly the absence of an incomes policy, and the failure to recognize that trade planning needs to be negotiated with our trade partners, with the clear exception of Japan. If the strategy is to be successful Labour needs to make a decisive break with the past, which includes Keynesianism as well as monetarism. Policy making needs to concentrate on the medium term and long term and to abandon the myopia of the Keynesian era. Ultimately it is the short-sightedness of policy makers, together with an obsolete ideological commitment to free trade, which are the biggest obstacles to industrial reconstruction and a long-term return to full employment.

Labour's social security plans

The major innovation in the plans for social security in the 1982 programme is the clear linkage which is made between social security benefits on the one hand and taxation on the other. Labour is committed to the reforming of taxation as well as benefits and this is a clear departure from the 1973 programme, which discussed these questions separately.

To consider the taxation proposals first, the main priority is to raise tax thresholds as a direct measure to help the low paid. The programme states: 'The basic tax threshold will be increased at least in line with inflation every year, with substantial additional increases over a 5 year period, the objective being to place the tax thresholds above supplementary benefit levels' (p. 89). A more long-term aim is to re-introduce reduced tax rates below the 30 per cent standard rate for those on low incomes. At the other end of the scale, there is a commitment 'to act to limit the open-ended nature of tax reliefs so that the better-off no longer benefit disproportionately' (p. 90); this is coupled with a commitment to reduce tax allowances on business perks. There is a plan to abolish the married man's additional personal allowance on the grounds that it discriminates against women, and this, together with the proposals for a wealth tax, represents a major step forward towards greater equality and justice in taxation.

The proposals for a wealth tax are fairly radical. The aim is 'to introduce an annual tax on personal wealth, applying to the most wealthy 1 per cent of the population. The exemption limit for Labour's wealth tax would be set around £150,000 in 1982 prices, and would of course be adjusted with inflation' (pp. 91–2). The aim is to keep exemptions to a minimum, so that owner occupied houses and future pension rights discounted to their present value would be eligible for tax. But rates would be set so as to remove from assessment 'the entire pension rights of the great majority of the working population' (p. 92). The anticipated revenue from the wealth tax is between £600 and £800 million per annum at current prices. In addition to the wealth tax, the capital transfer tax, which was introduced by the last Labour government as primarily a tax on inherited wealth, will be restored to full effectiveness, following its emasculation by the Conservatives.

On the issue of indirect taxation, there is a commitment to abolish VAT in the long run and replace it by a system of purchase taxes which will be less costly to collect, and which can be used to discriminate more easily between luxury goods and essentials. Finally, there is a commitment to crack down on tax avoidance, with the introduction of an important new

principle. This is the principle that 'artificial transactions' aimed principally at tax avoidance will be disregarded in assessments. This system
already operates in a number of European countries.

On the benefits side of social security, the most important objective
in the programme is the reduction in the numbers dependent on means
tested benefits. This will be done by increasing the value of national
insurance benefits, improving child benefit and improving and extending
various non-contributory benefits for the disabled. The aim is to link all
social security benefits to the rise in prices or earnings, whichever is the
greater. This was done by the last Labour government in the case of long
term national insurance benefits, but this was repealed by the Conservatives.

One of the largest groups in need in the future will be the unemployed. The programme involves extending the long-term rate of
supplementary benefits to the unemployed as a first step, but in the long
run the aim is to reduce their dependence on means tested benefits. The
programme restates the original Beveridge plan to pay benefits at a rate,
and for as long as needed, to ensure adequate maintenance without
means tested supplementation. Another group likely to be in poverty is
single parent families. The Finer Report suggested that they receive a
guaranteed maintenance allowance. Labour rejects this, however,
because it would be means tested. Instead there is a proposal to increase
the special single parent allowance of the child benefit.

The proposals for pensions are based largely on Labour's 1975
Pensions Act. In the long run this will ensure that total state retirement
pensions will be at least one-third of average earnings for a single person,
and half for a married couple. As we saw earlier, the problem with the
pensions plan is that it gives very little help to current pensioners or
pensioners who retire well before the full implementation of the scheme.
The plans to give additional help for this group are rather vague. The
programme suggests that the basic state pension could be supplemented,
but there is no firm commitment to do this. The reluctance to make any
firm commitment to pensioners stems, of course, from the huge cost of
doing so; there is an estimate in the programme that the cost of extending
full pension rights under the 1975 Act to all current pensioners would be
£8 billion per annum (p. 94), i.e. approximately 4 per cent of GDP. This
makes it difficult to achieve any substantial improvements in the position
of pensioners, at least in the short run. Thus pensioners in real need will
continue to depend on supplementary benefits under a future Labour
government. However, the commitment to index-link all benefits will
ensure that their value is retained over time.

There are no comprehensive new schemes in the 1982 programme
analogous to the pensions plan implemented in 1975. But the proposals
for index-linking benefits, for raising the tax threshold and for reforming

the tax system in other ways imply a substantial degree of redistribution. Ultimately the success of the social security programme depends upon the success of the economic strategy. If, for example, unemployment were halved within the lifetime of the Labour government this alone would enormously improve matters. It would reduce the large numbers of the people in poverty by getting them back to work, it would increase tax yields and considerably lighten the social security burden as claimants became wage earners. This would release resources for more generous benefits elsewhere. Ultimately social security policy, in common with other areas of policy, comes down to resources, and so the failure of the economic strategy would probably mean the failure of the social security strategy.

Reversing the Labour decline

This discussion leads to the following basic conclusion: if Labour can turn the economy round it can turn around its own postwar decline. There is an important historical lesson to be learned by Labour in the current situation from the experience of the Social Democratic Party in Sweden. When the Social Democrats took office in 1932 they were short of an overall parliamentary majority (Martin, 1979). They had developed what was essentially a Keynesian strategy for economic management aimed at getting Sweden out of the severe recession experienced by all European countries in the 1930s. The Right and Centre–Right opposed their plan for the expansion of demand for orthodox reasons; it was argued that the budget ought to be cut in a recession, rather than expanded to provide incentives for businessmen. Needless to say, in the absence of effective demand, budget cuts were the opposite to what was needed. The Social Democrats achieved a parliamentary majority by forming an alliance with the dissident wing of the Agrarian Party. They agreed to boost farm prices, and abandoned their previous opposition to tariffs on agricultural produce in exchange for support from the Agrarians for their new economic strategy. It was a great success, and largely because of the success of this strategy they stayed in power for forty-four years until 1976.

The moral of this story is not that Labour should revert to a simple Keynesianism, but that a decisive break with the past which transforms the economy can produce a long-term electoral re-alignment which benefits the party implementing the successful strategy. The only party which currently offers a new departure and a chance to rebuild our industrial base is the Labour Party. The Conservatives offered a radical new economic policy in 1979 which represented a decisive break with the past. But all this brought was the disaster of monetarism, which has now substantially been abandoned. The radical Right alternative has been tried by the Conservatives and found wanting by them, but at the time of writing they have no alternative, and this gives Labour a unique opportunity to chart a new course.

As we said earlier, the arrival of the Social Democratic Party and the new Liberal/SDP Alliance complicates the electoral picture in the immediate future. The problem facing the Alliance is that it has not developed any real alternative strategy to Keynesianism. The Alliance advocates policies which have been tried, and which worked successfully when they were allowed to, but which ultimately failed. Moreover, they share a romantic attachment to the Common Market, which is itself a barrier to trade planning. Contemporary liberalism, in so far as it exists, shares an ideological attachment to free trade along with the Conservatives which would prevent an Alliance government from implementing effective planned trade. The economic policy of an Alliance government would involve a return to 'stop–go' economic management, with no hope of preventing long-term decline. To make matters worse, the Social Democrats show every sign of being as hostile to the trade union movement as the Conservatives. For this reason, they would be unable to agree an incomes policy with the trade unions, which, as we have argued, is an essential part of the recovery programme. Of course, they might attempt to introduce an incomes policy by legislation but, as the experience of the Heath government demonstrated in 1973–4, a statutory policy without the agreement of the unions is worthless. Ultimately no government can send thousands of trade unionists to jail for breaking such a policy. For these reasons an Alliance government, or a coalition involving the Alliance is unlikely to agree an economic policy which will be an effective strategy for industrial regeneration.

The Labour Party stands at a crucial turning point in its existence. It has to decide whether to chart a genuinely new course, or whether to pursue the old orthodoxies whilst pretending to its dwindling band of supporters that it is doing something else. It will not survive a re-run of the Wilson or Callaghan governments as a major political party. If Labour can turn the economy round it can save itself, and Britain, from the long postwar decline. If it can stop the internal quarrelling, and unite around a credible economic strategy, it can win electoral success. But if it takes power and fails to chart a new course, it will be rightly condemned and abandoned by the millions of people who look to it to defend them and their interests. It is a heavy responsibility to bear, and it will not get a second chance.

9

Postscript:
The 1983 General Election

It would be an understatement to say that the 1983 General Election was a bad defeat for Labour. The statistics of this election have by now been well reviewed in the press. In terms of the share of the popular vote the result was Labour's worst since 1918; in terms of parliamentary seats the result was the worst since 1935; and if one cares to calculate the average Labour vote per candidate the results were worse than those of the 1930s. In this sense one has to look at the General Elections before the First World War when the party was in its infancy to see a worse performance.

The summary statistics of the 1983 election appear in Table 9.1, which also includes the results of the 1979 election. The most striking feature of these results, apart from the sharp decline in the Labour share of the vote, was the fact that the Conservatives increased their parliamentary representation by thirty-six seats with a smaller vote than in 1979. This result was of course produced by an electoral system which magnifies a lead in the popular vote, but also by the boundary reorganization which gave the Conservatives a distinct advantage. One of the most disturbing things about this reorganization was that although the boundary commissioners were politically independent they worked within a framework of boundaries arising from the local government reorganization of the early 1970s. It has been shown that this reorganization produced boundaries which clearly favoured the Conservatives, as it was designed to do so by the then minister, Peter Walker (Newton, 1983). Labour has suffered a loss of seats in the two General Elections since 1974 as a direct result of this. In the future Labour and others will have to look at this whole question again to ensure that boundaries fairly reflect political support in the country.

The task facing the Labour Party at the next General Election in the

Table 9.1 The results of the 1983 General Election in Great Britain

	Total vote	Percentage of all votes		Percentage of electorate	Seat changes	Total seats
		1983	1979			
Conservatives	12,991,377	43.5	43.9	31.6	+36	397
Labour	8,437,120	28.3	36.9	20.6	−44	209
Alliance	7,775,048	26.1	13.8	18.9	+8	23
SNP	331,975	1.1	1.6	0.8	0	2
Plaid Cymru	125,309	0.4	0.4	0.3	0	2
Others	183,877	0.6	1.2	0.4	—	—
Total vote	29,844,706					

Turnout: 72.7 per cent. Estimated swing to Conservatives using BBC/ITN calculations of 1979 vote = 3.8 per cent. Conservative overall majority = 144.

late 1980s is formidable. To win an overall majority Labour would need to capture 116 seats, assuming the Speaker remains Conservative. To achieve this would require a swing of 10.9 per cent from the Conservatives to Labour, which is just less than the swing of 11.8 per cent achieved in 1945. This task has been made more difficult by the fact that Labour has been pushed into third place by the SDP/Liberal Alliance in so many seats. Of the 397 Conservative seats in the new House of Commons following the election, the Alliance came second in 265 and Labour in 125. So the party has to capture nearly all the seats in which it was placed second in 1983, or it has to split the Conservative and Alliance votes sufficiently to capture seats in which it currently ranks third. By any standards this is a daunting task.

However, a careful analysis of the period immediately preceding the 1983 General Election shows that the electoral position of the Labour Party is far from hopeless. There were special factors at work in 1983 which are unlikely to occur in the future. This means that Labour can recover lost ground provided that it learns the lessons of the defeat. There is a good case for saying that Labour lost the election essentially in 1981, and had not the Falklands War occurred, it might well have recovered ground and run the Conservatives a much closer race in 1983. The evidence for this can be seen in the opinion polls. In Table 9.2 we can observe the voting intentions of the electorate at key times during the period 1979 to 1983 as measured in the Gallup Polls. In this table we can see that immediately following the 1979 General Election Labour was slightly ahead of the Conservatives in voting intentions, with the Liberals receiving rather less than their vote share of 13.8 per cent at the election. As time went on Labour gradually improved its position, so that by January 1981 it was some 13.5 per cent ahead of the Conservatives with a comfortable 46.5 per cent of the vote. During the same period the Liberals

Table 9.2 Levels of party support at key times from 1979 to 1983

Date	Conservatives	Labour	Liberal	SDP
June 1979	42.0	43.5	12.0	—
June 1980	40.5	45.0	11.5	—
January 1981	33.0	46.5	18.5	—
February 1981	36.0	35.5	20.0	—
March 1981	30.0	34.0	18.0	14.0
September 1981	32.0	36.5	11.5	17.5
December 1981	23.0	23.5	14.5	36.0
March 1982	31.5	33.0	11.5	19.5
May 1982	41.5	28.0	9.5	13.5
July 1982	46.5	27.5	7.5	13.0
May 1983	46.0	33.0	19*	
June 1983 (eve of poll)	45.5	26.5	26*	

* Denotes Alliance support

Source: Gallup Political Index, various issues.

had also improved their position at the expense of the Conservatives. If a General Election had been held at that time Labour would have achieved a substantial majority.

At that point the party embarked on the damaging series of public disputes over the deputy leadership, the split with the Social Democrats, and over entryism. The January 1981 special conference had a particularly significant impact on Labour support, reducing it by 11 per cent, according to the Gallup Polls, in a single month. By December 1981 the party was at the nadir of its electoral performance, reduced to an all-time low level of support of 23.5 per cent. It was in the same month that the Social Democratic Party reached the highpoint of their support at 36 per cent. However, another important feature of the polls in December 1981 was that, despite the bad Labour performance, the Conservative level of support was even worse at 23 per cent. Essentially the events of 1981 had damaged both major parties, but they had the effect of reducing the Labour lead over the Conservatives, which as we saw was substantial in January 1981, down to an insignificant 0.5 per cent. Interestingly enough, from December 1981 to May 1982, when the Falklands War had its first dramatic effect on public opinion, both major parties gradually improved their position, largely at the expense of the SDP, so that in March 1982 Labour's lead over the Conservatives was 1.5 per cent.

We shall of course never know what would have happened to public opinion had the Falklands War not occurred. But there are reasonable grounds for arguing that in this event Labour would have continued to gain ground slowly at the expense of the SDP, and to a lesser extent the Conservatives, and by 1983 would have gone into an election with a reasonably good chance of winning. At any rate the poll evidence should be kept in mind by those who try to argue that the Alliance has effectively replaced Labour as the party of opposition. It is clear that the Alliance star was already on the wane in early 1982 before the convulsions of the Falklands War.

The Falklands War changed everything and gave an immediate boost to the Conservatives, who by July 1982 had achieved a massive lead at the expense of both Labour and, more particularly, the Alliance: the Alliance support in that month was down to 20.5 per cent from over 50 per cent some seven months previously. From the summer of 1982 to the General Election the Conservative support was maintained at this high level. But this was not really surprising; an analysis of the polls over the period 1947 to 1975 has shown that a significant political event such as key strike or a major political row continued to influence public opinion for up to twelve months after the initial impact (Whiteley, 1979). It was obvious that an event of the political magnitude of the Falklands War would have an impact over a rather longer period, and this gave the Conservative government a wide 'window of opportunity' for calling a General Election. Thus, although it was not widely discussed during the election campaign, the Falklands War still had a very great influence on the outcome of the election.

We should not conclude from this, however, that Labour would have automatically won a General Election in 1983 or 1984 in the absence of the Falklands War. The fact remains that there were grave problems with Labour's campaign. We can see in Table 9.2 that the last pre-election campaign Gallup Poll gave Labour 33 per cent of the popular vote in May 1983, and the eve-of-poll support was 26.5 per cent. Although the poll share was rather larger than this at 28.3 per cent, the evidence points clearly to the conclusion that Labour lost ground substantially during the campaign itself. Why should this have occurred? We examine this question next.

Labour's election campaign: the credibility gap

We have argued in earlier chapters that performance, particularly in relation to economic management, is the main factor behind Labour's present crises. The 1983 General Election campaign strongly reinforced this conclusion.

We saw in Chapter 4 that economic performance rather than electoral promises was decisive in influencing electoral behaviour. In the 1983 election the key problem for the Labour Party was that neither its performance as an opposition nor its policy proposals for economic

Table 9.3   The electorate's evaluation of party performances in the 1983 General Election

If elected would the Labour/Conservative/ Alliance:	Labour		Conservatives		Alliance	
	All voters	Labour voters	All voters	Conservative voters	All voters	Alliance voters
reduce unemployment?						
would	50	84	30	58	44	79
would not	42	12	59	27	39	11
keep inflation down?						
would	22	46	68	89	36	61
would not	65	32	25	7	39	22
bring about better industrial relations?						
would	53	84	38	69	44	73
would not	37	9	50	17	33	10
care about the interests of people like you?						
would	50	86	45	74	63	91
would not	40	9	47	12	23	5
govern in the interests of the country as a whole?						
would	48	85	55	92	65	95
would not	40	8	38	4	21	4
keep its promises?						
would	34	72	46	80	46	79
would not	53	18	42	11	43	13

Source: The Observer, 22 May 1983, 29 May 1983 and 5 June 1983 (surveys based on quota samples of just over 1000 electors in 50 constituencies).

recovery were credible in the eyes of many voters. That coupled with widespread scepticism about the abilities of the Labour leadership meant that the party lost ground heavily during the election campaign.

The evidence for this conclusion comes from a series of polls carried out for *The Observer* by the Harris research agency during the election campaign. The results of these polls are given in Table 9.3. In this table the electorate were asked to say whether they thought a particular party would or would not do various things if they were elected. Thus the polls provide interesting evidence on voters' evaluations of the credibility of the different political parties.

In Table 9.3 we can see that Labour had a distinct advantage on the issue of unemployment, with 50 per cent of the electorate and 84 per cent of Labour voters believing that it would reduce unemployment. However,

Labour's advantage on this issue compared with the Alliance was not great, and in particular was not great amongst Conservative voters, 58 per cent of whom thought that the Conservative Party would reduce unemployment. By contrast, the Conservatives had a much greater advantage on the issue of inflation. Some 68 per cent of the electorate thought that they would keep inflation down, compared with a mere 22 per cent for Labour. On this issue Labour failed to obtain a majority even of its own supporters, since only 46 per cent of Labour voters thought it would succeed on inflation. The pattern of responses to the question on industrial relations is rather similar to the question on unemployment: Labour had a small advantage over the Alliance, but Conservative voters were not convinced that their own party would do a bad job on this issue.

The last three indicators in Table 9.3 are interesting because they do not focus closely on particular policy areas but ask more general questions which provide rough indicators of affective evaluations. As we saw in Chapter 4 these are particularly significant in influencing voting behaviour. In the three areas of looking after individuals' interests, looking after the interests of the country and in keeping promises, the SDP/Liberal Alliance did better than Labour. Labour did better than the Conservatives on individuals' interests, but not on the interests of the country as a whole. Most significant of all, barely a third of the electorate thought that Labour would keep its promises, a significantly smaller percentage than the Conservatives and the Alliance.

There are two broad conclusions to be drawn from this evidence. Firstly, Labour is still the preferred party on the question of unemployment, which was the most salient issue in the campaign. However, the electorate did not believe that Labour would significantly reduce unemployment without stimulating inflation. For this reason it lost any real advantage it might have had over the Conservatives on this issue, whose lead on the issue of inflation was impregnable. Secondly, Labour's promises were significantly less credible than those of the other parties, and it lost important ground to the Alliance in terms of voters' perceptions that it would look after their interests. Undoubtedly this credibility gap, which appears most clearly in the highly salient areas of economic management, also served to undermine Labour's appeal in other areas of policy.

The consequences of this credibility gap in terms of lost support among key groups in the electorate could be seen in a survey carried out by Gallup for the BBC which was reported in *The Guardian* (13 and 14 June 1983). The survey showed that 37 per cent of the electorate who supported Labour in 1979 switched their votes in 1983. Some 22 per cent switched support to the Alliance, 7 per cent switched to the Conservatives and 7 per cent did not vote at all. Of the group switching from Labour, some 33 per cent worked in the private sector compared with 29 per cent in the public sector. Thus production sector status marginally influenced the vote. However, the really striking impact was consumption sector status, particularly in relation to housing. No less than 59 per cent of the people who had voted Labour in 1979 and then bought their own council house switched from Labour in 1983, which testifies to the strength of consumption sector status. The party lost the largest percentage (12 per cent) amongst skilled manual workers, and the smallest percentage (4 per cent) amongst the unemployed.

The Gallup/BBC surveys show that the conclusions reached in Chapter 4 about the social class and sectoral composition of Labour support continued to apply in 1983. Relationships to the means of production were important, but they were eclipsed by consumption sector status, and the increasingly important claimant sector status.

Most significantly, the Conservatives were rewarded at the election for their success in reducing inflation, but they were not punished for their performance on unemployment in a way which helped Labour because Labour's strategy for dealing with this issue was not credible in the eyes of many voters.

In the light of these conclusions we can draw certain inferences about Labour's strategy in the future.

Labour's electoral future

In the face of such an electoral defeat there is bound to be much confusion about the way forward, and many suggestions, some of them foolish, will be made about what should be done. Some will take the view that the party should pursue a kind of centrist 'Poujadism' eschewing all policy positions which appear to be unpopular. A variation on this theme which is often not recognized as such is the tactic of promising large and increasing benefits to various minority groups in the belief that they will thereby vote Labour, and when all aggregated together form a majority. This is fundamentally mistaken because it produces what might be described as a 'maximalist' manifesto which, because it promises more for everyone, does not succeed in impressing anyone because it is not credible.

Others will take the view that nothing needs to be done since the party programme will at some undefined date in the future bring electoral victory because of the failures of the Conservative government. This is also fundamentally mistaken since it ignores the fact that the anti-Conservative vote need not come to the Labour Party but could easily go to the Alliance or some political descendant of it.

The starting point of a rethink of Labour's position is to recognize that electoral dealignment does not necessarily mean electoral realignment. That is, defectors from the Labour Party to the Conservative and

Alliance parties do not become strongly identified with these parties in a way which would prevent them from returning to Labour in the future. This is particularly true of the Alliance vote. There is convincing evidence that the Alliance vote is much more weakly attached than that of the other two parties, although it is also true that attachment to them has been declining significantly over time. In this respect support for the Alliance is very similar to the Liberal vote before 1981. This was confirmed in a series of Gallup Polls carried out in early 1982 when voters were asked how closely they identified with their preferred party. Some 31 per cent of Conservatives and 31 per cent of Labour voters identified very or fairly closely with their parties, whereas only 13 per cent of Liberals and 12 per cent of SDP voters did this (Crewe, 1982b, p. 290). Even more significantly, a total of 68 per cent of Liberals and 71 per cent of SDP voters thought that they were not close to any party at all. Thus Labour voters who have been lost to the Alliance in 1983 can be won back in the future.

The poll evidence together with our analysis in earlier chapters suggests some propositions which the party should take note of if it is to renew itself and avoid another electoral defeat on the scale of 1983. The first of these propositions concerns the question of constitutional reform which, as we noted earlier, divided the party after 1980. There should be no more constitutional changes for the foreseeable future, unless they are achieved by broad consensus. The constitutional changes made in 1981 should be left alone, even if they are not ideal from the point of view of intra-party democracy. Any other course of action will only serve to reopen the breaches made in 1981 and after.

A second proposition is that the party should avoid anything which appears to be a 'maximalist' manifesto of the type referred to earlier. This does not mean a wholesale revision of party policy, but it does mean abandoning extravagant commitments which cannot be credibly met. For example, it is right for the party to maintain a commitment to full employment on moral, on economic and on political grounds. But there can be little doubt that the commitment to reduce unemployment to under 1 million in five years was a mistake. This was not credible and it partly explains the evidence we can observe in Table 9.3. A similar point could be made about the commitment to complete unilateral nuclear disarmament within the lifetime of one Parliament. If there is wide support for unilateral disarmament in the party, it is right that this objective should be maintained. But it was folly to commit the party to a rigid timetable which ignored any developments in East–West negotiations on mutual force reductions. The commitment to cancel Trident and Cruise was electorally popular and credible, but not the undertaking to cancel Polaris whilst at the same time suggesting that it be included in East–West negotiations. This appeared to be confused and incoherent, and when the disagreements surfaced among the leadership over this issue during the campaign they did much harm.

A third proposition which derives from the second is that the party must develop and articulate a coherent economic strategy, since this is the centrepiece of any political programme. Without repeating the arguments of Chapter 8 this involves four separate but related issues. Firstly, it involves slow reflation, rather than a rapid reflation which will undoubtedly produce an inflationary wages explosion. Secondly, it involves negotiated trade planning which should be run in harness with the reflationary strategy. Thirdly, it involves a prices and incomes policy which is designed to prevent a wages explosion aborting recovery once reflation is underway. Finally, it involves an industrial policy which emphasizes intervention working with the market and concentrates on 'sunrise' industries, and not interventions working against the market propping up 'sunset' industries. At the broadest level, a coherent economic strategy involves policies which look at the medium and long term and which promote the growth of the real economy, and aims at removing constraints on this wherever they arise. The strategy should be worked out in opposition and presented to the electorate before the next election. It will not be easy, since it will involve subsuming all other economic objectives to the growth strategy, and in the case of incomes policy it will require long hours of hard work and persuasion to get the trade union movement to endorse and support it. But this is probably the single most important task facing the party in opposition.

A fourth proposition has not really been discussed very much, but it arises from the analysis of electoral behaviour in Chapter 4. It concerns the style of political debate and campaigning of the party, particularly during the election. It is far too confrontationist and negative, being concerned with vilifying opponents and abusing their policies rather than presenting a positive alternative. Despite the slogan 'Think positive, vote positive, vote Labour', which was used extensively in the election, Labour's campaign generally came across as sour and strident, and in at least one case was clearly counter-productive. This was Denis Healey's notorious attack on Mrs Thatcher for 'glorying in slaughter' over the Falklands War.

The argument that Labour's campaign should have been much more positive derives from an analysis of voters' affective evaluations of the party. It may be recalled that the strongest predictor of the probability of voting Labour in Chapter 4 was the affective evaluation scale. It is possible to probe in more detail the nature of this from replies to an open-ended question in the 1979 British Election Study about what people liked about the Labour Party. The answers to this question were very varied, but 63 per cent of respondents mentioned at least one thing they liked about the party, and many mentioned more than this. The most common thing cited in replies was that 'the party supports the working class'. This should be read in conjunction with another question asking individuals whether or not they thought of themselves as belonging to a particular social class. Some 28 per cent of the total sample agreed that they did, and thought of themselves as working class. A further 33 per cent also identified with the working class when they were probed about class affiliations. Class attachment may not be very strong in Britain, but nevertheless 61 per cent of the sample described themselves as working class. Thus the Labour Party would do much better if it stressed the need to help and support ordinary working people and their families, rather than abusing opponents or arguing within itself. It needs to listen more to its natural supporters so that it can learn from them, as well as appeal to their concerns and aspirations. One of the dangers of middle-class radical dominance in the party is that Labour can lose touch with these supporters and become preoccupied with symbolic and expressive questions when the working class are essentially instrumental in their approach to politics.

To summarize these points, the Labour Party needs to make its central economic strategy credible, and to present this positively so that it can appeal to the natural majority of people in the country who think of themselves as working class. It should avoid any more constitutional or symbolic arguments, which divide it and give voters the impression that the party is not fit to govern. Finally, it should avoid a strident anti-system type of rhetoric and instead emphasize the planning and caring aspects of party ideology.

It would be foolish to make any definite predictions about electoral behaviour in the late 1980s. But we can make inferences about the political and economic situation likely to face Britain on the assumption that the present policies of the government are maintained. The team at the University of Cambridge Department of Applied Economics have examined the prospects for 'spontaneous recovery' on existing policies before 1990. Their record in forecasting unemployment has been particularly good in the recent past. They point out that demographic trends, changes in female participation rates and deindustrialization imply that substantial economic growth will be required in the 1980s merely to stabilize the increase in unemployment. They conclude that 'well over 2 million jobs would have to be created by 1990 outside the manufacturing sector to stabilize unemployment at its present level. At least 1½ million jobs would probably be needed to prevent a further increase in the number officially registered as unemployed' (*Cambridge Economic Policy Review*, 1982, p. 7). Their prediction is that unemployment will reach 4.5 million by 1990 on present policies.

This kind of trend, together with the growth in other categories of claimants discussed in Chapter 7, will certainly produce a major fiscal crisis before the end of the 1980s. The government will be faced with the alternatives of making punitive reductions in the real value of benefits or allowing the burden of taxation to spiral upwards. The central question of British politics in the late 1980s will be claimant politics. Of course, if claimant politics were a substitute for class politics, then the Conservatives might hope to sustain a winning electoral coalition based upon rising real incomes for those in work, and falling real incomes for claimants. However, claimant politics is much more likely to reinforce class politics rather than become a substitute for it. This is because the fiscal crisis will imply large cuts in the health, housing and education services as well as in social welfare, in a way which is likely to reinforce class politics. The private sector–public distinction in health care, for example, is basically a class issue rather than a claimant issue; that is, the great bulk of the working class will never be able to afford private health care, so it will be difficult to construct a two-tier health service, one private and the other public, in the belief that this will be acceptable to most of the working population. A similar point can be made about further advances of the private sector in the housing field. We are rapidly reaching the financial limits of council house sales, due to the low incomes of the remaining council tenants. It seems plausible that the Conservatives have reaped the bulk of the political benefits to be gained from such sales. The evidence on dealignment suggests that newly privatized tenants will not necessarily remain loyalist Conservative voters in the future, particularly when they are increasingly likely to become unemployed. So it may be that the fiscal crisis will reverse some of the trends in consumption sector status which have benefited the Conservatives throughout the 1970s.

There is another, international, dimension to the economic crisis facing the British government in the 1980s. There are two aspects to this: firstly, the huge budget deficit in the United States produced by Reaganomics, specifically the policy of making tax cuts along with huge increases in defence spending. This will produce a secular trend rise in interest rates, unless the US administration radically changes course. This alone could abort any spontaneous recovery in the British economy as interest rates rise in order to stabilize the pound. The second aspect is the real possibility that one or more of the huge debtor nations in the international monetary system, such as Brazil and Mexico, will default on the repayment of loans. This will precipitate a major crisis in the international banking system as bad if not worse than the OPEC crisis of the early 1970s. It will also threaten the continued viability of some major British banks. In view of their profligate use of domestically generated funds to finance the growth of military dictatorships, there will be considerable political opprobrium attached to any government which decides to bail these institutions out. But the major problem for the domestic economy will come from the adverse consequences of such a crisis for world trade; it could severely damage exports, not to mention invisible earnings. Thus the international economic system does not appear to provide a favourable environment for spontaneous recovery in the 1980s.

This discussion implies that the political environment for a Labour Party resurgence in the late 1980s could be very favourable, provided the party learns the lessons of the 1983 defeat. The party has a long way to go to climb back to power, but this is not an impossible task provided that it knows where it is going.

Appendix I
A non-technical review
of the statistical methods

We use two types of statistical technique which may be unfamiliar to some readers. These are correlation and regression and factor analysis. In this appendix we give a basic introduction to these methods, aimed at the non-quantitative reader.

Correlation and regression

The starting point of an understanding of correlation and regression is the idea of a linear function. This is a relationship between two variables which traces out a straight line on a graph.

For example, let variable y be the distance travelled by a car in feet and variable x be time measured in seconds. Suppose we measure the relationship between distance and time and get the following observations:

y (feet)	x (seconds)
50	1
100	2
150	3
200	4

These can be represented in diagrammatic form as in Figure A.1.

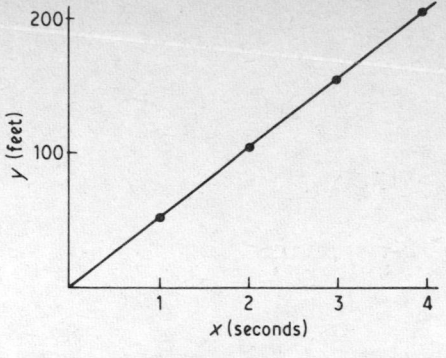

Figure A.1 The relationship between distance and time for a car starting from rest

All the points lie on a straight line, making this a linear function. Another way of describing such a function is to define it algebraically as a rule for transforming x observations into y observations. In this case the rule is:

$$y = 50x$$

If we multiply any x score by 50, this gives us the equivalent y score. More generally, this can be written as

$$y = bx$$

where b is a coefficient or parameter which measures the number of units by which y changes, in relation to a unit change in x. In our example the car travels 50 feet every second.

In the above diagram the car had travelled no distance at all before we started to measure its movement. However, it is more realistic to measure the car after it has attained a constant speed of 50 feet per second. Let us assume that it had to travel 100 feet before it reached this speed, so that the relationship between the variables is (see Figure A.2):

$$y = 100 + 50x$$

More generally

$$y = a + bx$$

where a is referred to as the intercept, because it measures the distance along the y axis at which the function intercepts the axis, and the b co-efficient measures the slope of the line (the change in y resulting from a unit change in x).

Regression analysis

Suppose there is a causal relationship between two variables; for example, the level of education of an individual influences his or her

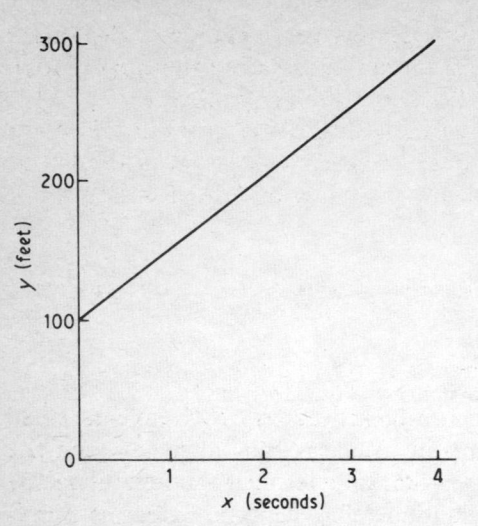

Figure A.2   The relationship between distance and time for a car measured after it
has attained a constant speed of 50 feet per second

earnings. A high level of education produces a high level of earnings, and
vice versa. It is often possible to model the relationship between variables
like these by a linear function, although not all the observations will lie on
a straight line (see e.g. Figure A.3).

In the case of Figure A.3 only one observation lies on a straight line,
but there is a broad association between these variables; that is, earnings
and education are related, but the relationship is not perfect. Regression
analysis is concerned with finding the linear function linking two
variables which is the line of best fit to the scatter of observations. This
line is found using calculus, but that need not concern us. The important

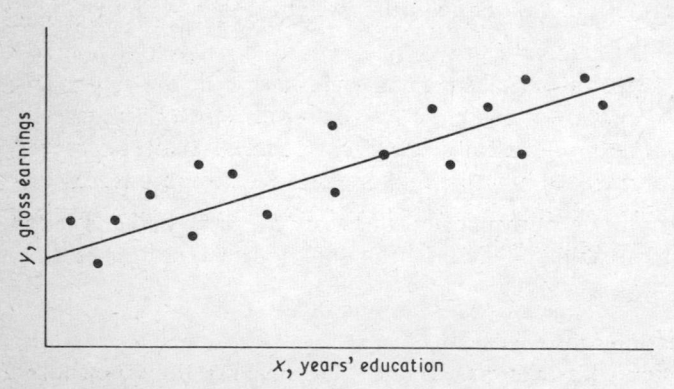

Figure A.3   The line of best fit, obtained by regression analysis, to the observed
values of x and y

point is that the regression analysis allows us to calculate the linear relationship between the variables, thereby estimating the quantitative influence of x on y, by a line that fits better than any other.

For example, suppose the y variable referred to gross hourly earnings, and the x variable referred to the number of years' education after the age of 11. Assume that the linear function which fits best is:

$y = 0.80 + 0.60x$

This model predicts that an individual who has 10 years' education after the age of eleven would earn

$y = 0.80 + 0.60 (10) = £6.80$ per hour

Similarly, an individual with no education after 11 would earn £0.80 per hour. This is essentially a model of the relationship between the variables for a particular sample. It is unlikely that the model will be 100 per cent accurate for any one individual. The important thing is that it should give a good overall fit, with not too much error.

The accuracy of the model is related to the scatter of observations about the line. If the scatter is very wide this makes the model inaccurate; if it is narrow the reverse is true. The correlation coefficient is directly related to the degree of scatter of the observations. If all observations lie on a straight line this gives a correlation of 1.0; if they are close to the line, a correlation of 0.80 to 0.90; if the scatter is very wide, a correlation of under 0.10; and, if there is absolutely no relationship between the variables at all, the correlation will be zero. The correlation coefficient is given the symbol r, and it can be shown that r^2 measures the percentage of variation in the dependent variable explained by the regression line. This is another way of defining the amount of scatter of the observations around the line. If the scatter is small then r^2 will approach 100 per cent, and if large it will approach 0 per cent.

Most models in social science are multivariate, rather than bivariate; that is, we need to consider many variables if we wish to explain the behaviour of a given variable. To do this we use multiple regression, which is a simple extension of the above example. Multiple regression allows us to examine the quantitative impact of each variable separately on the y variable or dependent variable. For example, suppose we include the dummy variable sex (males 1, females 0) as a predictor of earnings and get the following relationship:

$y = 0.80 + 0.50x_1 + 0.20x_2$

where x_1 is education and x_2 is sex.

The regression coefficients 0.50 and 0.20 measure the quantitative impact of x_1 and x_2 on y. This model tells us that men will obtain £0.20 more than women, even holding education constant. That is, on average men will be paid 20 pence per hour more than women, even when they have the same education. Obviously we could add other variables to the model and examine their impact on earnings.

Regression is important because it allows us to estimate quantitatively the causal relationships between variables. Correlation tells us how well (or badly) the regression models fit. Understanding these points is the essential starting point of interpreting a regression analysis. For a more advanced, but reasonably intelligible, discussion the reader should look at Koutsoyiannis (1973, Chapters 3–5).

Factor analysis

Factor analysis is a multivariate technique designed to explore the pattern of relationships underlying a set of correlations between variables. The object of factor analysis is to try to explain many correlations between many variables by a few correlations between those variables and a small number of underlying factors.

Factor analysis is best introduced by means of an example first used by Spearman, who wrote the first papers on this subject in the early part of the twentieth century. One of his examples involves a set of correlations between examination scores for a sample of children. The correlations were as follows:

Examination		1	2	3	4	5	6
Classics	1	1.0					
French	2	0.83	1.0				
English	3	0.78	0.67	1.0			
Mathematics	4	0.70	0.67	0.64	1.0		
Discrimination	5	0.66	0.65	0.54	0.45		
Music	6	0.63	0.58	0.51	0.51	0.40	1.0

Overall these correlations were quite high; for example, there was quite a strong linear relationship between performance in Classics and performance in French, having a correlation of 0.83. However, Pearson noticed that the correlations were smaller the lower one moved down the list of examination scores. Thus the correlation between Classics and Mathematics was 0.70, and between Mathematics and Music only 0.51. He reasoned that an underlying factor, which we might describe as 'intelligence', explained the relationship between these correlations, but that this underlying factor had a different impact on different subjects. In other words, the correlation between examination scores was composed of two parts:

correlation between examinations	=	relationship of 'intelligence' to the subject	+	skills unique to that subject

Thus Classics and French were highly correlated because individuals needed a lot of 'intelligence' to do well in them. But individuals did not need so much of this particular form of 'intelligence' to do well in Music, which was more a matter of other skills. This accounts for the difference in the correlations.

More generally, a factor analysis of the relationship between many variables will produce several factors to which the variables are related. These factors are interpreted by their relationship to the variables. The technique produces a set of correlations between factors and variables which we can use to interpret the meaning of the underlying factors. If, for example, the attitudes of respondents to a survey are significantly interrelated, so that individuals who favour nuclear disarmament also favour social security spending, and oppose racialism, then this 'consistency' in attitudes will emerge since all these items will be significantly correlated with an underlying factor. If, on the other hand, there is no such consistency, then no such factor would exist. Thus we can use factor analysis to estimate the degree of consistency between respondents with regard to their attitudes.

The percentage of variance explained by a factor refers to the extent to which a factor explains relationships between all the variables. If this is high, it means that a few underlying factors explain all the links between variables, much as 'intelligence' explained the correlation between examination scores in our example. If the percentage of variance explained is low, this means that there are no significant underlying factors which explain the associations between variables. A further, comprehensive discussion of factor analysis can be found in Harman (1976, Chapters 1 and 2).

Appendix II
A review of the surveys used in Part I

The following samples were used in Part I:

(1) A sample of 51 Labour Members of Parliament collected in 1975 by means of a postal survey. Questionnaires were sent to a random sample of 100 members of the parliamentary Labour party. There was an initial response rate of 31, which was increased to 51 by interviewing non-respondents. The sampling approach was used in anticipation of the need to interview non-respondents, following a low response rate to a pilot survey. An independent check on the representativeness of the sample was provided by the responses to the question: 'If Harold Wilson resigned the leadership of the Labour Party, whom would you like to see elected as leader?' The respondents' answers were compared with the voting behaviour of the entire parliamentary Labour party in the first ballot for the leadership in March 1976. The results were:

Preference	% MPs in survey (N = 51)	% MPs in parliamentary party (N = 314)
Michael Foot	25.0	28.7
Tony Benn	12.5	11.8
Denis Healey	15.0	9.5
Jim Callaghan	27.5	26.8
Tony Crosland	2.5	5.4
Roy Jenkins	17.5	17.8
Others	2.5	—

It can be seen that the left-wing candidates (Foot and Benn) received 37.5 per cent of the sample and 40.5 per cent of the parliamentary party.

The candidates from the centre–right (Healey, Callaghan and Crosland) received 45 per cent and 41.7 per cent respectively and the candidate from the right (Jenkins) 17.5 per cent and 17.8 per cent. This suggests that the sample is representative of the parliamentary party as a whole.

(2) A sample of 160 parliamentary Labour candidates from a population of 329 candidates who fought non-Labour constituencies in February 1974. Again the survey was carried out using a postal question-naire, which gave a response rate of 49 per cent. The brief biographical details published in *The Times Book of the House of Commons* (1974) made it possible to calculate the mean age of the population of candidates, and the proportion attending university. The mean age of the population was 37.6 years and the sample was 36.1 years. The proportion of the popu-lation who had attended university was 65 per cent and the sample was 71 per cent. Z tests of statistical significance showed no significant differ-ence between the sample and the population on these variables. In addition, the response rates of candidates in the different regions of the Labour Party were calculated. Again, no significant variations between regional response rates were discovered applying a χ squared goodness of fit test to the distribution of regional response rates and a rectangular distribution. All these tests suggest that the sample is representative of the population.

(3) A non-random sample of 89 Labour councillors. This was col-lected by a postal questionnaire sent to all Labour councillors in six differ-ent local authorities in England. These authorities were specifically chosen to be politically heterogeneous, varying from safe Labour to marginal Labour and marginal Conservative to safe Conservative. They were Durham, Hounslow, Harlow, Colchester, Surrey and Berkshire. Thus some authorities were County Councils and others Borough Coun-cils. The sample does not represent the population of all Labour councillors in a statistical sense, but the heterogeneity of these authorities should ensure that it gives a broad indication of their attitudes and back-ground.

(4) A sample of 254 delegates to the 1978 party conference. The population consisted of 623 constituency party delegates in Britain and approximately 550 trade union delegates. Two big unions with 120 delegates refused to co-operate, so there were 430 trade unionists in the target population. A random sample of 1 in 2 of these populations was selected. A sampling approach was used purely to reduce coding costs. From a mailing of 311 questionnaires to constituency delegates the response rate was 58.8 per cent, and from a mailing of 200 questionnaires to trade union delegates the response rate was 39 per cent. Tests of signifi-cance on the difference between the mean Labour vote for the respondent constituencies and the mean Labour vote nationally in 1974, and on the regional distribution of respondent constituencies, showed no statistically

significant differences. This suggests that the sample of constituency delegates is representative of the population of constituency delegates in Britain.

(5)   A multi-stage random sample of the British electorate in 1979 collected by the British Election Study at the University of Essex. The details of the sample are available from the British Election Study.

Bibliography

Abel-Smith, B. and Townsend, P. B. (1965) *The Poor and the Poorest* (London: Bell).

Abrams, M., Rose, R. and Hinden, R. (1960) *Must Labour Lose?* (Harmondsworth: Penguin).

Adorno, T. W., Frenkel-Brunswick, E., Levinson, D. J. and Sanford, R. N. (1964) *The Authoritarian Personality* (New York: Wiley).

Ajzen, I. and Fishbein, M. (1980) *Understanding Attitudes and Predicting Social Behaviour* (Englewood Cliffs, NJ: Prentice-Hall).

Allen, G. C. (1978) *How Japan Competes: A Verdict on 'Dumping'* (London: Institute of Economic Affairs).

Almond, G. A. and Powell, G. B. (1966) *Comparative Politics: A Developmental Approach* (Boston: Little, Brown).

Almond, G. A. and Verba, S. (1963) *The Civic Culture: Political Attitudes and Democracy in Five Nations* (Princeton, NJ: Princeton University Press).

Alt, J. (1979) *The Politics of Economic Decline* (Cambridge: Cambridge University Press).

Alt, J. and Turner, J. (1982) 'The case of the silk-stocking socialists and the calculating children of the middle-class', *British Journal of Political Science* 12, 239–48.

Ashford, D. E. (1981) *Policy and Politics in Britain* (Oxford: Basil Blackwell).

Atkinson, A. B. (1970) *Poverty in Britain and the Reform of Social Security* (Cambridge: Cambridge University Press).

Attlee, C. (1937) *The Labour Party in Perspective* (London: Gollancz).

Bacon, R. and Eltis, W. A. (1976) *Britain's Economic Problem: Too Few Producers* (London: Macmillan).

Ball, R. J. (1982) *Money and Employment* (London: Macmillan).

Ball, R. J. and Burns, T. (1976) 'The inflationary mechanism in the UK economy', *American Economic Review* 66, 467–84.

Balogh, T. (1982) *The Irrelevance of Conventional Economics* (London: Weidenfeld & Nicolson).

Banting, K. G. (1979) *Poverty, Politics and Policy* (London: Macmillan).

Baxter, R. (1972) 'The working-class and Labour politics', *Political Studies* **20**, 97–107.

Beackon, S. (1976) 'Labour Party politics and the working-class', *British Journal of Political Science* **6**, 231–8.

Bealey, F. (ed.) (1970) *The Social and Political Thought of the British Labour Party* (London: Weidenfeld & Nicolson).

Bealey, F., Blondel, J. and McCann, W. P. (1965) *Constituency Politics* (London: Faber).

Beckerman, W. (1972) *The Labour Government's Economic Record, 1964–1970* (London: Duckworth).

Beckerman, W. (ed.) (1979) *Slow Growth in Britain* (Oxford: Clarendon Press).

Berki, R. N. (1975) *Socialism* (London: Dent).

Bernstein, B. (1960) 'Language and social class', *British Journal of Sociology* **9**, 271–6.

Berrington, H. (1973) *Backbench Opinion in the House of Commons, 1945–1955* (Oxford: Pergamon Press).

Berrington, H. and Leece, J. (1977) 'Measurement of backbench attitudes by Guttman, scaling of Early Day Motions: a pilot study, Labour, 1968–1969', *British Journal of Political Science* **7**, 529–40.

Berry, D. (1970) *The Sociology of Grass Roots Politics* (London: Macmillan).

Berthoud, R., Brown, J. C. and Cooper, S. (1981) *Poverty and the Development of Anti-Poverty Policy in the UK* (London: Heinemann).

Bevan, A. (1961) *In Place of Fear* (London: MacGibbon).

Birch, A. H. (1959) *Small Town Politics* (London: Oxford University Press).

Bish, G. (1979) 'Drafting the manifesto', in K. Coates (ed.) *What Went Wrong?* (Nottingham: Spokesman), 187–206.

Bispham, J. A. (1975) 'The new Cambridge and "monetarist" criticisms of "conventional" economic policy making', *National Institute Economic Review* **74**, 39–59.

Black, D. (1958) *The Theory of Committees and Elections* (Cambridge: Cambridge University Press).

Blackaby, F. (ed.) (1979) *De-Industrialisation* (London: Heinemann).

Blank, S. (1977) 'Britain: the politics of foreign economic policy, the domestic economy and the problem of pluralist stagnation', *International Organisation* **31**, 673–722.

Blondel, J. (1963) *Voters, Parties and Leaders* (Harmondsworth: Penguin).

Bochel, J. M. and Denver, D. T. (1972) 'The impact of the campaign on the results of local government elections', *British Journal of Political Science* **2**, 239–43.

Bosanquet, N. and Townsend, P. (1980) *Labour and Equality* (London: Heinemann).

Bradley, I. (1981) *Breaking the Mould?* (Oxford: Martin Robertson).

Brand, J. (1973) 'Party organisation and the recruitment of councillors', *British Journal of Political Science* 3, 473–86.

Braybrooke, D. and Lindblom, C. (1963) *A Strategy of Decision* (New York: Free Press).

Brittan, S. (1964) *The Treasury under the Tories, 1951–1964* (Harmondsworth: Penguin).

Brittan, S. (1971) *Steering the Economy* (Harmondsworth: Penguin).

Budge, I., Crewe, I. and Farlie, D. (1976) *Party Identification and Beyond* (London: Wiley).

Budge, I. and Farlie, D. (1977) *Voting and Party Competition* (London: Wiley).

Buiter, W. H. (1980) 'The macroeconomics of Dr Pangloss. A critical survey of the new classical macroeconomics', *Economic Journal* 9, 34–50.

Butler, D. and Sloman, A. (1980) *British Political Facts, 1900–1979* (London: Macmillan).

Butler, D. and Stokes, D. (1974) *Political Change in Britain* (London: Macmillan).

Cairncross, A. (1979) 'What is de-industrialisation?', in F. Blackaby (ed.) *De-industrialisation* (London: Heinemann), 5–17.

Cambridge Economic Policy Review (1981) 'Economic policy in the UK', vol. 7 (Farnborough, Hants: Gower).

Cambridge Economic Policy Review (1982) vol. 8 (Farnborough, Hants: Gower).

Cameron, D. (1978) 'The expansion of the public economy: a comparative analysis', *American Political Science Review* 72, 1243–61.

Campbell, A., Converse, P. E., Miller, W. E. and Stokes, D. E. (1960) *The American Voter* (New York: Wiley).

Campbell, D. (1969) 'Reforms as experiments', *American Psychologist* 24, 409–29.

Campbell, D. and Cook, T. D. (1979) *Quasi-Experimentation: Design and Analysis for Field Settings* (Chicago: Rand McNally).

Castles, F. and McKinlay, R. D. (1979) 'Public welfare provision, Scandinavia, and the sheer futility of the sociological approach to politics', *British Journal of Political Science* 9, 157–72.

Caves, R. E. and Krause, L. B. (1980) *Britain's Economic Performance* (Washington, DC: Brookings Institute).

Clegg, H. (1971) *How to Run an Incomes Policy and Why We Made such a Mess of the Last One* (London: Heinemann).

Coates, K. (1975) *The Labour Party and the Struggle for Socialism* (Cambridge: Cambridge University Press).

Coates, K. (ed.) (1979) *What Went Wrong?* (Nottingham: Spokesman Books).

Coates, K. (1980) *Labour in Power?* (London: Longman).

Cohen, M., March, J. and Olsen, J. (1972) 'A garbage can model of organisational choice', *Administrative Science Quarterly* **17**, 1–25.

Cole, G. D. H. (1948) *A History of the Labour Party from 1914* (London: Routledge and Kegan Paul).

Converse, P. (1964) 'The nature of belief systems in mass politics', in D. Apter (ed.) *Ideology and Discontent* (New York: Free Press), 206–61.

CPAG (1978) *All Children Worse Off under Labour* (London: Child Poverty Action Group).

Craig, F. W. S. (1975) *British General Election Manifestos, 1900–1974* (London: Macmillan).

Crewe, I. (1974) 'Do Butler and Stokes really explain political change in Britain?', *European Journal of Political Research* **2**, 83–7.

Crewe, I. (1981) 'Why the Conservatives won', in H. R. Penniman (ed.) *Britain at the Polls, 1979* (Washington: American Enterprise Institute).

Crewe, I. (1982a) 'The Labour Party and the electorate', in D. Kavanagh (ed.) *The Politics of the Labour Party* (London: Allen & Unwin).

Crewe, I. (1982b) 'Is Britain's two-party system really about to crumble?', *Electoral Studies* **1**, 275–313.

Crewe, I. and Särlvik, B. (1980) 'Popular attitudes and electoral strategy', in Z. Layton-Henry (ed.) *Conservative Party Politics* (London: Macmillan).

Crewe, I., Särlvik, B. and Alt, J. (1977) 'Partisan dealignment in Britain, 1964–1974', *British Journal of Political Science* **7**, 129–90.

Crosland, A. (1956) *The Future of Socialism* (London: Jonathan Cape).

Crossman, R. H. S. (1964) *Planning for Freedom* (London: Hamish Hamilton).

CSO (1981) *Economic Trends*, Annual Supplement (London: HMSO).

Desai, M. (1974) *Marxian Economic Theory* (London: Gray-Mills).

Desai, M. (1981) *Testing Monetarism* (London: Frances Pinter).

Deutsch, K. (1963) *The Nerves of Government* (Glencoe, Ill.: Free Press).

Disability Alliance (1975) *Poverty and Disability* (London: Disability Alliance).

Donnison, D. V. and Plowman, D. E. G. (1954) 'The functions of local Labour politics: experiments in research methods', *Political Studies* **2**, 154–67.

Dow, J. C. R. (1964) *The Management of the British Economy, 1945–1960* (Cambridge: Cambridge University Press).

Downs, A. (1957) *An Economic Theory of Democracy* (New York: Harper & Row).

Dowse, R. (1973) 'The decline of working-class politics', *British Journal of Sociology* **24**, 264–5.

Drucker, H. (1979) *Doctrine and Ethos in the Labour Party* (London: Allen & Unwin).

Dunleavy, P. (1979) 'The urban basis of political alignment: social class, domestic property ownership, and state intervention in consumption processes', *British Journal of Political Science* 9, 409–44.

Dunleavy, P. (1980a) 'Some political implications of sectoral cleavages and the growth of state employment, Part I: The analysis of production cleavages', *Political Studies* 28, 364–83.

Dunleavy, P. (1980b) 'Some political implications of sectoral cleavages and the growth of state employment, Part 2: Cleavage structures and political alignment', *Political Studies* 28, 527–49.

Durbin, J. (1970) 'Testing for serial correlation in least squares regression when some of the regressors are lagged dependent variables', *Econometrics* 38, 410–21.

Easton, D. (1953) *The Political System* (New York: Alfred Knopf).

Easton, D. (1965) *A System of Analysis of Political Life* (London: Wiley).

Edwards, A. D. (1976) *Language in Culture and Class* (London: Heinemann).

Fay, S. and Young, H. (1978) *The Day the £ nearly Died* (London: Sunday Times Publications).

Fellowes, E. (1961–2) 'Review of backbench opinion in the House of Commons, 1955, 1959', *Parliamentary Affairs* 15, 244–5.

Festinger, L. (1957) *A Theory of Cognitive Dissonance* (Palo Alto, Calif.: Stanford University Press).

Festinger, L. (1967) 'An introduction to the theory of dissonance', in E. P. Hollander and R. G. Hunt (eds) *Current Perspectives in Social Psychology* (London: Oxford University Press).

Field, F. (1981) *Inequality in Britain: Freedom, Welfare and the State* (London: Fontana).

Field, F. (1982) *Poverty and Politics* (London: Heinemann).

Finer, S. (1980) *The Changing British Party System, 1945–1979* (Washington, DC: American Enterprise Institute).

Finer, S. E., Berrington, H. B. and Bartholomew, D. S. (1961) *Backbench Opinion in the House of Commons, 1955–1959* (Oxford: Pergamon Press).

Finney, D. J. (1964) *Probit Analysis* (Cambridge: Cambridge University Press).

Fiorina, M. (1977) 'An outline for a model of party choice', *American Political Science Review* 21, 601–23.

Fiorina, M. (1981) *Retrospective Voting in American National Elections* (New Haven, Conn.: Yale University Press).

Fishbein, M., Thomas, K. and Jaccard, J. (1976) *Voting Behaviour in Britain: An Attitudinal Analysis* (London: Social Science Research Council).

Forrester, T. (1976) *The Labour Party and the Working-Class* (London: Heinemann).

Freeman, C. (1979) 'Technical innovation and British trade performance', in F. Blackaby (ed.) *De-industrialisation* (London: Heinemann), 56–72.

Frey, B. and Schneider, F. (1978) 'A politico-economic model of the United Kingdom', *Economic Journal* **88**, 243–53.

Friedman, M. (1968) 'The role of monetary policy', *American Economic Review* **63**, no. 1, 1–17.

Galbraith, J. K. (1978) *The New Industrial State* (Boston: Houghton Mifflin).

Gallup Polls (1981) *The Gallup Political Index*, no. 256, December (London: Gallup Polls).

Gamble, A. (1981) *Britain in Decline* (London: Macmillan).

Glasgow Media Group (1976) *Bad News* (London: Routledge & Kegan Paul).

Godley, W. (1975) minutes of evidence to Expenditure Committee (General Subcommittee), 3 November, 'The Financing of Public Expenditure', pp. 101–2.

Godley, W. (1979) 'Britain's chronic recession – can anything be done?', in W. Beckerman (ed.) *Slow Growth in Britain* (Oxford: Clarendon Press), 226–33.

Goldthorpe, J. H. (1980) *Social Mobility and Class Structure in Modern Britain* (Oxford: Clarendon Press).

Goldthorpe, J. H., Lockwood, D., Bechofer, F. and Platt, J. (1969) *The Affluent Worker, II: Political Attitudes* (Cambridge: Cambridge University Press).

Gordon, I. and Whiteley, P. (1977) 'The political ideology of Labour councillors', *Policy and Politics* **5**, 1–26.

Gordon, I. and Whiteley, P. (1979) 'Social class and political attitudes: the case of Labour councillors', *Political Studies* **27**, 99–113.

Gordon, I. and Whiteley, P. (1981) 'Swings and roundabouts: an ecological analysis of the European and general election results in Great Britain', *Political Studies* **29**, 586–603.

Gould, J. and Kolb, W. L. (1962) *A Dictionary of Social Science* (New York: Free Press).

Grant, W. (1982) *The Political Economy of Industrial Policy* (London: Butterworth).

Grant, W. and Marsh, D. (1977) *The CBI* (London: Hodder & Stoughton).

Greenstein, F. I. (1968) 'Political socialisation', in D. Sills (ed.) *International Encyclopaedia of the Social Sciences* (New York: Free Press).

Habermas, J. (1976) *Legitimation Crisis* (London: Heinemann).

Hahn, F. H. (1980) 'Monetarism and economic theory', *Economica* **47**, 1–17.

Hanby, V. T. (1974) 'A changing Labour elite: the National Executive of the Labour Party, 1900–1972', in I. Crewe (ed.) *British Political Sociology Year Book*, vol. 1 (London: Croom Helm), 126–58.

Harman, H. (1976) *Modern Factor Analysis* (Chicago: Chicago University Press).

Harrod, R. (1972) *The Life of John Maynard Keynes* (Harmondsworth: Penguin).

Harrop, M. (1980) 'The urban basis of political alignment: a comment', *British Journal of Political Science* 10, 388–97.

Harrop, M. (1982) 'Labour-voting Conservatives: policy differences between the Labour Party and Labour voters', in R. M. Worcester and M. Harrop (eds) *Political Communications* (London: Allen & Unwin).

Hatfield, M. (1978) *The House the Left Built* (London: Gollancz).

Heclo, H. and Wildavsky, A. (1974) *The Private Management of Public Money* (London: Macmillan).

Henry, S. G. B. (1981) 'Incomes policy and aggregate pay', in J. L. Fallick and R. F. Elliot (eds) *Incomes Policies, Inflation and Relative Pay* (London: Allen & Unwin), 23–44.

Hibbs, D. A. (1977) 'Political parties and macro-economic policy', *American Political Science Review* 71, 1467–87.

Hibbs, D. and Fassbender, H. (eds) (1981) *Contemporary Political Economy* (Amsterdam: North Holland).

Himmelweit, H., Humphreys, P., Jaeger, M. and Katz, M. (1981) *How Voters Decide* (London: Academic Press).

Hindess, B. (1971) *The Decline of Working-Class Politics* (London: Paladin).

Hirsch, F. and Goldthorpe, J. H. (eds) (1978) *The Political Economy of Inflation* (Oxford: Martin Robertson).

Hirschman, A. O. (1970) *Exit, Voice and Loyalty* (Cambridge, Mass.: Harvard University Press).

HMSO (1942) *Social Insurance and Allied Services* (the Beveridge Report), Cmnd 6404 (London: HMSO).

HMSO (1944a) *Employment Policy*, Cmnd 6527 (London: HMSO).

HMSO (1944b) *Social Insurance*, Cmnd 6550 (London: HMSO).

HMSO (1959) *Committee on the Working of the Monetary System*, Cmnd 827 (London: HMSO).

HMSO (1974a) *Better Pensions Fully Protected against Inflation: Proposals for a New Pensions Scheme*, Cmnd 5713 (London: HMSO).

HMSO (1974b) *DHSS Social Security Provision for Chronically Sick and Disabled People*, Cmnd 276 (London: HMSO).

HMSO (1974c) *Report of the Committee on One-parent Families* (the Finer Report), Cmnd 5629 (London: HMSO).

HMSO (1974d) *The Regeneration of British Industry*, Cmnd 5710 (London: HMSO).

HMSO (1975) *An Approach to Industrial Strategy*, Cmnd 6315 (London: HMSO).

HMSO (1976a) *Cash Limits on Public Expenditure*, Cmnd 6440 (London: HMSO).

HMSO (1976b) *Report of the Committee on Financial Aid to Political Parties, Chairman Lord Houghton*, Cmnd 6601 (London: HMSO).

HMSO (1979) *Supplementary Benefits Commission Annual Report, 1978*, Cmnd 7725 (London: HMSO).

HMSO (1980b) *Inland Revenue Statistics, 1979* (London: HMSO).

HMSO (1980c) *Social Trends* (London: HMSO).

HMSO (1981) *DHSS Social Security Statistics* (London: HMSO).

HMSO (1982) *The Government's Expenditure Plans, 1982–83 to 1984–85*, Cmnd 8494–1 (London: HMSO).

Holland, S. (1975) *The Socialist Challenge* (London: Quartet Books).

Houghton, D. (1967) *Paying for the Social Services* (London: Institute of Economic Affairs).

House of Commons (1967–8) *Debates* 762, 240–1.

House of Commons (1971–2) *Debates* 806, 253.

House of Commons (1974) *Report of the House of Commons Expenditure Committee*, HC 328.

House of Commons (1980–1) *Report of the House of Commons Treasury and Civil Service Committee on Monetary Policy*, HC 163–1, Session 1980–1.

Howard, M. C. and King, J. E. (1975) *The Political Economy of Marx* (London: Longman).

Howell, D. (1976) *British Social Democracy* (London: Croom Helm).

Janosik, E. G. (1968) *Constituency Labour Parties in Britain* (London: Pall Mall Press).

Jenkins, R. (1972) *What Matters Now* (London: Fontana).

Johnson, C. (1982) *MITI and the Japanese Miracle: The Growth of Industrial Policy, 1925–1975* (Palo Alto, Calif.: Stanford University Press).

Johnson, R. W. (1973) 'The British political elite, 1955–1972', *European Journal of Sociology* 14, 35–77.

Johnston, J. (1972) *Econometric Methods* (Tokyo: McGraw-Hill Kogakusha).

Jones, A. (1973) *The New Inflation* (Harmondsworth: Penguin).

Kaldor, N. (1982) *The Scourge of Monetarism* (Oxford: Oxford University Press).

Keegan, W. and Pennant-Rea, R. (1979) *Who Runs the Economy?* (London: Maurice Temple Smith).

Kennedy, M. C. (1976) 'The economy as a whole', in A. R. Prest and D. S. Coppock (eds) *The UK Economy: A Manual of Applied Economics* (London: Weidenfeld & Nicolson), 6th edn, 1–53.

Keynes, J. M. (1936) *The General Theory of Employment, Interest and Money* (London: Macmillan).

Kindelberger, C. P. (1976) 'Systems of international organisation', in P. Calleo *et al.* (eds) *Money and the Coming World Order* (Chicago: Aldine).

Kinder, D. R. and Kiewet, D. R. (1981) 'Sociotropic politics: the American case', *British Journal of Political Science* **11**, 129–62.

King, M. A. (1975) 'The United Kingdom profits crisis: myth or reality?', *Economic Journal* **85**, 1492–3.

Klein, R. (1976) 'The politics of public expenditure: American theory and British practice', *British Journal of Political Science* **6**, 401–32.

Kogan, D. and Kogan, M. (1982) *The Battle for the Labour Party* (London: Fontana).

Kornberg, A. and Frasure, R. C. (1971) 'Policy differences in British parliamentary parties', *American Political Science Review* **65**, 694–703.

Koutsoyiannis, A. (1973) *Theory of Econometrics* (London: Macmillan).

Kravis, I. and Lipsey, R. E. (1977) 'Export prices and the transmission of inflation', *American Economic Association Proceedings*, 155–73.

Labour Party (1918) *Labour and the New Social Order* (London: Labour Party).

Labour Party (1928) *Labour and the Nation* (London: Labour Party).

Labour Party (1933) *Socialism and the Condition of the People* (London: Labour Party).

Labour Party (1952) *One Way Only* (London: Labour Party).

Labour Party (1957a) *Annual Conference Report, 1957* (London: Labour Party).

Labour Party (1957b) *National Superannuation, Labour's Policy for Security in Old Age* (London: Labour Party).

Labour Party (1959) *Annual Conference Report, 1959* (London: Labour Party).

Labour Party (1963) *New Frontiers for Social Security* (London: Labour Party).

Labour Party (1973) *Labour's Programme for Britain, 1973* (London: Labour Party).

Labour Party (1980) *Annual Conference Report, 1980* (London: Labour Party).

Labour Party (1981) *Labour's Plan for Expansion* (London: Labour Party).

Labour Party (1982a) *Conference Agenda, 1982* (London: Labour Party).

Labour Party (1982b) *Labour's Programme, 1982* (London: Labour Party).

Laidler, D. (1976) 'Inflation in Britain: a monetarist perspective', *American Economic Review* **66**, 485–500.

Land, H. (1977) 'The child benefit fiasco', in *The Yearbook of Social Policy in Britain, 1976* (London: Routledge & Kegan Paul).

Lane, R. (1962) *Political Ideology* (New York: Free Press).

Lapping, B. (1970) *The Labour Government, 1964–1970* (Harmondsworth: Penguin).

Lasswell, H. (1936) *Politics, Who Gets What, When, How?* (New York: McGraw-Hill).

Layard, R. (1982) 'Is incomes policy the answer to unemployment?' *Economica* **49**, 219–40.

Layard, R., Piachaud, D. and Stewart, M. (1978) *The Causes of Poverty*, Background Paper no. 5, Royal Commission on the Distribution of Income and Wealth (London: HMSO).

Leijonhufvud, A. (1968) *On Keynesian Economics and the Economics of Keynes* (London: Oxford University Press).

Lewis-Beck, M. and Alford, J. (1980) 'Can government regulate safety? The coal mine example', *American Political Science Review* **74**, 745–56.

Lindblom, C. (1959) 'The science of "muddling through"', *Public Administration Review* **19**, 79–88.

Lindblom, C. (1968) *The Policy-Making Process* (Englewood Cliffs, NJ: Prentice-Hall).

Longstreth, F. (1979) 'The city, industry and the state', in C. Crouch (ed.) *State and Economy in Contemporary Capitalism* (London: Croom Helm), 157, 190.

Lucas, R. E. (1972) 'Expectations and the neutrality of money', *Journal of Economic Theory* **4**, 103–24.

McKenzie, R. T. (1963) *British Political Parties* (London: Mercury Books).

McKenzie, R. T. (1982) 'Power in the Labour Party: the issue of "intra-party democracy"', in D. Kavanagh (ed.) *The Politics of the Labour Party* (London: Allen & Unwin).

Maddala, G. S. (1977) *Econometrics* (Tokyo: McGraw-Hill Kogakusha).

Mannheim, K. (1936) *Ideology and Utopia* (London: Kegan Paul).

Marsh, D. (1971) 'Political socialisation: the implicit assumptions questioned', *British Journal of Political Science* **1**, 453–65.

Marshall, T. H. (1975) *Social Policy in the Twentieth Century* (London: Hutchinson).

Martin, A. (1979) 'The dynamics of change in a Keynesian political economy: the Swedish case and its implications', in C. Crouch (ed.) *State and Economy in Contemporary Capitalism* (London: Croom Helm), 88–121.

Meade, J. E. (1982) *Stagflation*, vol. 1: *Wage-Fixing* (London: Allen & Unwin).

Merelman, R. (1969) 'The development of political ideology', *American Political Science Review* **63**, 750–67.

Metcalf, D. and Richardson, R. (1976) 'Labour', in A. R. Prest and D. S. Coppock (eds) *The UK Economy: A Manual of Applied Economics* (London: Weidenfeld & Nicolson), 6th edn, 238–96.

Miller, W. (1977) *Electoral Dynamics* (London: Macmillan).

Milne, R. S. and Mackenzie, H. C. (1954) *Straight Fight* (London: Hansard Society).

Minkin, L. (1978) *The Labour Party Conference* (London: Allen Lane).

Modigliani, F. (1977) 'The monetarist controversy, or, should we forsake stabilisation policy?', *American Economic Review* **67**, 1–19.

Mueller, D. C. (1979) *Public Choice* (Cambridge: Cambridge University Press).

Mughan, A. (1981) 'The cross-national validity of party identification: Great Britain and the United States compared', *Political Studies* **29**, 365–75.

Muth, J. F. (1961) 'Rational expectations and the theory of price movements', *Econometrica* **29**, 315–35.

Neild, R. R. (1979) 'Managed trade between industrial countries', in R. Major (ed.) *Britain's Trade and Exchange-Rate Policy* (London: Heinemann), 5–23.

New Society (1976) 'Killing a commitment: the Cabinet *versus* the children', *New Society* **36**, no. 715 (June), 630–2.

Newton, K. (1976) *Second City Politics* (London: Oxford University Press).

Newton, K. (1983) 'Votes count, but boundaries decide how votes count', mimeo (Department of Politics, University of Dundee).

Nie, N., Verba, S. and Petrocik, J. R. (1976) *The Changing American Voter* (Cambridge, Mass.: Harvard University Press).

Niskanen, W. A. (1971) *Bureaucracy and Representative Government* (New York: Aldine-Atherton).

O'Connor, J. (1973) *The Fiscal Crisis of the State* (New York: St Martin's Press).

OECD (1978) *Public Expenditure Trends* (Paris: OECD).

Olson, M. (1965) *The Logic of Collective Action* (Cambridge, Mass.: Harvard University Press).

Ormerod, P. (ed.) (1979) *Economic Modelling: Current Issues and Problems in Macro-economic Modelling in the UK and US* (London: Heinemann).

Parkin, F. (1968) *Middle Class Radicals* (Manchester: Manchester University Press).

Parkin, F. (1971) *Class Inequality and Political Order* (London: Paladin).

Peacock, A. R. and Wiseman, J. (1961) *The Growth of Public Expenditure in the United Kingdom* (London: Allen & Unwin).

Pelling, H. (1965) *The Origins of the Labour Party* (Oxford: Clarendon Press).

Peston, M. H. (1974) *Theory of Macroeconomic Policy* (Deddington, Oxford: Philip Allan).

Petit, P. (1982) 'Reflation and industrial policy in France', in *Cambridge Economic Policy Review* vol. 8, chap. 3 (Farnborough, Hants: Gower).

Phillips, A. W. (1958) 'The relationship between unemployment and the rate of change of money wage rates in the UK, 1861–1957', *Economica* **25**, 283–99.

Pindyck, R. S. and Rubinfeld, D. L. (1976) *Econometric Models and Economic Forecasts* (New York: McGraw-Hill).

Pissarides, C. A. (1980) 'British government popularity and economic performance', *Economic Journal* **90**, 569–81.

Pliatzky, L. (1982) *Getting and Spending* (Oxford: Basil Blackwell).

Pollard, S. (1982) *The Wasting of the British Economy* (London: Croom Helm).

Pond, C. (1982) 'Taxation and public expenditure', in A. Walker (ed.) *Public Expenditure and Social Policy* (London: Heinemann), 49–70.

Posner, M. (ed.) (1978) *Demand Management* (London: Heinemann).

Posner, M. and Steer, A. (1979) 'Price competitiveness and the performance of manufacturing industry', in F. Blackaby (ed.) *Deindustrialisation* (London: Heinemann), 141–65.

Pulzer, P. (1967) *Political Representation and Elections* (London: Macmillan).

Putnam, R. (1971) 'Studying elite political culture: the case of ideology', *American Political Science Review* **65**, 651–81.

Putnam, R. (1973) *The Beliefs of Politicians* (New Haven, Conn.: Yale University Press).

Rallings, C. S. (1975) 'Two types of middle-class Labour voter?', *British Journal of Political Science* **5**, 107–11.

Rapoport, A. (1960) *Fights, Games and Debates* (Ann Arbor: University of Michigan Press).

Rees, A. (1970) 'The Phillips curve as a menu for policy choice', *Economica* **37**, 227–38.

Riker, W. H. (1980) 'Implications from the disequilibrium of majority rule for the study of institutions', *American Political Science Review* **74**, 432–46.

Riker, W. H. and Ordeshook, P. (1973) *An Introduction to Positive Political Theory* (Englewood Cliffs, NJ: Prentice-Hall).

Roberts, K., Cook, F. G., Clark, S. C. and Semeonoff, E. (1977) *The Fragmentary Class Structure* (London: Heinemann).

Robertson, D. (1976) *A Theory of Party Competition* (London: Wiley).

Robinson, D. (1974) *Solidaristic Wage Policy in Sweden* (Paris: OECD).

Rose, R. (1962) 'The policy ideas of English party activists', *American Political Science Review* **56**, 360–71.

Rose, R. (ed.) (1974) *Comparative Electoral Behavior* (New York: Free Press).

Rose, R. (1980) *Do Parties Make a Difference?* (London: Macmillan).

Rothwell, R. and Zegveld, W. (1981) *Industrial Innovation and Public Policy* (London: Frances Pinter).

Rowntree, B. S. (1941) *Poverty and Progress: A Second Social Survey of York* (London: Longman).

Rowntree, B. S. and Lavers, G. R. (1951) *Poverty and the Welfare State: A Third Social Survey of York dealing only with economic questions* (London: Longman).

Runciman, W. G. (1966) *Relative Deprivation and Social Justice* (London: Routledge & Kegan Paul).

Samuelson, P. (1954) 'The pure theory of public expenditure', *Review of Economics and Statistics* **36**, 387–9.

Satterthwaite, M. A. and Sonnenschein, H. (1981) 'Strategy-proof allocation mechanisms at differentiable points', *Review of Economic Studies* **48**, 587–97.

Schofield, N. (1978a) *General Relevance of the Impossibility Theorem in Dynamical Social Choice*, mimeo (University of Texas, Austin).

Schofield, N. (1978b) 'Instability of simple dynamic games', *Review of Economic Studies* **45**, 575–94.

Schofield, N. (1982) 'Instability and development in the political economy', in P. C. Ordeshook and K. A. Shepsle (eds) *Political Equilibrium* (Boston and The Hague: Kluwer-Nijhoff Publishing), 96–106.

Searing, D., Wright, G. and Rabinowitz, G. (1976) 'The primacy principle: attitude change and political socialisation', *British Journal of Political Science* **6**, 83–113.

Seyd, P. and Minkin, L. (1979) 'The Labour Party and its members', *New Society* **49**, no. 885, 613–15.

Sharpe, L. J. (1964) 'Elected representatives in local government', *British Journal of Sociology* **13**, 169–209.

Shonfield, A. (1958) *British Economic Policy since the War* (Harmondsworth: Penguin).

Shonfield, A. (1969) *Modern Capitalism* (Oxford: Oxford University Press).

Simkins, J. and Tickner, V. (1978) *Whose Benefit? Uncertainties of Cash Benefits for the Disabled* (London: Economist Intelligence Unit).

Simon, H. (1959) 'Theories of decision making in economics and the behavioural sciences', *American Economic Review* **49**, 253–83.

Skidelsky, R. (1979) 'The decline of Keynesian politics', in C. Crouch (ed.) *State and Economy in Contemporary Capitalism* (London: Croom Helm).

Stewart, M. (1978) *Politics and Economic Policy in the UK since 1964* (Oxford: Pergamon Press).

Stout, D. K. (1977) *International Price Competitiveness, Non-Price Factors and Export Performance* (London: National Economic Development Office).

Strachey, J. (1936) *The Theory and Practice of Socialism* (London: Gollancz).

Tawney, R. H. (1931) *Equality* (London: Gollancz).

Tawney, R. H. (1933) *The Acquisitive Society* (London: Bell).

Titmuss, R. M. (1963) *Essays on 'The Welfare State'* (London: Allen & Unwin).

Titmuss, R. M. (1974) *Social Policy: An Introduction* (London: Allen & Unwin).

Townsend, P. B. (1954) 'Measuring poverty', *British Journal of Sociology* **5**, 130–7.

Townsend, P. B. (1962) 'The meaning of poverty', *British Journal of Sociology* **13**, 210–17.

Townsend, P. B. (1979) *Poverty in the United Kingdom* (Harmondsworth: Penguin).

TUC (1982) 'Programme for recovery', *TUC Economic Review, 1982* (London: TUC).

Tufte, E. R. (1978) *Political Control of the Economy* (Princeton, NJ: Princeton University Press).

Walker, A. (1982) 'Public expenditure, social policy and social planning', in A. Walker (ed.) *Public Expenditure and Social Policy* (London: Heinemann), 3–26.

Webb, A. (1975) 'The abolition of national assistance: policy changes in the administration of assistance benefits', in P. Hall, H. Land, R. Parker and A. Webb, *Change, Choice and Conflict in Social Policy* (London: Heinemann), chap. 14.

Webb, N. L. and Wybrow, R. J. (1981) *The Gallup Report* (London: Sphere Books).

Weissberg, R. (1974) *Political Learning: Political Choice and Democratic Citizenship* (Englewood Cliffs, NJ: Prentice-Hall).

Whiteley, P. (1978) 'The structure of democratic socialist ideology in Britain', *Political Studies* **26**, 209–31.

Whiteley, P. (1979) 'Electoral forecasting from poll data: the British case', *British Journal of Political Science* **9**, 219–36.

Whiteley, P. (ed.) (1980) *Models of Political Economy* (London: Sage).

Whiteley, P. (1981) 'Who are the Labour activists?', *Political Quarterly* **52**, 160–70.

Whiteley, P. (1983) 'The political economy of economic growth', *European Journal of Political Research* **11**, 197–214.

Whiteley, P. and Gordon, I. (1980) 'Middle class, militant and male', *New Statesman* **99**, 41–2.

Whiteley, P. and Winyard, S. (1983) 'Influencing social policy: the effectiveness of the poverty lobby in Britain', *Journal of Social Policy* **12**, 1–26.

Wildavsky, A. (1975) *Budgeting, a Comparative Theory of Budgetary Processes* (Boston: Little, Brown).

Williams, S. (1981) *Politics Is for People* (London: Allen Lane).

Willis, J. R. M. and Hardwick, P. S. W. (1978) *Tax Expenditures in the United Kingdom* (London: Heinemann).

Wilson, G. D. (1973) *The Psychology of Conservatism* (London: Academic Press).

Wilson, H. (1974) *The Labour Government, 1964–1970: A Personal Record* Harmondsworth: Penguin).

Wilson, H. (1979) *Final Term* (London: Weidenfeld & Nicolson/Michael Joseph).

Worcester, R. M. and Harrop, M. (eds) (1982) *Political Communications* (London: Allen & Unwin).

Index

Abel-Smith, B., 167–8
Abrams, M., 94, 125
activists: and ideological structuring, 66–9; as ideologues, 30; and membership, 56; role of, 7–10; and social class, 13, 14, 42, 62, 63–4; and unemployment, 78
Adorno, T. W., 22
affective evaluations: measurement of, 95; notion of, 92; and social class, 79; and voting behaviour, 96–106
affiliated membership figures, 70–1, 77–8
affluent workers, 63, 86, 106
Ajzen, I., 88
Alford, J., 154
All Children Worse Off under Labour, 186
Allen, G. C., 199
Almond, G. A., 10, 90
Alt, J., 2, 9, 24, 26, 62, 83, 84, 85, 105
'anti-controllers' class, 84
Ashford, D. E., 166
Atkinson, A. B., 181
attendance allowance, 184
attitude coherence, 13, 45
attitude constraint, 24, 35
attitude indicators, 33–4, 37
attitude structuring, 28, 34, 50
Attlee, C., 112
autocorrelation, 74

Bacon, R., 141

balance of payments, and postwar economy, 134–5, 144–5, 146, 147, 148, 160
Ball, R. J., 119, 131, 137
Balogh, T., 137
bank rate, 155, 157*tab*.
Banting, K. G., 171, 181, 182
Barber, Anthony, 149
'Barber boom', 148, 149
Baxter, R., 62
Beackon, S., 42
Bealey, F., 21, 29, 112
Beckerman, W., 131, 145
benefits: earnings related, 174–5, 178–9, 183; means tested, 163, 165, 170–2, 182; and number of beneficiaries, 171; relative value of over time, 173–4; *see also individual benefits*
Benn, Tony, 4, 149, 150
Berki, R. N., 112
Bernstein, B., 64
Berrington, H., 31
Berry, D., 29
Berthoud, R., 172
Bevan, A., 112, 121, 163
Bevanite revolt, 121–2
Beveridge Report, 17, 120, 164, 165–70
Birch, A. H., 29
Bish, G., 129
Bispham, J. A., 148
Black, D., 87

Blackaby, F., 140
Blank, S., 197
Blondel, J., 8
Bochel, J. M., 9
Bosanquet, N., 41, 63, 131
Bradley, I., 5
Brand, J., 62
Braybrooke, D., 194
Bretton Woods, 196
British Election Study Survey (1979),
    13, 25, 94–5
British Leyland, 47
British National Oil Corporation, 14,
    47
Brittan, S., 131, 144, 146
Brookings Institute, 132
Brown, George, 145–6
Budge, I., 86, 87, 88
budgetting process, 140
Buiter, W. H., 137
Bullock Report, 203
Burns, T., 137
Butler, D., 7, 11, 12, 24, 25, 54, 69, 75,
    81, 82, 83, 95, 117, 118, 200

Cairncross, A., 141
Callaghan, Jim, 3, 4, 129, 147, 182,
    185–6
Cambridge Economic Policy Review, 141
Cambridge School, 148, 190, 199
Cameron, D., 140
Campaign for Democratic Socialism,
    50
Campaign for Labour Party
    Democracy, 3, 4, 8, 129–30
Campbell, A., 81
Campbell, D., 154
canvassing, 9
capitalism: changes in, 122–3; and
    socialism, 112, 113
car ownership, and voting behaviour,
    95, 96, 100, 102, 104
Castle, Barbara, 185, 186
Castles, F., 140
Caves, R. E., 104, 132
child benefit, 164, 170, 172, 173, 180,
    183, 185–6

Child Poverty Action Group, 172, 182,
    185, 186
Chronically Sick and Disabled Persons
    Act (1970), 185
City, the, 197
Clause Four, 4, 59–61, 67–8, 79–80n.,
    125
'clawback', 182, 183
Clegg, H., 131, 139
Coates, K., 22, 41
cognitive dissonance, 66
'cohabitation rule', 181
Cohen, M., 194
Cole, G. D. H., 112, 113, 115–16
collective action, paradoxes of, 58, 91,
    93, 138
collectives, 90
Common Market negotiations, and
    trade planning, 198
Common Market policy: and Social
    Democratic Alliance, 5; and voting
    behaviour, 96, 99
Common Market Referendum (1975),
    5, 150
Communist Party, 6
conference delegates, 33, 34, 53, 55,
    66–9, 220–1
conference resolutions, 29–30
Conservative share of the vote, 11–12
constituency boundaries, 12
constituency parties, membership of,
    55, 62
constitution, Labour Party, 6, 51
'constraint', and ideology, 22–3
consumption, means of, and social
    attributes, 89
consumption, modes of, 15
consumption indicators, and voting
    behaviour, 96
consumption locations, and voting
    behaviour, 91
consumption sector variables, 95, 106
consumption sectors, 84–5
'controllers' class, 84
Converse, P., 22–3
Cook, T. D., 154
core classes, 84
corporate sector, 127–8

corporate sector membership: and trade union membership, 104; and voting behaviour, 95, 100
corporate taxation, decline in, 175
correlation and regression, 213–14
Council for Social Democracy, 5
council tenants, and voting behaviour, 96
councillors, 43–4, 62, 65, 220
covert trade controls, 198
Craig, F. W. S., 115, 117, 124, 125, 128, 185
Crewe, I., 9, 24, 26, 62, 82, 83, 84, 85, 86, 89
Cripps, F., 143
'crisis offset' decision making, 194
Cromer, Lord, 145
Crosland, A., 5, 49, 111, 112, 122–4, 163
Crossman, R., 180
currency crises, 202

dealignment: effects on Labour Party, 105–6; and evaluations, 94, 105; and objective needs, 93; and partisanship, 83–5; and sectoral analysis, 85–6
decision making, 194
defence spending, 143, 147
deflation, 134, 135, 136
de-industrialization, 140–1, 193, 194
demand management, 132–4
'democratic control of industry', the, 114
democratic socialism, doctrine of, 112
Denver, D. T., 9
Department of Economic Affairs, 125, 145
depression, the, and economic theory, 118–19
deputy leadership, the, 4
Deutsch, K., 2, 90
Desai, M., 120, 136
devaluation, 142, 144, 147, 152
Disability Allowance, 184
disabled: and Beveridge, 166–7; Labour's record, 184–5
Disablement Income Group, 184

'dominant ideology', 44, 92, 94
Donnison, David, 186
Donnison, D. V., 29
Dow, J. C. R., 131, 143
Downs, A., 81, 86–7, 93
Dowse, R., 62
Drucker, H., 30
dummy variables, 95, 106–7n.
Dunleavy, P., 84, 85, 94
Durbin, J., 75
Durbin–Watson statistic, 74

Early Day Motions, 31–2
earnings related benefits, *see* benefits
earnings related pension scheme, 178–9, 180
earnings related supplement (ERS), 174, 177, 181
Easton, D., 2, 89
economic decline, 133*tab.*
economic expectations of electorate, 105
economic policy: and changes within an administration, 154; and foreign trade, 141–2; and Labour in office, 142–3; and Labour's 1982 programme, 189–204; since the Second World War, 132–42
economic series, 155
Economic Theory of Democracy, An, 81
economic variables, as predictors of membership, 75–6
economists, 196
Edwards, A. D., 64
EEC, *see* Common Market
election manifestos: (1918), 115; (1955), 124; (1959), 124; (1964), 16, 125–6, 179; (1974), 128–9
electoral behaviour, *see* voting behaviour
electoral college, for leadership, 3, 4, 130
electoral crisis, the, 10–12
electoral system, the, 188–9
elite, of the Labour Party: defined, 12, 13; and factor analysis, 36*tab.*, and ideology, 30–9; and policy, 46–50; and social class, 62

Eltis, W. A., 140
employment, Labour's 1982
    programme for, 191
employment policy 1944, 133, 138
employment sector variables, and
    voting behaviour, 95
Engels, Friedrich, 21
Ennals, David, 185
entryism, 2, 5–6
European Monetary System, 200
European Nuclear Disarmament
    Campaign, 9
evaluation indicators, 95–6, 100–2
evaluations, 92–4
exceptional needs payments, 172, 173
exchange controls, 190–1, 197, 199
exports, 142, 190
expressive motives, 58

Fabian Society, 21
faction fighting, 71, 78
factor analysis, 25–8, 217–18
false consciousness, 92
Family Allowance Act (1945), 166
family allowances, 177, 181–2
Family Expenditure Survey, 172
family income supplement, 171, 172,
    183
Farlie, D., 86, 87, 88
Fassbender, H., 90
Fay, S., 152
Featherstone, K., 148
Fellowes, E., 32
female employment, 141
Field, F., 167, 171, 172, 176–7, 182,
    185, 186
Finer, S. E., 31, 154
Finer Report, 170
'fine tuning', policy of, 136
Fiorina, M., 92, 100
Fishbein, M., 88
floating pound, 145
Foot, Michael, 4
Ford, President, 153
foreign trade, and the economy,
    141–2; *see also* trade planning
Forrester, T., 41, 42, 62
'four week rule', 181

France, 198, 199–200
Frasure, R. C., 31
Freeman, C., 142
Freeman, John, 121
'free rider' problem, 57, 58, 79
free trade, 195
Frey, B., 105
Friedman, M., 135, 137, 138
Future of Socialism, The, 5, 122–3

Gaitskell, Hugh, 122, 124, 125
Galbraith, J. K., 122–3
Gallup Polls 1981, 4–5, 71
Gamble, A., 2, 129
GDP: increase in 1945–51, 143; and
    indirect taxation, 160; and public
    expenditure, 133, 139, 153; and
    trade, 190; and TUC's programme
    for recovery, 199
General Agreement on Tariffs and
    Trade (GATT), 190
General Elections: (1929), 117; (1931),
    4, 118; (1951), 70; (1955), 70, 124;
    (1964), 70; (1966), 147; (1970), 3, 70,
    126; (1979), 2, 3, 10, 81, 86; (1983),
    see postscript
General Household Survey, 168
General Strike, 115, 116
*General Theory of Employment, Interest
    and Money*, 118, 132
Glasgow Media Group, 94
Godley, W., 148, 152, 196
Goldthorpe, J. H., 62, 63, 86, 106, 131
Gordon, I., 32, 57, 62, 65, 84
Gould, J., 22
Grant, W., 135, 150, 151, 197
grassroots party members, 28–30
Greenstein, F. I., 41
growth, and Labour government, 160,
    161, 193

Hahn, F. H., 136
Hanby, V. T., 62
'hands off' intervention, 127, 135, 150
Hardie, James Keir, 21
Hardwick, P. S. W., 176
Harman, H., 26
Harrod, R., 120

Harrop, M., 10, 84, 85, 86
Hatfield, M., 3
Hayward, Roan, 6
Healey, Denis, 4–5, 148, 185, 186
Health Service, reorganization of, 149
Heath, Edward, 140, 147
Heclo, H., 140
Heffer, Eric, 182
Henry, S. G. B., 139
Herbison, Margaret, 171, 182
Hibbs, D., 90, 160
'hidden welfare state', 176
Himmelweit, H., 24–5, 88
Hinden, R., 125
Hindess, B., 29, 42, 62, 63
Hirsch, F., 131
Hirschman, A. O., 63
Holland, S., 41, 63, 127–8
home ownership, and voting
  behaviour, 96, 100, 102, 104
Houghton Commission, 55–7
Houghton, Douglas, 171, 181, 182
House of Lords, abolition of, 3
Howard, M. C., 120
Howell, D., 22
h statistic, 75–6
Hughes, David, 6
Hyndeman, H. M., 21
hyper-inflation, 138

ideological coherence, 43–6, 79
ideological crisis, nature of, 2–6
ideological schism, sources of, 46–50
ideological structuring, 32, 66
ideologue, the, 23–4
ideology: defined, 13, 22–4; and
  Labour voters, 24–8; and party
  membership, 28–30, 64–9
IMF crisis, 152–3, 194
import controls, 142, 190, 196; and
  retaliation, 197–9
imports, 134
incomes policy: and collective
  paradox, 93; and elite preferences,
  47; problems of, 138–9; and trade
  unionists, 9; (1965), 146; (1974),
  151–2, 153; (1982), 200–1

incumbency, and membership, 73, 76,
  78
Independent Labour Party (ILP), 21,
  116, 118
indirect taxation, 204–5
industrial democracy, 191, 195, 202–3
industrial policy, 135, 149–51
Industrial Reorganization Corporation,
  147, 150
industrial strategy, Labour's
  programme 1982, 191–2
industry, White Paper on 1974,
  149–50
Industry Act (1972), 150
industry act, proposals for 1973, 127–8
inflation: and expenditure cuts, 140;
  and incomes policies, 138, 151, 153;
  and money supply, 137; and
  paradox of collective action, 91; and
  party membership, 72–4, 76, 78;
  and 1982 programme, 191; and
  voting behaviour, 95, 96
instrumental electorate, 106
instrumental evaluations, and policy
  outcomes, 92, 93
instrumental motives, 58, 79
invalid care allowance, 185
invalidity pension, 184, 185
issue indicators, 26*tab.*
issues, importance of in electoral
  behaviour, 84

Jaccard, J., 88
Janosik, E. G., 31
Japan, 196, 198
Jay, Peter, 122
Jenkins, Roy, 49, 147
Johnson, C., 196
Johnson, R. W., 62
Johnston, J., 74, 75
Joint Statement of Intent, 144
Jones, A., 131, 139
Jones, Aubrey, 146
Jones, Jack, 151
Joseph, Keith, 171

Kaldor, N., 136, 137

Keegan, W., 151, 152, 153
Kennedy, M. C., 136
Keynes, J. M., 118, 119, 132–3
Keynesianism: and classical economic
    theory, 119–20; and Labour's 1982
    programme, 190; and Mosley, 118;
    problems of, 16, 135
Kindelberger, C. P., 196
King, J. E., 120
King, M. A., 175
Klein, R., 140
Kogan, D., 3, 22, 47, 129
Kogan, M., 3, 22, 47, 129
Kiewet, D. R., 91
Kinder, D. R., 91
Kolb, W. L., 22
Kornberg, A., 31
Koutsoyannis, A., 74
Krause, L. B., 104, 132
Kravis, I., 142

Labour Co-ordinating Committee, 3
Labour governments: (1924), 115–16;
    (1929–31), 115, 117; (1945–51), 121,
    142–3, 166; (1964–70), 41, 144–8,
    177–83; (1974–9), 41, 148–9
Labour and the Nation, 115, 116–17
Labour and the New Social Order,
    113–14
Labour Party: foundations of, 21–2;
    origins to 1945, 112–21
Labour Representation Committee, 21
Labour's Plan for Expansion (1981), 189
Labour's Programme 1982, 17, 189–206
Labour's Programme for Britain 1973, 3,
    17, 126–8, 149
Laidler, D., 137
Land Commission, 147
Land, H., 185
Lane, R., 22
language codes, 64
Lapping, B., 131
Lasswell, H., 90
Lavers, G. R., 167
Layard, R., 168, 201
law and order, 95, 96, 102
Leece, J., 31
Left, strategies of, 3–4, 51

left–right continuum, 87
left–right dimension, 35–9, 87
left–right ideology scale, 38
'less eligibility' rule, 166
Lewis-Beck, M., 154
Leijonhufvud, A., 119
Lever, Harold, 152
liberalism, 207
Limehouse Declaration, 5
Lindblom, C., 90, 194
Lipsey, R. E., 142
Livingstone, Ken, 47
Lloyd, Selwyn, 135
local elections, 9
local government, reorganization of,
    149
London Business School, 137
Longstreth, F., 197
Lucas, R. E., 137

MacDonald, Ramsay, 115, 116
Mackenzie, H. C., 94
macroeconomic management, 120,
    125, 190, 191, 202
mandatory reselection of MPs, 2, 3, 4,
    8, 129
manifesto, control of, 3, 4
manifestos, *see* election manifestos
Mannheim, K., 22
Manpower Services Commission, 191
manual workers, decline in numbers,
    62
manufacturing industry, decline in,
    see de-industrialization
March, J., 194
marginal rates of taxation, 176
market sector, 141
market sector membership: and trade
    union membership, 104; and voting
    behaviour, 95
Marsh, D., 41, 197
Marshall Aid, 143
Marshall, T. H., 163
Martin, A., 206
Marx, Karl, 21
Marxist economics, 120
Marxist Social Democratic Federation,
    21

mass media, influence of, 10
Meade, J. E., 138, 201
means tested benefits, *see* benefits
media bias, 94
membership, of the Labour Party: and
  activism, 53–7; decline in, 7*fig*.,
  54*fig*., 61–4; figures, 70–1, 77–8;
  and inflation, 72*fig*., reasons for,
  57–61, 63, 65; and unemployment,
  73*fig*.
membership crisis, 6–10
Merelman, R., 23
Metcalf, D., 138, 146
microeconomic intervention, 126
microelectronics, 203
middle class, and Party membership,
  61, 62
middle-class vote, 85
Militant Tendency, 2, 6, 8
Miller, W., 84
Milne, R. S., 94
Ministry of Technology, 126
minimum income guarantee, 179–80
Minkin, L., 57, 79
misspecification, 74, 80n.
mobility allowance, 185
monetarism, 136–7, 161
money supply, 137, 155, 157*tab*.
Morris, Alf, 185
Mosley, Oswald, 118, 119
MPs, and ideology, 43–6
Mueller, D. C., 87
Mughan, A., 86, 89
multinationals, control of, 192
multiple interrupted times series
  analysis (MITS), 154–5
multiple regression analysis, 40
multivariate analysis of vote model,
  100–6
Muth, J. F., 137

national assistance, 165
National Assistance Act (1948), 166
National Assistance Board, 166, 167,
  180
National Economic Development
  Council, 126, 135, 193

National Enterprise Board, 47, 128,
  150, 151, 203
National Executive Committee, 3, 62
National Government, 118
National Health Service, 121, 122,
  165, 203
National Insurance Act (1946), 166
national insurance benefits, 163
national investment bank, proposals
  for, 192, 193
nationalization: and attitudes of
  Labour elite, 47, 49*tab*., and
  Campaign for Labour Party
  Democracy, 3; and manifesto 1974,
  128; and Labour's programme 1982,
  192–3, 203; and revisionism, 123–4;
  and voters' attitudes, 24
national minimum, 113, 114
National Plan (1965), 126, 135, 140,
  146, 192
*National Superannuation, Labour's
  Policy for Security in Old Age*, 178
NATO, 122
Neild, R. R., 196
New Frontiers for Social Security, 179
New Society, 185
Newton, K., 10
Nie, N., 86
Niskanen, W. A., 140
North Sea oil, 154

objective indicators, in model of
  voting behaviour, 104
objective needs and interests, and
  Labour Party support, 90, 92, 93, 94
occupational mobility, 62
occupational pensions, 183
occupational status: and ideology, 40,
  41–3; and voting behaviour, 95, 102,
  103*tab*., 104
OECD, 132
oil crisis (1975), 77
Olsen, J., 194
Olson, M., 57, 91, 138
One Way Only, 122
Ordeshook, P., 82, 87
ordinal variables, 96
Ormerod, P., 131

Parkin, F., 8, 44, 92
parliamentary candidates, and ideology, 43–6
partisanship, 82–3, 84
party competition, theory of, 87
party conferences: (1918), 114–15; (1930), 118; (1934), 118; (1959), 125; (1960), 125; (1979), 129; (1981), 189; (1982), 189
party identification, concept of, 82, 84, 86, 89
party leader, election of, 2, 3
Peacock, A. R., 140
Pelling, H., 21
Pennant-Rea, 151, 152, 153
pensions, Labour's record, 183–4
Pensions Act (1975), 183, 205
performance hypothesis, 12–18, 106
PESC, 140
Peston, M. H., 131, 155
Petit, P., 198, 200
pharmaceuticals, 203
Philips curve, 136
Pindyck, R. S., 100
Pissarides, C. A., 105
Pliatsky, L., 133, 139, 152, 153, 155
Plowman, D. E. G., 29
policy aims space, 87–8
policy cycles, 87
policy discussions, at grassroots level, 29
policy goals, failure to achieve, 12–13, 46–50, 63
policy making, and activists, 8–9
policy methods space, 88
policy performance, and decline of membership, 69–79
policy preferences of Labour voters, and party policies, 94
political education, 10
political status, and ideology, 43–6
Pollard, S., 134–5
Pond, C., 175, 176
Poor and the Poorest, 167
Posner, M., 131, 142
poverty, 166, 167, 168–70, 174–5; and the Labour Party, 178
'poverty trap', 172

Powell, G. B., 90
pressure groups, 79
price controls, 186, 191
Prices and Incomes Board, 146, 147
principal components analysis, 35
probit analysis model, 100, 107n.
production locations, and electoral behaviour, 91
production, means of, and social attributes, 89
production sectors, 84–5
production sector variables and voting behaviour, 95, 96
productivity, 161
'Programme for Recovery', 199
'programme of joint control', 128
proscribed organizations, 6
prospective evaluations, 92, 93, 94, 95–6, 102, 104
public expenditure, 139–40, 149, 151–2, 160, 190
public investment, 190
public ownership, *see* nationalization
public sector borrowing requirement (PSBR), 148–9, 152–3, 155, 157tab.
public sector employment, 85, 141
public service sector membership, 95, 104
Pulzer, P., 82
Putnam, R., 22, 31

Rabinowitz, G., 41
Radcliffe Committee, 137
radicalism, 41
Rallings, C. S., 85
Rapoport, A., 138
rational choice models, 88–9, 92–3
recruitment, 8, 55
redistribution, 163, 177, 182, 206
Rees, A., 136
reflation, 199
register of non-affiliated groups, 6
regression analysis, 214–17
relative deprivation, 167
retirement pensions, 164, 170, 171, 173, 174, 177
retrospective evaluations, 92–3, 95, 96, 100, 102, 104, 106

revisionism, 5, 50, 121–30
Richardson, R., 138, 146
Right, long-term prospects for, 51
Riker, W. H., 82, 87
Roberts, K., 63
Robertson, D., 87–8
Robinson, D., 139
Rose, R., 30, 84, 125, 154
Rothwell, R., 142, 143
Rowntree, B. S., 166, 167
Royal Commission on the Distribution of Income and Wealth, 168
Rubinfeld, D. L., 100
Runciman, W. G., 167

'safety-net', 165, 166
Samuelson, P., 58
Särlvik, B., 9, 24, 26, 62, 83, 84
Satterthwaite, M. A., 196
'Says Law', 133
Scanlon, Hugh, 151
Schneider, F., 105
Schofield, N., 87, 196
Searing, D., 41
sectoral analysis, 85–6
sector, notion of, 84–5
Seyd, P., 57
Sharpe, L. J., 62
Shonfield, A., 131, 135
sickness benefits, 164, 174, 177–8, 183
Simkins, J., 184
Simon, H., 194
single parent families, 167, 170, 205
Skidelsky, R., 133
Sloman, A., 7, 12, 54, 75, 117, 118, 200
Snowden, Philip, 117
social attributes, 89, 92–3, 94, 95, 100, 102, 105
social background, and ideology, 39–43
social class: and ideological structuring, 66–9; and language, 64; and membership of Labour Party, 59, 60; and occupational status, 82–3; as a predictor of voting behaviour, 88; as a stabilizing influence on politics, 87

Social Democratic Alliance, 5
Social Democratic Party, 2, 5, 50, 207
Social Insurance and Allied Services, 120
social policy, scope of, 163
Social Security Act (1966), 180, 181
social security benefits, *see* benefits
social security: Labour's programme for 1982, 204–6; Labour's record, compared with Conservative, 177–8; and taxation, 175–7, 204
social services, cuts in, voters' attitudes to, 96
socialism: democratic, 112; and the early Labour Party, 112–13; and *Labour's Programme for Britain*, 127; nature of, 111; and revisionism, 130
Socialism and the Condition of the People, 16, 115, 118–19
sociological paradigm, and voting behaviour, 86
sociotropic voting, 91
Sonnenschein, H., 196
spatial model of electoral behaviour, 87–8
stabilization policy, 132–3, 137
'stagflation', 141, 144
state, role of, 122
statutory wage freeze, 146
Steer, A., 142
Stewart, M., 131, 144, 145, 147
Stokes, D., 12, 24, 25, 69, 81, 82, 83, 95
'stop–go', 134–5, 143, 146–7
Stout, D. K., 142
Strachey, J., 111, 112, 120
strikes, voters' attitudes to, 95, 96
subjective evaluations, 89
subjective indicators of voting behaviour, 104
subjective needs and interests, 90, 91, 92, 93, 94
supplementary benefit, 164, 169, 172–8, 183, 205
Supplementary Benefits Commission, 167, 175, 181
Sweden, 139, 206
system models of politics, 89–90
systems theory, 2

take-up, of benefits, 171, 180–1
Tawney, R. H., 111
tax, and incomes policy, 201
tax allowances, 176–7
tax avoidance, 204–5
tax threshold, 175, 204
taxation, 96, 160, 204
'techno-structure', 122
television, 79
Thatcher, Margaret, 161
Thomas, K., 88
three year rule, 4
Tickner, V., 184
Titmuss, R. M., 163, 167, 176
Townsend, P. B., 41, 63, 131, 167–8
trade planning, 195, 197–9
Trades Disputes Act (1927), 116, 117
trade union power, and dominant
    ideology, 94
trade unions: and incomes policies,
    139, 201; legal curbs on, 96, 99, 102,
    104; membership of, 43, 95, 100,
    104; and socialism, 112–13
transfer payments, 176
Treasury econometric model, 199
Trotskyite Fourth Internationale, 6
t statistics, 74, 76, 80n., 100
TUC, 151, 182, 191, 199
TUC/Labour Party Liaison Committee,
    186
training programme, 191
Tufte, E. R., 140
Turner, J., 85
'twelve month rule', 154

unemployment: Labour's record, 117,
    160; Labour's 1982 programme, 190,
    199, 200; and party membership,
    72–4, 76–8; and voting behaviour,
    95, 96
unemployment benefit, 170–4, 177–8,
    183
unilateral disarmament, 8–9
unilateralism, 125
unionization, 100–3
US Treasury, 152

Varley, Eric, 150
VAT, abolition of, 204
Verba, S., 10
vested interests, 197
voluntary organizations, support for,
    57
vote, share of, 10–12
voting behaviour: economic theory of,
    86–9; explanations of, 81–2;
    sociological account of, 82–6; and
    state of economy, 105; theoretical
    model of, 89–106

wage explosion, risk of, 200–1
'wage stop' rule, 166, 181
Walker, A., 175
Wass, Sir Douglas, 152
wealth tax, 114, 117, 204
Webb, N. L., 4, 179
Weissberg, R., 41
Whiteley, P., 32, 41, 57, 62, 65, 71, 78,
    84, 105, 172, 195
widows, 181
Wildavsky, A., 140
Williams, S., 49
Willis, J. R. M., 176
Wilson, G. D., 32
Wilson, Harold, 3, 16, 77, 121, 125,
    144–5, 149, 179
'winter of discontent', 4, 99
Winyard, S., 172
Wiseman, J., 140
Worcester, R. M., 10
workers' participation, 195
working class, and party membership,
    61, 62
working-class vote, decline in, 85–6
Wright, G., 41
Wybrow, R. J., 4

Young, H., 152
Young Socialists, 6

Zegfeld, W., 142, 143